Using PowerPoint ®

James G. Meade

que ®

Carmel, Indiana

Using PowerPoint®

Library of Congress Catalog No.: 90-64395
ISBN: 0-88022-698-6

93 92 91   4 3 2 1

Interpretation of the printing code: the rightmost double-digit number is the year of the book's printing; the rightmost single-digit number, the number of the book's printing. For example, a printing code of 91-1 shows that the first printing of the book occurred in 1991.

The graphics in this book were created by artists at Genigraphics Corporation using Microsoft® PowerPoint®.

Screen shots: Microsoft® PowerPoint,® ©1987-1991 Microsoft Corporation. Reprinted with permission from Microsoft Corporation.

This book is based on Microsoft PowerPoint Version 2.0.

Publisher: Lloyd J. Short

Associate Publisher: Karen A. Bluestein

Acquisitions Manager: Terrie Lynn Solomon

Product Development Manager: Mary Bednarek

Managing Editor: Paul Boger

Book Designer: Scott Cook

Production Team: Sandy Grieshop, Howard Peirce, Joe Ramon, Tad Ringo, Johnna Van Hoose, Lisa Wilson, Christine Young

DEDICATION ▼

To my mother,
for (among other things) letting me
use the new Impala, circa 1962.

Product Director
Shelley O'Hara

Production Editor
Gregory Robertson

Editors
Sharon K. Boller
Frances R. Huber

Technical Editor
Dana Schmeller

*Composed in Garamond
and Macmillan
by Que Corporation*

ABOUT THE AUTHOR ▼

James G. Meade

When he is not playing basketball in his backyard, Jim Meade spends most of his time writing Que books. His previous Que titles are *Using Freelance Plus, Using MultiMate, Using Peachtree,* and *Using Andrew Tobias' TaxCut.* His company, Meade Ink, has been providing writing services since 1983 to companies such as Lotus Development Corporation, Digital Equipment Corporation, and MCI Communications Corp. His monthly column, "Raw Ink," appears in *Digital Desktop Magazine.* He is a regular software reviewer for *HR Magazine* and has written dozens of columns and articles for computer and technical magazines, such as *Data Communications Magazine* and *Information Week.*

TRADEMARK ACKNOWLEDGMENTS

Que Corporation has made every effort to supply trademark information about company names, products, and services mentioned in this book. Trademarks indicated below were derived from various sources. Que Corporation cannot attest to the accuracy of this information.

Ami Professional is a registered trademark of SAMNA Corporation.

Epson is a registered trademark of Epson Corporation.

Genigraphics is a registered trademark and GraphicsLink is a trademark of Genigraphics, Inc.

Hayes is a registered trademark of Hayes Microcomputer Products, Inc.

ITC Zapf Dingbats is a trademark of International Typeface Corporation.

LaserJet and HP are registered trademarks of Hewlett-Packard, Inc.

Lotus, 1-2-3, Manuscript, and Symphony are registered trademarks of Lotus Development Corporation.

Microsoft, Microsoft Excel, PowerPoint, and Multiplan are registered trademarks and Windows is a trademark of Microsoft Corporation.

PC Paintbrush is a registered trademark of ZSoft Corporation.

Trademarks of other products mentioned in this book are held by the companies producing them.

ACKNOWLEDGMENTS ▼

Que publishing, in Indiana and in the heart of basketball country, lives up to the spirit of that game. A Que book is truly a team effort. Credit on the title page may to go the author, but the team makes the author. The author is nothing without the Que team.

At Que I want to thank Scott Flanders, Lloyd Short, and Karen Bluestein for the opportunity to write this, my fifth Que book. I thank Product Director Shelley O'Hara for reminding me always to have the reader in mind and for keeping a view of the whole as I worked on the parts. Sandy Blackthorn also provided steady direction for several weeks. Greg Robertson was most skilled in leading the project through editing and into production. Dana Schmeller of Microsoft provided a knowledgeable, sure technical review. I also want to thank all the others at Que—editors Fran Huber and Sharon Boller, the production and business departments, everyone—for being the team that made this book possible.

In my own home region of Iowa, I want to thank my associate Philip Magnier for major contributions throughout the project. Kirk Neff contributed to the chapters on using text. Elise Van Looy worked on the book as a student intern and helped with the quick starts and the chapters on color. I also want to thank Jeff Fitz-Randolph at Iowa Computer for outstanding, quick hardware assistance whenever I needed it.

Above all, as always, I want to thank Nina, Molly, Ben, and Josh for keeping me company and for laughing at my jokes (if I said them over and over enough times).

CONTENTS AT A GLANCE

TABLE OF CONTENTS ▼

Part II   PowerPoint Advanced Features

14 Using Advanced Features of Color 347

15 Creating Standard Business Charts 365

Introduction

Microsoft® PowerPoint® is aptly named. The "power" in the name refers to all the capabilities loaded into the program. PowerPoint is not one program, but several.

- PowerPoint is a highly efficient drawing program. You can create lines, rectangles, and ovals, and combine them into any shape you want.

- PowerPoint is a graphing program. You write down the data you want to present (for example, sales for the third and fourth quarters), then click one of the 45 predefined graph styles to choose the one you want.

- PowerPoint is an executive word processor. You can add text and choose different fonts and type sizes, and you can word wrap. You can indent bulleted lists. You also can use PowerPoint's search and replace feature. PowerPoint can even check your spelling.

- PowerPoint is an artist's palette that offers you 5,000 professionally designed color schemes. If these built-in color combinations don't satisfy you, PowerPoint enables you to create your own colors and combinations.

- PowerPoint is an output program. You can output to your screen, and you can create color slides and overhead transparencies. If you want professionals to create the final output, you can use the GraphicsLink program (included with PowerPoint) to send your file to Genigraphics, a company that will make the slides for you. (The PowerPoint documentation includes the Genigraphics phone number.) PowerPoint, therefore, is also a communications program.

PowerPoint has the power of all those programs loaded into memory and at your service *all at once*. When you use all that power to create your graphics, you do not work with a single chart or drawing, as you might have done with a DOS program. Instead, you can work with an entire multiple-slide presentation at one time. On-screen you can have miniatures of all the slides in your presentation (as many as the memory on your computer can hold).

If you have 16 slides, you can rearrange them, delete them, add to them, change the color scheme, move words and objects from one to the other—all without ever exiting one file or opening another. If you want, you can view all the slides at once by title, or you can view them individually, and then work on them in detail.

PowerPoint, therefore, certainly has immense power, and using this power in your business presentations can help you make your point to your audience. The power available in this program would overwhelm most users without the rest that PowerPoint offers, described by the "point" in its name. You can use all that immense capability by using a mouse to point to options on menus as well as to manipulate the images on-screen.

You may have a task that calls for many different steps, such as creating a scatter chart; importing data from a Lotus 1-2-3 worksheet; using 48-point Helvetica text for the title, a 16-color pastel color scheme, and a rounded rectangle as a frame; importing clip art; setting up the format as a new default; and so on. Your task would be complicated indeed if you had to specify each step by name. When you use PowerPoint, however, you do not have to specify all those steps by name or even know the names of all those steps. You just point and click with the mouse. Anybody can do it.

When you point to the feature you want and select it, you are using the graphical user interface (GUI), a user interface that uses the mouse and a graphics display to simplify your use of computer operations. When you review what you see on the screen to decide whether you like it, you are using another advanced capability—WYSIWYG ("what you see is what you get"). In PowerPoint, all the colors, typefaces, sizes, and proportions you work with on-screen are those you will see in your final slide.

Thanks to the graphical user interface, PowerPoint is at once powerful and easy to use. What about artistic features for your presentations? You can point to those easily, too. If at first you are not comfortable with the thought of designing the aesthetic aspects of an entire presentation, PowerPoint has found a way to do that for you. Genigraphics artists have created 40 sample templates that have all the features of an outstanding slide show, such as color scheme, fonts for the titles, placement of graphics objects, and the flow of the whole presentation. You can copy the presentation, change the words or objects to suit your purposes, and create a slide show that is just as professional as the one from Genigraphics—without having to know graphic arts.

If the template does not include the image that you need, you probably can find the one you do want. PowerPoint has a clip art library of 400 color images, drawn by those professional artists at Genigraphics. You can browse through the images, copy one that you want, and paste it into the program.

PowerPoint is immense power that you can use to make your point in presentations. You are an expert almost as soon as you begin, and using PowerPoint soon becomes second nature. At first, however, you can learn much by reading about the program. PowerPoint offers so much concentrated power that you are almost certain to miss some of its capabilities unless you take a little time to seek them out. Helping you discover PowerPoint's possibilities is the purpose of this book.

What Is in This Book

Like the PowerPoint program itself, *Using PowerPoint* attempts to make the power of the program readily accessible. The book begins with basic features and moves toward more advanced features. Start by learning the basics, and then later, when you feel at home with the fundamentals, you can move to advanced features.

Three quick starts get you started using PowerPoint. Other chapters provide detailed explanations and additional tips so that you not only use the features, but understand them and their relation to each other and to the whole program.

Part I, "PowerPoint Basics," introduces you to the basics of PowerPoint.

Chapter 1, "Getting Acquainted with PowerPoint," shows you how to use the mouse and the keyboard, work with the menus, get help, and take advantage of PowerPoint as a Windows program.

Chapter 2, "Quick Start: Creating Your First Presentation," takes you step-by-step through the process of creating a presentation, adding text and graphic objects, and saving the presentation.

Chapter 3, "Creating a Presentation," shows you in detail how to start PowerPoint, create a presentation from scratch, create a presentation by copying a template, view and rearrange the presentation, and save the presentation.

Chapter 4, "Adding Text to a Presentation," demonstrates how to create text with the labeler and word processor tools, change typefaces and styles, and set up margins and tabs. This chapter also explains how to find and change text and how to use the spelling checker.

Chapter 5, "Drawing Objects," familiarizes you with the drawing tools available in PowerPoint. You draw and delete lines and shapes, move objects, add frames and shadows, and change fill patterns. You learn how to use guides and grids to help you put your drawings exactly where you want them to be on the slide.

Chapter 6, "Quick Start: Choosing Color Schemes," gives you hands-on experience in choosing color schemes, entering data into a graph, and changing the colors within a chart.

Chapter 7, "Using Basic Color," explains in detail the procedures you learned in Chapter 6. You also see how to color individual objects and text and how to work with patterns.

Chapter 8, "Creating Basic Graphs," shows you how to put your data into a datasheet, choose a graph form from the Chart menu, and include the graph in your slide.

Chapter 9, "Creating Output," shows you how to set up your printer. You learn how to output in every possible way—to your screen, to a film recorder, to a transparency, to paper, or to the Genigraphics slide service. You also see how to create and print notes and handouts.

Part II, "PowerPoint Advanced Features," takes you beyond the basics and helps you become familiar with some of the advanced power in PowerPoint.

Chapter 10, "Quick Start: Working with Pictures," demonstrates how to turn objects into a picture and how to retrieve a finished picture from the clip art file and put the picture into your slide.

Chapter 11, "Manipulating Pictures for Special Effects," takes you a step beyond the capability to work with multiple slides at once. Thanks to Windows, you can work easily with multiple *presentations* at once, or even with multiple applications. This chapter shows you how.

Chapter 12, "Using Advanced Features of Text," acquaints you with text capabilities that were not covered in Chapter 4. You see how to use the ruler to set indentations and tabs and how to set line and paragraph spacing. You also learn how to create a custom dictionary for your spelling checker, and you find out how to set up a new text style.

Chapter 13, "Using Advanced Features of Graph," discusses advanced graphing capabilities available in PowerPoint. You find out here about capabilities such as creating new number formats on the datasheet and customizing your graphs with special effects.

Chapter 14, "Using Advanced Features of Color," introduces you to advanced color capabilities. You learn how to work with colors that are not in the color scheme, such as those you create yourself. You find out how to recolor a picture you bring in from outside your presentation.

Chapter 15, "Creating Standard Business Charts," gives guidance on how to create standard charts you may need in your business, such as organization charts. Explicit step-by-step instructions are not given, but you learn how to approach these various charts and which tools to use to create them.

Appendix A, "Installing PowerPoint," shows you how to install PowerPoint. Appendix B, "PowerPoint Defaults," reviews the PowerPoint default settings—initial settings that are changed (sometimes by accident) as you use the program, but which you may want to restore. Appendix C, "The Clip Art Slides by Presentation," lists the clip art that comes with PowerPoint.

Who Should Use This Book

If a program is "intuitive," as PowerPoint is, why read a book about it? You can use almost anything in PowerPoint—even the most advanced capability, like setting up the color scheme—by browsing through possibilities and making choices. PowerPoint does not require you to know sophisticated commands, as do many non-Windows programs. Nor does PowerPoint require you to know graphic arts.

Read this book to become acquainted with the many possibilities that are available in PowerPoint. You easily can copy a presentation template and use it as your own. To use a presentation template, however, you must know that it is available to use. Any book about PowerPoint, therefore, is more a catalog of possibilities than an instruction manual.

If you start using PowerPoint and never read anything about it, you can perform well. Much of the power in the program, however, almost certainly will be lost to you. Gradually, you may make discoveries. You can continue to make them for months and months, because the program has so much to offer.

If you read this book, though, you do not need to wait until you happen upon such capabilities by accident. You can find out about PowerPoint's easy-to-use possibilities, learn the simple steps for using them, and discover shortcuts and special tips.

This book is not aimed toward the software expert or the graphic artist, although either one can profit by reading it. A software expert can learn about PowerPoint and receive advice on doing graphics well. A graphics expert can learn about the software and get advice on using it well. *Using PowerPoint*, however, is written primarily for business presenters who want to create their own presentations. *Using PowerPoint* shows you how to use the program step-by-step in a business context. Simple guidelines and explanations keep you steadily on course and help you get the most out of PowerPoint in the least amount of time.

How To Use This Book

PowerPoint is not difficult. You do not have to think hard about each feature to be able to use it. You do need to know, however, what the feature is and understand what it does for you. (A slide master, for example, is a great concept, but you must know what it is and how to use it.) Read this book to find out what PowerPoint has to offer.

You probably will not read this book as you would a novel, from beginning to end. Keep it available as a reference whenever you use the program. You may use some features often, others only rarely. *Using PowerPoint* can serve as a reference for features you only partially remember. Even if you use a feature often, you may want to check this book for shortcuts and special tips. A feature-rich program, no matter how easy to use, deserves a feature-rich book to help you get the most from it.

No matter how intuitive the program, you still must go through a series of steps to perform even the most basic operations. Before you create a slide, for example, you should install and set up your printer, because your printer setup influences how the slide looks on the screen and determines what fonts are available. If you do not follow a procedure step by step, you may find out that you have omitted a step and must go back. When you read a Que book such as *Using PowerPoint*, you learn all the right steps to follow and the sequence in which to follow them.

Conventions Used in This Book

Several conventions are used in this book to help you learn to use Microsoft PowerPoint quickly and easily. These conventions are as follows:

1. The names of dialog boxes and their options as well as menu names and their options are in initial capital letters.

2. Tips for using Microsoft PowerPoint are included in gray boxes. These tips can help you become more efficient in using the program.

3. Cautions are included in outlined boxes with a drop shadow. Pay close attention to these warnings, because they may save you from losing data or creating other problems for yourself.

4. Anything the user should type is in *italic type* or on a line by itself.

5. Messages that appear on-screen are `in a special typeface`.

Part I

PowerPoint Basics

Includes

Getting Acquainted with PowerPoint

Quick Start: Creating Your First Presentation

Creating a Presentation

Adding Text to a Presentation

Drawing Objects

Quick Start: Choosing Color Schemes

Using Basic Color

Creating Basic Graphs

Creating Output

1

Getting Acquainted with PowerPoint

The beauty of any Windows application is that you probably know a great deal about using the application before you even begin. Windows' greatest value is that it establishes a graphical user interface (GUI). Known as "gooey" around the industry, the GUI is a common interface for all Windows applications.

Chances are that PowerPoint is not your first Windows application. Many people use a Windows word processor or a Windows spreadsheet before they begin to use a Windows graphics program. You probably already know how to move the cursor with the mouse or keyboard, how to make menu selections, how to save your document, and much more. You probably know how to use the Windows File Manager for copying files and directories. And you probably know the basics about using the Program Manager to work with multiple programs.

If you know how to use Windows for your word processing or your spreadsheet or for managing files, you also know how to use it for your graphics application. You move the cursor in the same way for any Windows application. You choose from menus in the same way. You shrink and expand windows on the page in the same way. After you know any Windows 3.0 application, then in a sense you truly do know *any* Windows 3.0 application. Navigating in PowerPoint is like navigating in other Windows applications.

If you don't know how to use Windows or a Windows application, learning to do so is easy. This chapter reviews Windows features—using the mouse, changing and moving windows, using the Maximize and Minimize buttons—

and explains how to start PowerPoint. As you become comfortable with these capabilities, you will become increasingly comfortable with PowerPoint and all other Windows applications.

In the following sections, you become acquainted with the PowerPoint screen and with certain tools that you find in PowerPoint but not elsewhere in Windows—such as the Slide Changer and the Slide Sorter. As you work in PowerPoint, you often make changes to slides on the screen, and in this chapter you see how to change the text on a slide. You become familiar with the basic capabilities PowerPoint brings to all your presentations. You learn how to use PowerPoint menus and discover menus that are useful to know as you get started—the File, View, Window, and Help Menus. (You must have Windows and PowerPoint installed on your computer before you can do any of the exercises in this chapter. Appendix A tells you how to install PowerPoint.)

Using Standard Windows Features

Certain basic screen features are standard to Windows—clicking with the mouse, dragging, choosing from menus with the mouse or keyboard, controlling the size of windows, and so on. These features are the basis of Windows' considerable power. You may be familiar with these features already. If not, this section teaches you how to perform these tasks. By getting to know all the basic Windows features at the outset, you can use Windows most efficiently as you go along.

The following sections give brief descriptions of Windows features you will find valuable when you use PowerPoint. Refer to your Windows manual for complete explanations of all Windows features.

Using the Mouse

For most PowerPoint activities, you can use either a mouse or the keyboard. (For some of the drawing activities, explained in Chapter 5, "Drawing Objects," you must use the mouse.) The keyboard sometimes provides valuable shortcuts, but the mouse is the instrument of choice in Windows.

In fact, because you can do some things in PowerPoint *only* with a mouse, a mouse is required for PowerPoint.

To move the mouse pointer on the screen, move the mouse on your desktop. As you slide the mouse, the pointer moves accordingly. To point with the mouse, move the mouse until the tip of the on-screen pointer is in the position you want. To select an item, click the left mouse button once. When you have selected the item, it appears highlighted on the screen. To choose an item, double-click it (click the left mouse button twice quickly).

When you choose an item rather than highlight it, you initiate an action. For example, when you start PowerPoint (explained in the following section) you do not just highlight PowerPoint. You choose it by double-clicking.

You also can drag with the mouse, a capability that saves a great deal of time over using the keyboard. If, for example, you want to move the title of a slide, you can use the keyboard. Alternatively, as you see in Chapter 5, "Drawing Objects," you can point to the object, then hold down the mouse button while you slide the mouse to a different position. The cursor changes to a four-pointed arrow as you move the object. Another way to drag an object is to highlight it first, point to any edge of the box, and then drag it.

You can move to any place that is visible on the screen by moving the pointer to that position and clicking. Your entire slide may not be completely visible on-screen, particularly if you have been moving windows around and changing their sizes. To "scroll" through a slide, use the scroll bars on the right and bottom sides of the window.

The mouse pointer can take several shapes as you use it. The arrow is the most common shape. Use the arrow for "pointing"— choosing from menus, selecting objects, and similar operations. When the mouse pointer is a straight line (the I-beam), use it for typing or highlighting text. For drawing rectangles, lines, ovals, and text boxes, the pointer appears as a crosshair. As you see in Chapter 11, "Manipulating Pictures for Special Effects," the mouse pointer assumes a special shape when you use the cropping tool to crop (cover over) the outer parts of a graphic. When the program is completing some task and you have to wait, the pointer appears as an hourglass. When you are resizing windows, the pointer appears as a two-headed arrow. The two-headed arrow appears diagonally when you are resizing horizontally and vertically at the same time. A four-headed arrow is for moving objects with the keyboard instead of dragging them with the mouse.

Manipulating Windows

Just as you do not truly receive the benefit of Windows unless you use a mouse rather than the keyboard, so you do not truly put Windows to use unless you use multiple windows at one time. You can have PowerPoint running in one window and a word processor running in a second window. You also can have several PowerPoint windows open at the same time.

Two especially valuable Windows capabilities, maximize and minimize, are explained in this section. At the top right of each window you find the Maximize and Minimize buttons, identified by black pointers against white backgrounds (see fig. 1.1). As their names imply, these buttons enlarge or shrink windows currently on-screen. The important point to remember with PowerPoint is that the two buttons on the very top line refer to the PowerPoint application itself. Another Maximize/Minimize button, with two black pointers on the same button (one pointing up, the other down), refers to the presentation currently on-screen and affects only that particular window. (If the presentation screen has not been maximized, this button has only one arrow pointing up.)

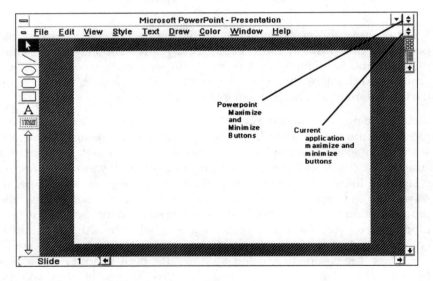

Fig. 1.1. The Maximize and Minimize buttons.

You can perform the operations of opening and closing windows, changing the "view" of the window (from full size to 50 percent size, for instance), and arranging windows with the PowerPoint menus, as explained in the sections on File, View, and Window later in this chapter.

Starting PowerPoint

Because PowerPoint is a Windows application, you can use it only within Windows. You can install PowerPoint from within Windows, as you find out in Appendix A. After you install PowerPoint, the Windows Application group window contains an icon called PowerPoint, which you use to invoke PowerPoint.

Starting PowerPoint is a simple matter of double-clicking icons with the mouse.

To start PowerPoint, follow these steps:

1. At the DOS prompt, type *win* and press Enter to enter Windows, if Windows is not already running.

   You see the main group window of Windows, called the Program Manager (see fig. 1.2). One of the icons in the Program Manager group window is Windows Applications.

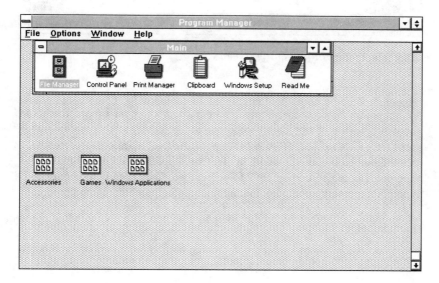

Fig. 1.2. The Windows Program Manager.

2. Double-click (press the left mouse button twice quickly) the Windows Applications group icon to open that menu.

3. Double-click the PowerPoint icon within the Windows Applications window.

The PowerPoint program starts. Figure 1.3 shows the PowerPoint opening screen.

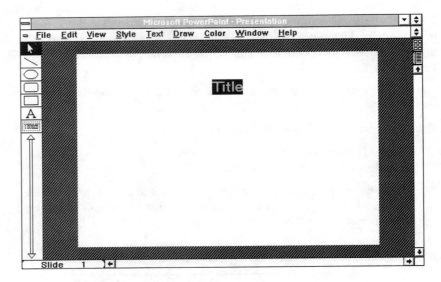

Fig. 1.3. The PowerPoint opening screen.

Tip: To start PowerPoint from the keyboard, type *win* from the DOS prompt to enter Windows. When you see the Main group window, press Ctrl-F6 to select (highlight) the Windows Applications group. Press Enter to open the window. In the Windows Applications window, press the arrow keys to select the PowerPoint icon, and then press Enter.

Getting Familiar with the PowerPoint Screen

If you know how to use Windows, you have a good idea of how to use PowerPoint. You can click and drag. You can expand and contract windows. You can choose from menus. Even though PowerPoint is a Windows application, it is nevertheless a separate application with certain features of its own. In this section, you look at the PowerPoint screen and begin to understand some of its features, as distinct from Windows features.

Across the top, the PowerPoint screen displays the words Microsoft PowerPoint. On the second line, you see the PowerPoint menu bar, with the choices File, Edit, View, Style, Text, Draw, Color, Window, and Help. On the third line (or next to the words Microsoft PowerPoint on the first line after you maximize a presentation so that it fills the window), you see the word Presentation. Figure 1.4 shows these parts of the PowerPoint display. When you name and save a presentation to disk, the name you give the presentation replaces the word Presentation.

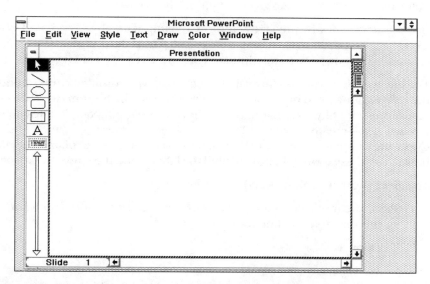

Fig. 1.4. *The top three lines of the PowerPoint screen.*

When you first start PowerPoint, the middle of the screen is blank except for the word Title. When you invoke PowerPoint, you see an unnamed presentation with one slide already created—the slide you see on the first screen. On the bottom left you see the words Slide 1. The current slide number always appears in this location.

Above and to the left of Slide 1 is a vertical line with arrows on the ends; this line is called the Slide Changer. You use it to change slides within a presentation by clicking the arrows or by dragging the marker, much as you do with vertical and horizontal scroll bars, as explained in Chapter 3, "Creating a Presentation."

Locating the Object Tools

Above the Slide Changer on the left side of the screen, you see the object tools: the arrow, the line, the oval, the rounded rectangle, the rectangle, the labeler, and the word processor. The top tool, shaped like an arrow, is the default tool. When you first enter a presentation, the arrow is selected, as indicated by the black background behind the arrow.

Use the default tool—the arrow tool—to manipulate already-created objects. See the section "Changing a Text Title" later in this chapter for an example showing how to manipulate text you already have created.

The line tool draws lines. The oval, the rectangle with rounded corners, and the conventional rectangle draw their own shapes. The bottom two tools—one represented by a capital A, the other by a broken rectangle enclosing minute text—create words and text in slides. Chapters 6, "Quick Start: Choosing Color Schemes," and 8, "Creating Basic Graphs," explain in detail how to use these tools, which are called the labeler and the word processor.

To select another tool, proceed as follows:

1. Place the mouse pointer arrow over the box for the tool you want, in this example the line tool.

2. Click once.

Tip: For the correct keyboard commands, select Keyboard from the Help menu (press Alt-H, then K). There you can choose Constraint Keys for Rectangles and Ovals and Constraint Keys for Lines—lists of keyboard equivalents to the tools.

The black background moves to the line tool from the arrow tool. The line changes to white, to distinguish it from the background. The arrow tool you used earlier changes to a white background with a black arrow. You select all other tools in the same way.

The shape of the cursor changes to a cross when you position it over the slide.

Using the Title Sorter and Slide Sorter

On the upper right side of the screen you see two icons that you may not have seen in other Windows applications. The icons are PowerPoint icons that enable you to work with more than one slide on your screen at the same time. The top icon, the Slide Sorter, enables you to work with your presentation as a series of slides. After you are in the Slide Sorter view, you can change the sequence of slides, delete them, or copy them.

If you prefer to work with the text names of slides rather than with pictures of the slides, you can copy, change the sequence, and delete slides with the Title Sorter, the second button on the upper right. See Chapter 3, "Creating a Presentation," for details on using the Title Sorter and Slide Sorter.

Changing the Title Text

When you first enter PowerPoint, `Title` appears in a black box. The Title is selected and available for you to change or delete. To manipulate this text, follow the steps described here. Notice that the tool in use is the arrow tool.

1. To deselect `Title`, click anywhere outside the black box and below the menu bar with your mouse pointer.

   The black box disappears, indicating that `Title` is no longer selected.

2. Next, reselect `Title` by placing the mouse pointer over the word `Title` and clicking once.

   This time the black box does not appear. You see a broken rectangle surrounding the word. The word `Title` is highlighted again, but now as part of an object within a selection box. Chapter 5 deals with manipulating objects. Here, you are looking at selecting text only.

3. Place your mouse cursor over the word `Title` and double-click.

   The black box reappears. The clicks need to be fast and close together or this procedure does not work.

4. Press the Backspace key to delete the word `Title`, leaving a large blinking vertical-line cursor.

   You then can type any new word that you want for the title. Alternatively, you can begin to type when the text is selected. The old text disappears. To distinguish this first slide from others, type *This is the first slide*. The words appear on the screen as shown in figure 1.5.

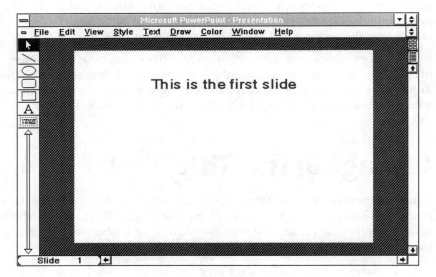

Fig. 1.5. Changing text on-screen.

After you type the text, change the vertical blinking cursor back to the arrow cursor.

5. Click anywhere on the screen below the line of menu titles and away from the text you just typed.

   The arrow pointer returns to the screen.

You now have seen the basic steps for changing text on the screen. In later chapters, you see in detail how to change both objects and text.

Reviewing the PowerPoint Menus

The basic menu in any Windows application is the Control menu in the upper left corner. You identify the Control menu by the horizontal line against a white background. You can use the menu options, shown in figure 1.6, to close, resize, and move the window (which is the presentation in PowerPoint).

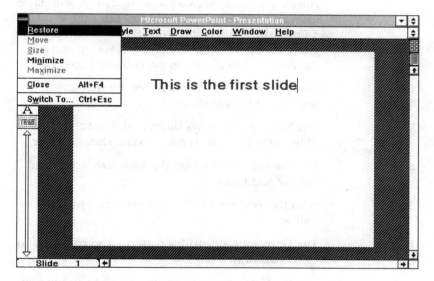

Fig. 1.6. *The Control menu.*

To select any menu with the mouse, point to the menu and click the left mouse button once. To select a menu with the keyboard, hold down the Alt key and press the underlined letter in the menu, such as the F key for the File menu. To select the presentation Control menu, press Alt-Hyphen. To select the application (PowerPoint) Control menu, press Alt-Space bar. To cancel any menu, click the file name again or click the mouse anywhere in the screen outside the menu. To cancel a menu from the keyboard, press the Esc key.

If a menu command appears in dimmed type, the command is not available. If three dots appear after the name of a command, choosing that command brings a dialog box on-screen. A check mark next to a command name indicates that the command is active. If a command has a key combination listed after it, you can use that key combination as a shortcut. If a menu command has a triangle to its right, clicking on that command leads to a drop-down menu with additional available commands.

Table 1.1
PowerPoint Menu Bar—Summary of Functions

Menu	Function
File	This menu provides access to the disk and gives the capability to open a new or existing presentation, close a presentation, save a presentation, and paste from another presentation. From this important menu, you also start the PowerPoint Graph program, set up the slide dimensions, set up and run the printer, run a slide show, and exit PowerPoint.
Edit	The Edit menu provides options for manipulating text and objects in slides.
View	The View menu shows slides in different sizes and different aspects, including several slides at once.
Style	Use this menu to change the font, size, color, and style of text in a slide.
Text	With the Text menu, you can place and find text in a slide.
Draw	The Draw menu provides patterns and background effects for drawn objects.
Color	Use the Color menu to color your slide and drawn objects.
Window	You can use this menu to move between windows and arrange windows.
Help	This menu provides the PowerPoint help facility.

After the menu is open, you can use one of several methods to select the command:

- Point to the command with the mouse and click
- Use the arrow keys to highlight your selection and then press Enter
- Press the underlined letter in the menu command
- Press the keyboard shortcut (when listed)

Table 1.1 gives a short description of the options each menu provides.

You will become familiar with all the menu options as you read this book. The following three sections discuss three menus that are useful to know from the outset—File, View, and Help. You are likely to use these menus during any PowerPoint session.

Using the File Menu

When you save a presentation in PowerPoint, the presentation becomes a file. The File menu enables you to access files. The File menu is the means PowerPoint provides to interact with presentations and with other files and to save the presentation that is on-screen. In this section, you learn how to use the most common functions of the File menu.

To access the File menu, click on the word File with your mouse pointer or press Alt-F on the keyboard. The menu drops down as shown in figure 1.7.

You now can choose any of the options from the File menu. One of the most useful options is Save, which is explained in the next section.

Saving Your Presentation

After you have started PowerPoint, you have a slide before you on the screen. The presentation is not a file on the disk, however, until you save it. After you have saved the file once, using Save replaces the original file with the current file. Save often as you work, to preserve your changes and to avoid losing them in case of a power failure. Follow these steps to save a presentation:

1. Select Save from the File menu, or press Alt-F-S. You see a dialog box, as shown in figure 1.8.

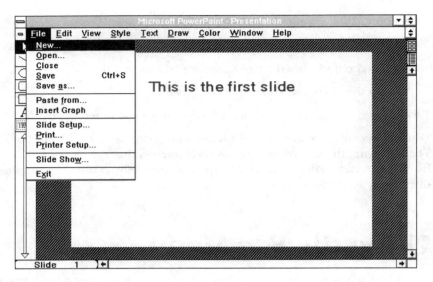

Fig. 1.7. *The File menu.*

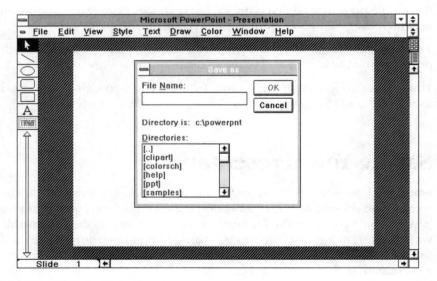

Fig. 1.8. *The Save dialog box.*

A line cursor is blinking under File Name. Type a file name here to save the file. The normal DOS file name rules apply: you can use up to eight characters before the dot separator and up to three after the dot separator. PowerPoint gives all its presentation files the extension PPT, unless you specify otherwise. Using this extension is best, because otherwise PowerPoint doesn't recognize the file as a PowerPoint presentation. See the section "Opening a Presentation" for more information on this point.

2. Type up to eight characters to name the presentation. For example, type *test*. (You can type in upper- or lowercase letters; DOS makes no distinction between them in file names.)

   Below the name you see `Directory is:`, followed by the current directory. The current directory should be C:\POWERPNT, created automatically when you installed PowerPoint. You can change to another directory by navigating in the Directories box using standard Windows procedures. Any file you save goes into the directory displayed in the dialog box.

   Change the current directory in PowerPoint the same way that you change the current directory in Windows and all its applications. To move up to a higher level (from the \POWERPNT subdirectory back up to C:\), double-click the [..] line in the directory box. To get into a lower subdirectory, double-click the line showing the subdirectory name in the directory box. For this example, use the displayed directory, C:\POWERPNT. From the keyboard, press Alt-D to select the Directories list box and use the arrow keys to change directories.

3. Click on the OK button to save the file to disk.

   The menu box disappears.

   To use the keyboard shortcut for Save, press Ctrl-S.

> *Tip:* To organize your "desktop," create a subdirectory called PPT within the PowerPoint directory and save all your presentation files to that subdirectory.

After you have saved the new presentation with the designated name, TEST.PPT in this example, the new name replaces the word `Presentation` at the top of the screen.

The Save As function works like the Save function except that Save As always asks for a name. Save asks for a name only when you save the new presentation for the first time. After that, using Save always saves the file on disk with the name displayed on top of the screen.

Use Save As when you want to create a new presentation similar to one already on file. Open the existing presentation and, as soon as it comes on-screen, use the Save As option to rename the presentation and save it to disk. (The original presentation remains unchanged under its original name.) Change the presentation as necessary. You now can keep the two presentations on file separately.

Opening and Closing Files

The Open, Close, and New options on the File menu work similarly to Save. Like all Windows applications, PowerPoint enables you to have multiple files open at the same time. You cannot, however, have two copies of the same file open at the same time (unless one of the two is untitled). The next section shows you how to open a presentation.

Opening a Presentation

PowerPoint opens a new presentation whenever you start the program. Often, however, you need to open an existing presentation. To do so, follow these steps:

1. Select Open from the File menu. (From the keyboard, press Alt-F-O.)

    You see the dialog box shown in figure 1.9.

    The Open dialog box functions much like the Save and Save As dialog boxes. The directory is the one you specified the last time you used any of the File menu options— C:\POWERPNT, in this example. The Files box on the left displays the PPT files in this directory—COLUMBUS.PPT and TEST.PPT. Other presentations in this directory may have extensions other than PPT, but PowerPoint does not recognize them. If you want to see a presentation file with an extension other than PPT, type the full name in the File Name box and click OK. If the file exists, PowerPoint brings it to the screen.

    To see a copy of the file COLUMBUS.PPT, continue following these steps.

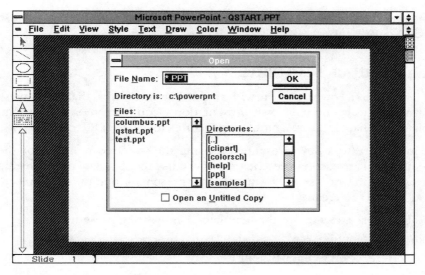

Fig. 1.9. *The Open dialog box.*

2. Click the empty square box (the check box) next to Open an Untitled Copy.

    An X appears in the box, indicating that this option is selected. If you open COLUMBUS.PPT without creating an untitled copy, the actual COLUMBUS.PPT file appears on the screen. When you select the Open an Untitled Copy option, a copy of the file appears on-screen. If you want, you can save the copy under another name.

3. Select COLUMBUS.PPT. (From the keyboard, press Alt-F, then press the down-arrow key until COLUMBUS.PPT is highlighted.)

    The black box around the title indicates that this file is selected. COLUMBUS.PPT appears in the File Name box.

4. Click OK or press Enter.

    The COLUMBUS.PPT file opens and is displayed on-screen.

    To open a file quickly, highlight the file name and double-click. The file opens and appears on-screen.

Closing a Presentation

The Close command on the File menu closes the presentation currently on display. Select Close from the File menu. If you have made any changes to the presentation, PowerPoint asks whether you want to save them. Choose Yes, No, or Cancel.

Opening a Template

A template is a PowerPoint file with an existing slide format that you can use or modify to create your own presentations. You learn more about templates in Chapter 11, "Manipulating Pictures for Special Effects."

You can create a new presentation using the standard template or the template of an existing presentation. If you use the template of an existing presentation, you use the format for that presentation in the new presentation that you create.

Follow these steps to use the template of an existing presentation:

1. Open a copy of the presentation that uses the template you want. Here, open COLUMBUS.PPT.

2. When the copy appears, select New from the File menu. You see the box shown in figure 1.10.

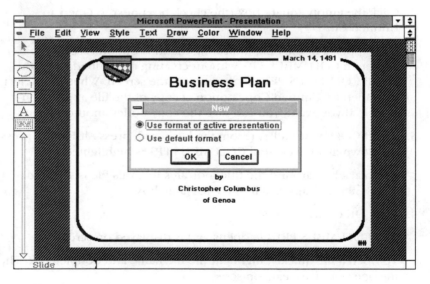

Fig. 1.10. The New dialog box under the File menu.

On the screen you see these two options: Use Format of Active Presentation (Alt-A) and Use Default Format (Alt-D). The default format is the initial PowerPoint settings, as explained in Chapter 3 and Appendix B. The first option, Use Format of Active Presentation, opens a new presentation using the template of the active (on-screen) presentation—in this case COLUMBUS.PPT. The blackened circle to the left of the option name shows that the option is currently active.

3. Click OK to accept the first option. You see the screen shown in figure 1.11.

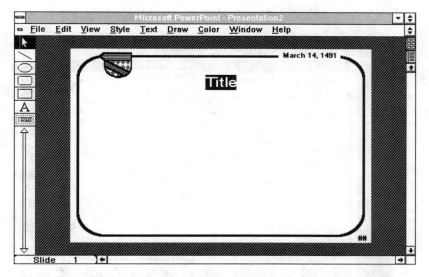

Fig. 1.11. *The template of COLUMBUS.PPT.*

This new presentation, using the template of COLUMBUS.PPT, has one slide (unlike COLUMBUS.PPT, which has many) and no text except Title. This template also has the background (the emblem, date, and black outline) of the original COLUMBUS.PPT.

The template option can save you a great deal of time if your company always uses a standard template. You need not re-create the standard elements from scratch. Just put the information into a template and use the template as the master for a presentation, as explained in Chapter 3, "Creating a Presentation."

Using the Window Menu

After you have used the File menu to open more than one presentation at a time, you can use the Window menu to manage those presentations.

In this chapter, you have created three separate presentations. To move among a number of presentations, do the following.

1. Open the Window menu (press Alt-W).

   In this example, you see five options, shown in figure 1.12.

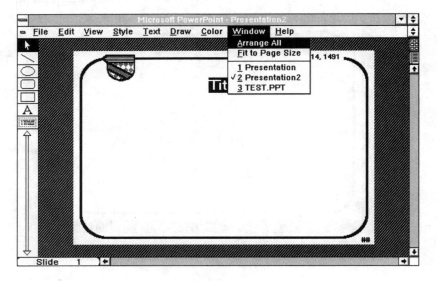

Fig. 1.12. *The Window menu in PowerPoint.*

Above the line are two commands that are always present—Arrange All and Fit to Page Size. Arrange All stacks your open presentations in the order in which you created them. Fit to Page Size resizes the active window to the same size as the slide in view.

Below the line is a list of all open presentations. In the example, three presentations are open: TEST.PPT, PRESENTATION, and PRESENTATION2. The check mark to the left of PRESENTATION2 indicates that it is the active presentation. PRESENTATION is the copy of COLUMBUS.PPT that you opened earlier and PRESENTATION2 is the template of that copy. Until you name the presentations, PowerPoint supplies them with these temporary identifications.

2. To activate another presentation, click the name in the Window menu, or press the underlined number in front of the name. For this example, select TEST.PPT.

To arrange all the presentations on-screen, click Arrange All in the Window menu or press Alt-A. All open presentations are stacked neatly on top of one another, with the titles showing above in the title bar, as illustrated in figure 1.13. You also see the main PowerPoint screen with the menu bar. If you close all open presentations, this main screen remains on-screen until you exit PowerPoint or open a new presentation.

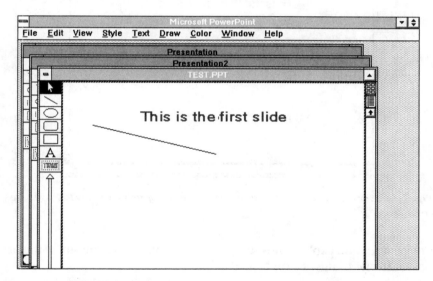

Fig. 1.13. Stacked screen presentations after using Arrange All from the Window menu.

You can move quickly between presentations when they are stacked in this way. Click once on any presentation window to activate the presentation. Whenever a portion of a presentation screen is visible, you can click it to make that presentation the active screen. To use the keyboard to move quickly between windows, press Ctrl-F6 to move down through the presentations in order. Although the preceding window disappears from view, it is still open and you can reselect it from the Window menu.

The other command on the Window menu, Fit to Page Size, makes the active presentation expand to fill the available room on-screen—a useful capability when you want to give all your attention to one presentation and want to have the maximum space in which to work. Open the Window menu and select Fit to Page Size. The result should be similar to that shown in figure 1.14.

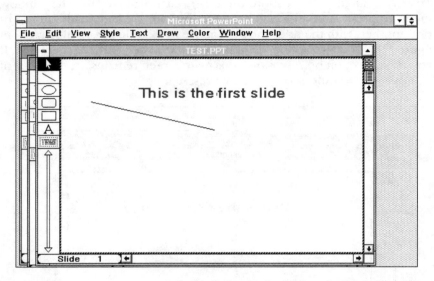

Fig. 1.14. *A presentation screen showing the result of using the Fit to Page Size command.*

The next section explains how to use the View menu to manipulate the on-screen image to fit your own needs.

Using the View Menu

Windows has exploded the old 640K barrier that limited DOS graphics applications to the use of 640K of random-access memory (RAM) at a time. When you use PowerPoint, you can load much more into memory at one time than you can when you use a DOS graphics application. With PowerPoint, you can load a multiple-slide presentation into memory and work with the entire presentation, instead of one slide or a small number of slides at a time.

The View menu controls how PowerPoint displays your slides. This menu is valuable when you work with multiple slides in a single presentation. The View menu, like the Window menu, enables you to see a display of several slides at a time. You can move among slides by choosing slides from the display. With the View menu, you also can see a list of your slide titles and use it to move among slides. Chapter 3 shows in detail how to use the View menu when you create your own presentations.

With the View menu, you control whether you view a slide master or a regular slide. (A slide master controls the format for all other slides in a presentation.) You also can choose to view notes, a notes master, or a handout page, all explained in Chapter 9. You can use the View menu to see whichever item you are viewing—a slide in this example—at Full Size, 66% Size, 50% Size, or 33% Size.

Changing the View

As you work with a presentation, you may want to change your "view" of the presentation and of individual slides. You may want to see slides at full size or in reduced size. You may want to view a master rather than slides. To change the slide view, follow these steps:

1. With the presentation on-screen, open the View menu (press Alt-V from the keyboard).

   The first four options are Full Size, 66% Size, 50% Size, and 33% Size. The check mark to the left of 50% Size indicates that this size is active. The display you see on-screen is 50 percent of the largest scale you can display on-screen.

2. Select Full Size (press F). The result should be similar to that shown in figure 1.15.

Use the scroll bar tools to scroll through the slide. (The keyboard has no alternative for scrolling.) For example, click the upward-pointing arrow (the scroll bar arrow) on the right scroll bar. The screen "moves down." Click as many times as necessary to see what is above the current view. The words Business Plan should come into view. Now try the other arrow. Each arrow "moves" the screen in the direction the arrow points.

Between the arrows on the right (and also between the arrows on the bottom), you see a white box. The position of this box indicates which portion of the screen is on display. If the block is near the bottom arrow on the right scroll bar, then the bottom portion of the slide is displayed. Click the arrow and notice how the white blocks move.

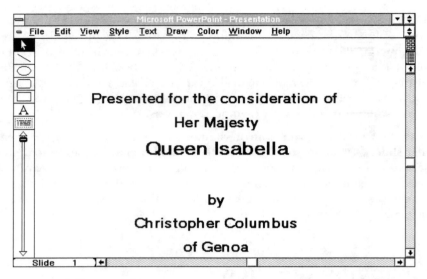

Fig. 1.15. A full-size screen.

To try other views, click again on View and then on any of the remaining sizes—66% Size and 33% Size—to see how the screen changes.

Displaying Many Slides

As you create new slides and develop full slide shows, you may want to see an overview of what you have created. You can use two options in the View menu to get an overview: the Slide Sorter and the Title Sorter.

To use the Slide Sorter, select Slide Sorter from the View menu. Use Alt-V-L from the keyboard.

The slides are displayed in order, top to bottom and left to right (see fig. 1.16). To make any of the nine slides on display the active (on-screen) presentation, place the mouse pointer over the slide you want to see and click twice. The slide comes on-screen, filling the entire window. Double-clicking a slide in the Slide Sorter has no keyboard equivalent.

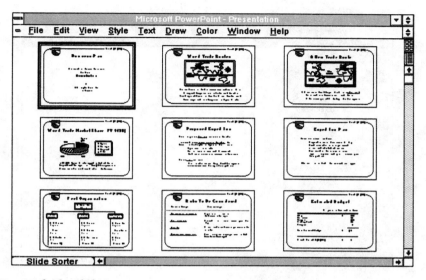

Fig. 1.16. *The Slide Sorter screen showing many slides at one time.*

You can summon the multiple-slide view in another way. On the right side of the screen, directly above the scroll bar arrow, you see two boxes that are actually buttons. The top button is the Slide Sorter button. Place the mouse pointer over the Slide Sorter button and click. You see the Slide Sorter view.

You also can use the Title Sorter view to get an overview of your slides. Like the Slide Sorter, you can access the Title Sorter through the View menu or with a button. The Title Sorter button is directly underneath the Slide Sorter button on the right side of your screen.

To use the Title Sorter, follow these steps:

1. Click the Title Sorter button. PowerPoint replaces the slides with a list (11 entries in this example) of slide titles, as shown in figure 1.17. Alternatively, select the Title Sorter from the View menu (Alt-V-T if you are using a keyboard).

2. To see a particular slide, place the mouse pointer over the title and click twice. (This step has no keyboard equivalent.)

The View menu is very useful when you are working with multiple slides in a presentation. See Chapter 3, "Creating a Presentation," for a full discussion of how to use the View menu commands in a presentation.

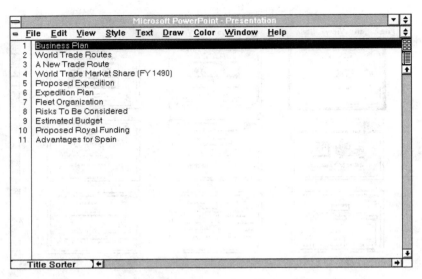

Fig. 1.17. The Title Sorter screen showing a list of your slide titles.

Getting Help

The Help menu, at the far right of the menu bar, is useful for looking up individual topics quickly. The Help menu has four options—Index, Keyboard, Using Help, and About.

To get help, click the Help menu in the menu bar or press Alt-H. You see the drop-down menu shown in figure 1.18.

The About option lists copyright and version information about PowerPoint. The Using Help option displays a small drop-down box with a message to look for help in the Index option, and then offers you the choice of going to the Index option.

Using the Help Index

The Index option prompts you through a series of menus to break down your topic into the smallest unit. Suppose that you want to look up the menu topic Slides (#1) from the View menu. Follow these steps to find out about this topic:

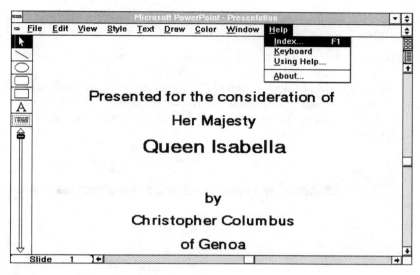

Fig. 1.18. The Help menu options.

1. Select Index from the Help menu. If you are using the keyboard, press Alt-H-I.

    The drop-down Help Index screen shows a list of topics that begins with Using Help (see fig. 1.19). To the right of the list is a scroll bar.

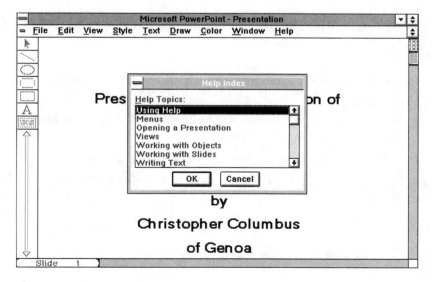

Fig 1.19. The Help Index screen.

2. Find the topic you want. Click the down arrow to see the rest of the topics.

3. To get to the next level of help, place the mouse pointer over the topic you want and click twice. Alternatively, click once over the topic to highlight it and then click OK. From the keyboard, select the topic by highlighting it using the up- or down-arrow key and then press Enter. For example, if you select Menus, the list in figure 1.20 appears.

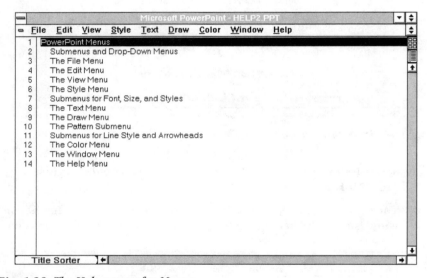

Fig. 1.20. The Help screen for Menus.

All 14 topics on this screen cover menus. Select the topic you want to see.

4. Place the mouse pointer over your choice and click twice. (This step has no keyboard equivalent.)

If you choose The View Menu, you see the screen shown in figure 1.21.

Help briefly explains each menu option on the View menu. The explanation for Slides (#1) is Shows the current slide.

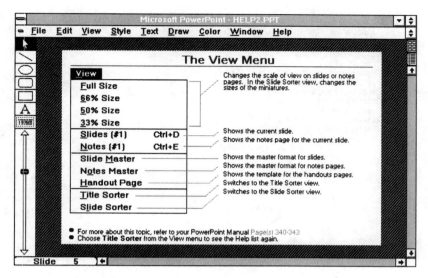

Fig. 1.21. *The Help screen for the View menu.*

You must close the file to exit this Help screen. Select Close from the File menu or press Alt-F-C. Your presentation slide appears on-screen. Use similar steps to investigate other topics on the Index menu.

Using the Keyboard Help Option

You use the Keyboard option in the same way that you use the Index option. The Keyboard option gives keystrokes that are useful shortcuts to using the mouse or for drawing objects. To access keyboard help, follow these steps:

1. Select Keyboard from the Help menu or press Alt-H-K (see fig. 1.22). A list of topics appears on-screen.

2. Select the topic for which you want help. For example, click twice on the Zapf Dingbat Keyboard (1 of 6) option. A screen showing Zapf Dingbat characters appears (see fig. 1.23).

If you have changed the font to Zapf Dingbat, you produce the character shown in the Character column when you press the key shown in the KeyCap column. (Fonts and Zapf Dingbats are explained in Chapters 4 and 12.)

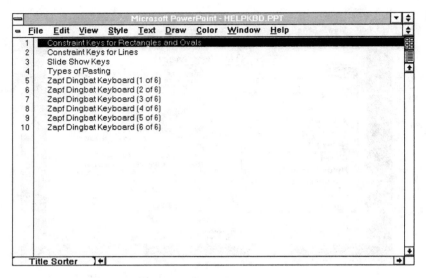

Fig. 1.22. The Keyboard Help options.

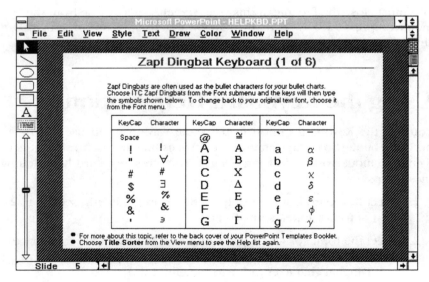

Fig. 1.23. The Zapf Dingbat Keyboard (1 of 6) screen in Keyboard help.

Chapter Summary

In this chapter, you learned how to start PowerPoint. You reviewed standard Windows features, such as using the mouse and using the Maximize and Minimize buttons. You became familiar with the icons on the PowerPoint screen, and you also learned how to change text on the screen. This chapter showed you how to make selections from PowerPoint menus and helped you become familiar with the menus that you are likely to use in most of your presentations—File, Window, and View. Finally, you saw how to turn to the Help files for on-line guidance with your activities.

Now that you have become familiar with Windows, you are ready to put your knowledge to use by creating an actual presentation. You do that in the next chapter.

2

Quick Start: Creating Your First Presentation

In this quick start, you create a new presentation and perform some of the basic functions available in PowerPoint. If you work through this quick start and try all the steps, you will get practice in learning how to use PowerPoint.

You learn how to open a new presentation and change the title of the first slide. Next, you learn how to add multiple lines of text to your screen. To do that, you need to manipulate one of the object tools available in PowerPoint. You use one object tool to draw a text block and another to draw a rectangle around your text to improve the appearance of the slide. You finish this quick start session by saving your work and exiting PowerPoint.

Starting PowerPoint

You should have installed PowerPoint before using this quick start. See Appendix A of this book if you need help with installation. PowerPoint works through Windows, so before you can use PowerPoint, you must open Windows. To start PowerPoint, follow these steps:

1. At the DOS prompt, type *win* to start Windows.

    Windows opens and displays the Program Manager group window with the title `Program Manager` across the top of the first window (see fig. 2.1). Your own screen will be similar to the screen shown here, but not necessarily identical.

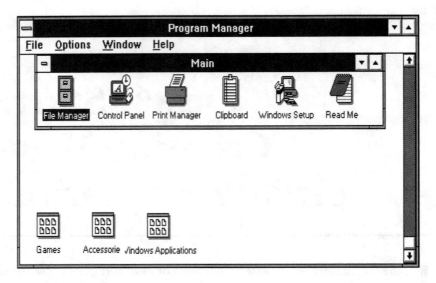

***Fig. 2.1.** The Windows Program Manager.*

2. Activate the Window menu.

   To open a menu, place the mouse pointer over the menu name and click once, or press Alt and the underlined letter in the menu name. Here, press Alt-W to open the Window menu.

   The Window menu drops down, showing you the available choices, as shown in figure 2.2.

3. Select Windows Applications.

   To select a menu command, use your mouse pointer to point to the option, then click once. With the keyboard, use the arrow keys to highlight the option and then press Enter, or press the underlined letter (the underlined numeral, in this case).

   The Windows Applications group window opens up. In it, you see a drawing that looks like a letter with two stamps. Underneath the drawing is the title `PowerPoint`. This drawing is the PowerPoint icon.

4. Position your mouse pointer on the PowerPoint icon and double-click.

You see the screen shown in figure 2.3.

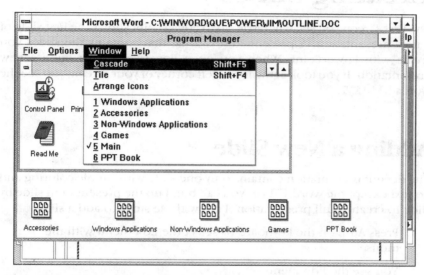

Fig. 2.2. *The Window menu.*

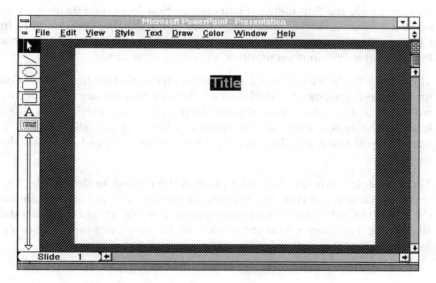

Fig. 2.3. *The PowerPoint screen.*

PowerPoint is now up and running.

Creating Slides

The first screen you see when you open PowerPoint shows the first slide of a new presentation. A presentation is a file that contains the slides you create with PowerPoint. When you open PowerPoint, you open a new presentation. If you look at the lower left corner of your screen, you see the words Slide 1.

Adding a New Slide

The default presentation contains only one slide with simple coloring and no text except the word Title. You can build up the presentation slide by slide to create a full presentation. Follow these steps to add a slide:

1. Press Alt-E on the keyboard or select the Edit menu with the mouse.

   You see the Edit menu.

2. From the Edit menu, choose New Slide (or press N).

Be sure to use the Edit menu. If you choose New from the File menu, you open a new presentation, not a new slide in the existing presentation. In Chapter 3, "Creating a Presentation," you find out more about how PowerPoint works in presentations, as well as with slides.

The new slide, shown in figure 2.4, is almost identical to the first slide. If you look at the slide number in the lower left, you see that you are now working with Slide 2. If you had entered something on the slide master (discussed later in the quick start, in the section "Changing the Slide Master"), whatever you entered—a logo or a date, for example—would appear on the new slide.

The new slide's title is in the same place as the preceding slide's title. The text in the title is selected. PowerPoint encourages you to create a title for the new slide right away. When you create a new title, PowerPoint lists the slide in the Title Sorter. You can work with the slide from the Title Sorter, as you see in the next section.

Moving from One Slide to Another

In PowerPoint, you do not work with a single slide, as was often the case with pre-Windows graphics programs, but with a complete presentation made up of more than one slide. You can move from one slide to another in a number of ways. The simplest way is to scroll through the slides one at a time.

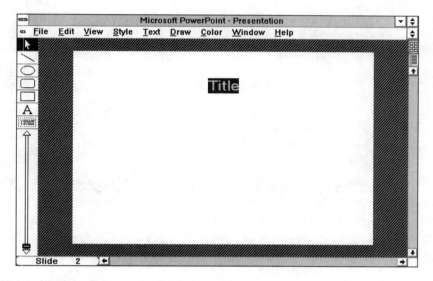

Fig. 2.4. *A new slide created from the preceding slide.*

To return to the first slide, click on the top arrow of the Slide Changer, located at the lower left of the PowerPoint screen, as shown in figure 2.5.

Slide 1 returns to the screen. When you have more than one slide, you can drag the rectangle in the Slide Changer until the slide you want is on-screen. The Slide Counter shows the number of the slide currently selected.

Rather than use the Slide Changer, you can press PgUp or PgDn on the keyboard to move up or down one slide at a time. To choose a slide by name, click on the Title Sorter (explained in Chapter 1), and then choose the title that you want. To select the slide you want by viewing, use the Slide Sorter and from there choose the slide you want.

You now can create slides one at a time and move from one slide to another. The next section explains how you can begin with a finished, professional presentation and adapt it to your own needs.

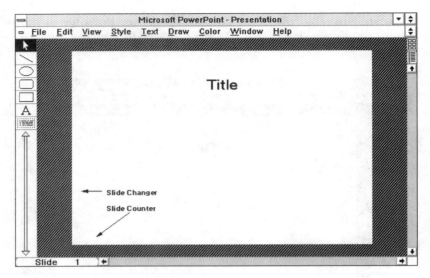

***Fig. 2.5.** The Slide Changer and Slide Counter.*

Adapting an Existing Template

An easy way to start a presentation is to use the presentation templates provided with PowerPoint. Templates are skeleton presentations with professionally designed backgrounds, color schemes, and text formatting. Using templates gives you a head start in creating your presentation.

First, close the on-screen presentation. Choose Close from the File menu by clicking File with the mouse pointer and then clicking Close. Alternatively, press Alt-F on the keyboard and then press C. Your window goes blank except for the title bar and the menu bar. Now, use the following steps to access a template.

1. Choose Open from the File menu.

   You see the dialog box shown in figure 2.6.

   The box labeled Files shows all PowerPoint files in the current directory that have a PPT extension. If you have not created another presentation, you see only the sample presentation, COLUMBUS.PPT, listed here. The Directory Is line shows the current directory, C:\POWERPNT.

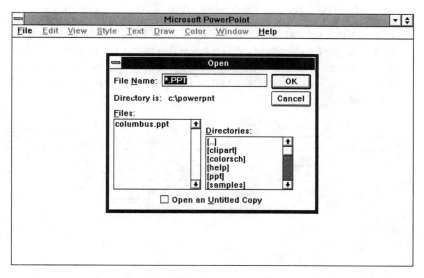

Fig. 2.6. The Open dialog box.

You want to get to the template subdirectory. A box to the right, called Directories, lists the subdirectories within PowerPoint. If TEMPLATE is not visible, scroll down using the scroll bar, as explained in Chapter 1.

2. Go to the TEMPLATE subdirectory by clicking on the line that says [template] and then click OK. Alternatively, you can double-click [template]. You also can use the Tab and Enter keys on the keyboard to navigate through the screen. Press Tab to move forward from one field to the next, Shift-Tab to move backward one field at a time, and Enter to accept the selection.

The Directories box now shows another list of subdirectories: 35MM, GRAPHS, OVERHEAD, and STRYBRDS. These subdirectories contain templates for different uses, as explained in Chapter 3, "Creating a Presentation." In this example, suppose that you want to create 35 millimeter slides.

3. Select the 35MM subdirectory.

A list of presentations that starts with BLUEDIAG.PPT appears in the Files box, as shown in figure 2.7.

These presentations are the templates that PowerPoint provides to help you set up a new presentation. When you have time, go through the presentations to see which ones you like best. Suppose that you want to use the presentation template CIRCLES.PPT. If you open CIRCLES.PPT and change it, you no longer can use CIRCLES.PPT as a template. To keep the template intact, activate the Open an Untitled Copy option, located at the bottom of the dialog box. You now open a copy of the file rather than the original.

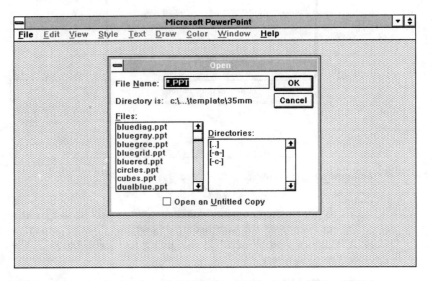

Fig. 2.7. *The Open dialog box showing the template files in the 35MM subdirectory.*

4. Select the Open an Untitled Copy option by clicking it or by pressing Alt-U from the keyboard. *Note:* To use the keyboard to select from the menu bar, press Alt and the underlined letter. To select from a submenu, press the underlined letter by itself. To select from a dialog box, press Alt and the underlined letter.

   Now you can open the presentation.

5. Open the copy CIRCLES.PPT presentation template. Click twice on CIRCLES.PPT or click CIRCLES.PPT once and then click OK.

You now see the screen shown in figure 2.8.

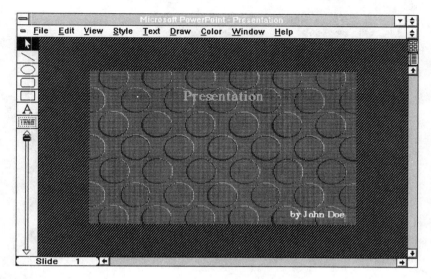

Fig. 2.8. The first slide of the copy of the CIRCLES.PPT presentation template.

You can make changes to this set of slides without altering the original template, as you see in subsequent sections of this quick start.

Saving a Presentation

The presentation now exists only in RAM, the working area of the computer. To make the presentation permanent, you must save it to disk. To save the presentation, follow these directions:

1. Choose File from the menu bar.

2. Choose Save.

   After you save a file for the first time, you only need to select Save to save the file. In this example, however, the file, or presentation, that you are saving has no name. PowerPoint prompts you for the information through a dialog box, shown in figure 2.9.

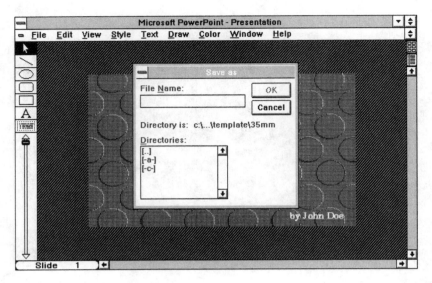

Fig. 2.9. The Save dialog box.

A cursor is blinking under File Name. Type a file name here before you save the file. PowerPoint gives all its presentation files the extension .PPT, unless you specify otherwise.

3. Type *qstart*.

   Next, you must specify the directory into which the file should go. PowerPoint specifies the current directory after the words Directory Is. Any file that you save goes into the current directory. If you have been following the steps in this chapter, the screen should read `C:\...\template\35mm`. The three dots in the middle stand for PowerPoint; in this case, the Directory Is line is too small to display the full directory location. You should keep this particular directory for template presentations, so save your new file to another directory. For this example, suppose that you want to save the file to the main PowerPoint directory, POWERPNT.

4. To go up one directory level, double-click [..] in the Directories box or navigate with the keyboard.

   Now the Directory Is line reads `c:\powerpnt\template`.

5. Go up one more directory level by clicking twice on [..].

   You now are in C:\POWERPNT.

6. Click OK to save the file to disk. Alternatively, press Enter.

The menu box disappears. You have created the file QSTART.PPT in the POWERPNT directory. The name of the new file now appears along the top of the PowerPoint window. Now you are ready to work on your new presentation. In the next section, you learn how to modify your slide master—the slide that acts as a background to all other slides on the presentation.

Changing the Slide Master

You can save a great deal of time and duplicated effort by using a slide master. Everything on a slide master appears on each slide in the presentation, unless you deliberately block out something on an individual slide. For example, if you put the date of the presentation or the company name on the slide master, you need not copy that information to each individual slide. For this example, suppose that you want to put the company name, Golden Dome Landscaping, and a design rectangle on each slide. To achieve this goal, choose View from the menu bar (Alt-V). Click Slide Master or press M. You see the screen shown in figure 2.10.

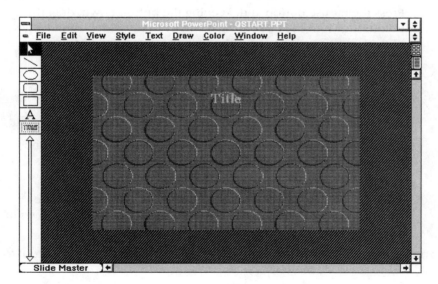

Fig. 2.10. The Slide Master of the new presentation.

In this case, the master is almost identical to Slide 1, as shown in figure 2.8. The word `Title` is at the center of the screen, instead of the word `Presentation`, as on Slide 1. The style of the title, including font and size, is the same for other slides as for the master. Whatever text you type on the master also appears on every other slide. Here, leave `Title` as the text.

The next step in creating this slide master is to create a rectangle as a border around the slide, as shown in the next section.

Drawing a Rectangle

The tool bar, explained in Chapter 1, runs along the left side of each PowerPoint screen. Each tool appears in a separate box. The top tool is the arrow tool. The third tool down from the arrow tool is the round-cornered rectangle tool. Select this tool by following these steps:

1. Click on the round-cornered rectangle tool in the tool bar.

2. Place the mouse pointer (now in the shape of a crosshair) in the upper left corner of the slide, still on the part of the screen with circles in the background, but quite close to the corner.

3. Press the mouse button and, keeping the button down, drag the pointer down to the bottom right corner of the slide. Don't let go of the button until you want the shape to be permanent.

4. Release the mouse button.

   The rectangle is selected after you first draw it. If you are not satisfied with the rectangle, press Del to delete it, then repeat steps 2 and 3.

   The newly drawn rectangle remains selected, as indicated by the dotted rectangle with black dots in each corner that surrounds the line rectangle.

5. Click the pointer anywhere outside the selected rectangle. The dotted rectangle disappears, and you see the rectangle, as shown in figure 2.11.

You have created a drawn object. Next, you learn to use the labeler tool to add text to the slide master.

Adding Text with the Labeler Tool

Using the labeler tool is the simplest way to put text on a slide. Here, because you want to write only the company name on the slide master, use the labeler rather than the word processing tool, both of which are discussed in Chapter 4, "Adding Text to a Presentation." To add the company name, follow these steps:

1. Select the labeler tool by clicking on the button with the letter A in the row of tools.

2. Place the cursor (now in the shape of a vertical line) in the upper left corner of the slide, just inside the rectangle you drew previously. Click the mouse button.

3. Type *Golden Dome Landscaping*.

4. Click on the arrow tool to deselect the labeler.

You now have your company name on the slide, surrounded by a border.

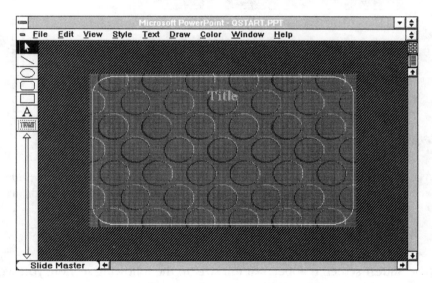

Fig. 2.11. A drawn rounded-corner rectangle around a slide.

Viewing the Slides

Use the Slide Sorter button to check to see that everything you drew and typed on the slide master appears on all the other slides.

1. Click on Slide Sorter, located on the right side of the screen just under the Maximize/Minimize buttons.

Your screen now displays the seven slides that make up this presentation and that you copied when you copied the template (see fig. 2.12). Remember that the slide master is only background and never appears as a slide in your presentation.

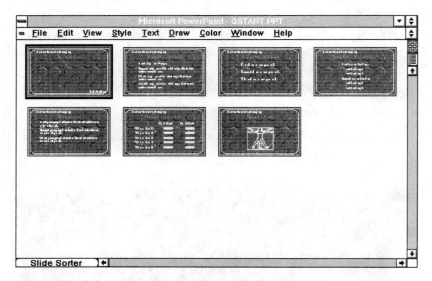

Fig. 2.12. The Slide Sorter view after changing the slide master.

Each slide has a white rectangular border. The text that you typed appears in the upper left corner, although the individual words are indistinguishable in this view. Now return to Slide 1.

2. Place the pointer over the slide in the upper left portion of the display and click twice.

The Slide 1 screen reappears at full size. In the following section, you see how to add text to this slide.

Editing Text

Each slide comes with a title. You can delete the words in the title or you can change them. To change the title, do the following:

1. Double-click on the word `Presentation`.

   If you double-click quickly enough, a yellow box encloses the word. (On black-and-white screens, the box is black.) You now can edit the text. If you click only once, the text box itself becomes selected, and a dotted rectangle surrounds the word. You then can move or resize the text box as an object. If the dotted rectangle appears on your screen, double-click again on the word.

   The yellow box indicates that the word is highlighted, or selected. In PowerPoint, you can change anything that is selected. Now change the title.

2. Type *Improving Your Home*.

You don't need to erase the word `Presentation`. Any character key that you press replaces the entire highlighted section. After you finish typing, click anywhere outside the text box to deselect it. Now your screen should look like figure 2.13.

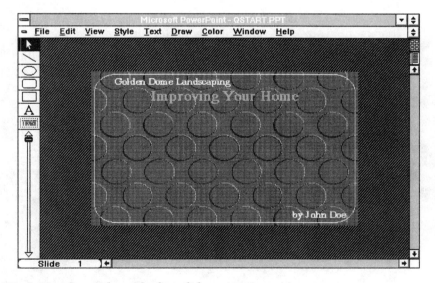

Fig. 2.13. *A new title on the first slide.*

Now you can add additional explanatory text to this slide, as explained in the next section.

Adding Text with the Word Processor Tool

You can use the word processor tool to add text of any length to a slide. The word processor tool is the bottom tool. Use it to draw a text box and then enter text in the box. A text box is the approximate area where you plan to enter text. The text box need not be exact: it expands if you type more text than it can hold as originally drawn.

To use the word processor tool, follow these steps:

1. Place the mouse pointer over the word processor tool and click once to select it.

   Move the mouse pointer to the slide. The pointer takes the shape of a crosshair, as it did earlier when you used the rounded-corner rectangle tool. Drawing a text box—a container to hold your writing—is similar to drawing any shape.

2. Position your mouse pointer about one line down from the words Improving Your Home and directly under the G in Golden.

3. Hold down the mouse button and drag the crosshair down to the right until you almost reach the D in John Doe.

4. Release the mouse button.

   The result is a dotted rectangle similar to that shown in figure 2.14.

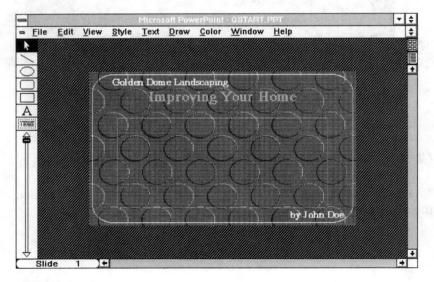

Fig. 2.14. *A text box.*

On your screen, notice the I-beam blinking in the upper left portion of the new text box. This cursor indicates that PowerPoint is ready for you to begin typing. As soon as you draw the text box, the arrow tool replaces the word processor tool as the selected tool. Whenever you finish using one of the other tools, you return to the arrow tool, which is the default tool. Nevertheless, the cursor remains in the form of the I-beam. You are ready to enter text.

Because you want certain words to appear on certain lines for formatting reasons, use the Enter key rather than automatic word wrap to determine your line breaks.

5. Type the following text: *This is a brief slide presentation by*.

6. Press the Enter key and type the following: *The Golden Dome Landscaping Company*.

7. Press Enter again and type the last line: *showing the benefits of using our expertise*.

The result is shown in figure 2.15.

Fig. 2.15. *Text in a text box.*

Now that your text is on the screen, you can format it to look better.

Formatting Text

The text on your slide at this point looks uneven on the screen. This section shows you how to improve its appearance.

After you have typed the text, the cursor is located after the period following the word expertise. You want to center the text lines in the text box. First, select all the lines, as follows:

1. Hold down the mouse button, and drag the mouse pointer to the top left word of the text: This.

   If you are using a color monitor, the background of the area over which you drag the pointer changes to a different color, yellow in this presentation. On a monochrome monitor, the selected text appears in reversed video. This color change indicates that the text is selected.

2. Release the mouse button after you have selected all the text.

3. If you are using a mouse, click on the Text menu. From the keyboard, press Alt-T. The Text menu drops down, as shown in figure 2.16.

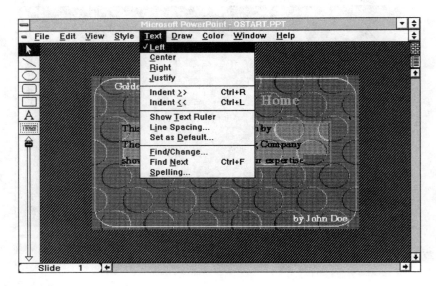

Fig. 2.16. The Text menu.

4. Select Center by clicking on the option. From the keyboard, use the arrow keys to highlight the Center option and then press Enter, or press C.

   The menu disappears, and each line of text centers itself within the text block. The text remains selected. Next, you want to italicize the words of the text block to distinguish them from the title.

5. Choose Italic from the Style menu. Your text is now centered and italicized.

   Both the Style and Text menus offer options to alter the text on your slide. Use the Style options to affect the appearance of your text by making it plain or italic or to change the fonts or text size. Use the Text menu to affect the positioning of your text.

6. Click outside the text box with the mouse pointer to deselect the text.

The black background and the dots outlining the text box disappear. The result is shown in figure 2.17.

Fig. 2.17. *Centered and italicized text within an invisible text box.*

This first slide of your presentation is your introductory slide. It has a title, `Improving Your Home`, and a brief explanation in the text block of what the viewers will see in your presentation.

Deleting an Object

Keep your slides uncluttered to make them more readable. You now can delete from Slide 1 the text block containing the words by John Doe, located in the bottom right corner of the slide. To remove these words, follow these steps:

1. Select the text block by clicking once over the words by John Doe. A dotted selection rectangle appears around the text. Alternatively, you can double-click to select the text itself, and then drag the mouse to select all the text.

2. Press the Del key.

   The object disappears.

You now have seen the basic techniques for creating and editing text in PowerPoint. When you create your own presentations, you will continue to add text, objects, and additional slides until you have your full presentation, as explained in Chapters 3 and 4.

Exiting PowerPoint

After you have completed your session, you can save the presentation and exit the program. If you choose Exit before you choose Save, PowerPoint prompts you to see whether you want to save what you have created since the last session. To exit PowerPoint, follow these steps:

1. Press Ctrl-S to save the changes you made in the presentation.

   After you finish and save a presentation, you can close the presentation and remain in PowerPoint or you can quit PowerPoint altogether. In this case, you now want to exit PowerPoint.

2. Open the File menu.

3. Select Exit.

   You exit PowerPoint.

Chapter Summary

This chapter introduced you to some basic procedures you need to know to use PowerPoint. You saw how to enter PowerPoint through Windows, create a new slide, and move through slides in a presentation. You closed the default presentation and copied a PowerPoint template from the template subdirectory, and then you named and saved the new presentation. You drew a rectangle and wrote the company name on the slide master, so that both would appear on each individual slide in the presentation. You then changed the title of the first slide and used the word processor tool to create a text box and to enter text. You centered and italicized the text and saved the whole presentation for future use. Finally, you exited PowerPoint.

You are now able to use PowerPoint. You can begin to see how the program lives up to its name—*Power*Point—when you learn how to manage entire presentations in the next chapter.

3

Creating a Presentation

Y ou cannot put the true power of PowerPoint to use until you work with overall presentations rather than with individual slides. In DOS, the basic unit you work with in any program is almost always the individual graph, drawing, or slide, not the overall presentation consisting of multiple graphs, drawings, and slides.

DOS-based graphics programs may encourage you to work with presentations and may attempt to provide tools for doing so. Because of the 640K memory restriction, however, DOS graphics programs can go only so far in enabling you to work with multiple slides—an overall presentation.

In PowerPoint, you work with all the slides in the presentation as a single Windows file that you can see all at once on the screen. Because PowerPoint has so much more memory than a DOS-based graphics program and puts the memory to use to handle large numbers of slides, this Windows program is a "paradigm shift" from DOS graphics programs. That is, you operate in a new environment with possibilities not available in a DOS-based graphics program, which causes you to think about the graphics-creation process in a new way. With PowerPoint, you not only do what you used to do but perhaps you do it faster and better.

Windows-based graphics programs offer you more than the capability to "point and click" and otherwise use the graphical user interface "intuitively." Programs like PowerPoint enable you to work with the overall presentation rather than with the individual slides (although, as later chapters show, you can work with the individual slides with more power in PowerPoint than in a DOS-based program).

You begin this chapter by finding out how to start PowerPoint and how to set the defaults (the settings that apply to every slide in a presentation). Next, you see how to create a presentation one slide at a time.

You also see how to create a presentation "from the outside in," beginning with the template of a finished presentation. Presentation templates are highly polished, finished presentations. They already apply most of the things you will know about PowerPoint after you become an expert, and they apply the knowledge you would have if you took the time and training to become a professional artist. Using templates can save you much time and give superior results.

After you see how to choose a template, you find out how to create the slide master, the slide that is the heart of any template and that controls the appearance of every slide in the presentation. You then see how to view the presentation in different ways—the slide view, the title view, and a view of an individual slide.

After you see how to change the views of a presentation, you find out how to use those views when you rearrange the presentation, add slides, and delete slides. Finally, you find out how to save a presentation and exit PowerPoint.

With these tools, you have the capability, for the first time in PC graphics programs, to work with entire presentations at once. The templates enable you to work with an entire presentation that looks professional even before you begin. After you learn how to work with an entire presentation, you learn in later chapters how to change text and objects on the individual slides in a presentation.

Creating a Presentation

PowerPoint makes working with an overall presentation and adapting a finished product to your needs easy. A basic PowerPoint presentation, however, consists of the familiar ingredients that you know from your own presentations: individual slides that you create one at a time.

To create a PowerPoint presentation, you follow these general steps:

1. Start PowerPoint and open a new presentation or make an untitled copy of an existing presentation.

2. From the File menu, choose Printer Setup and set up your printer, as explained in Chapter 9, "Creating Output." The printer that you choose determines the fonts that you have available.

3. If you want, from the File menu, choose Slide Setup, explained in Chapter 9. You use Slide Setup to specify the dimensions and numbering of your slides. In most cases, however, you can use the defaults.

4. Review templates to see if one matches your needs, as explained in this chapter in the section "Selecting a Template." If you find a template that suits your needs, all your design considerations are set before you begin. You need change only the content.

5. If you want to use the PowerPoint defaults (the initial settings that apply to every presentation you create), go to the next step. If you want to change the defaults for color scheme, the specific colors in the color scheme, font sizes and styles, indents, tabs, and line spacing, change them now. See the section "Setting PowerPoint Defaults" in this chapter for more information on defaults.

6. Review the slide master and, if necessary, make changes, as explained in this chapter in the sections "Creating a New Slide Master" and "Copying an Existing Slide Master."

7. Create the slides for your presentation by adapting them from the template or by creating them fresh. Chapters 4 and 5 cover working with text and graphics. Chapter 7 shows you how to add color, and Chapter 8 explains the Graph feature. Part II of this book covers advanced text, graphics, color, and graph features.

8. Manage the slides as you go along. Use the Slide Sorter and Title Sorter to rearrange the slides.

9. Create the notes pages for each slide, as explained in Chapter 9, "Creating Output."

10. Print the presentation or create other output, as explained in Chapter 9.

11. Save the presentation. See the section "Saving and Exiting" in this chapter.

Starting PowerPoint

If you know how to use Windows, you know how to start PowerPoint. Choose PowerPoint from the Windows Applications group window (or from the window where you have it stored). You see the PowerPoint opening screen—a window with the name Presentation at the top. You have started PowerPoint and are now in a presentation. From here you can create slides, rearrange slides, and save the presentation.

Most of the time you will work with a presentation by creating an original presentation or by working from a template. To create a new presentation, you do not have to do anything more. You can work with the initial presentation, titled Presentation, that PowerPoint gives you. Often, however, you will want to give your presentation a more descriptive name. To name a presentation, do the following:

1. Choose File from the menu bar.

   You see the File menu, shown in figure 3.1

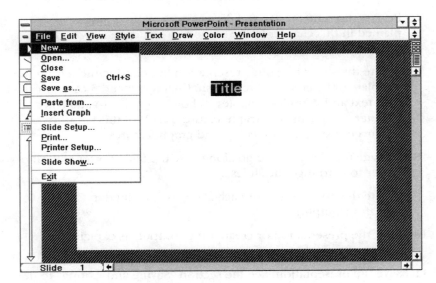

Fig. 3.1. The PowerPoint File menu.

2. Choose New from the File menu.

   You see the dialog box called New, with two choices, shown in figure 3.2. If you are not familiar with using a dialog box, refer to

Chapter 1 and to your Windows documentation. If you choose Use Format of Active Presentation, you use the slide master format and the other defaults of the currently active presentation. If you choose Use Default Format, you use the PowerPoint default format, explained later in this chapter. (When you first start PowerPoint, the active presentation also uses the default, so the two choices are the same.)

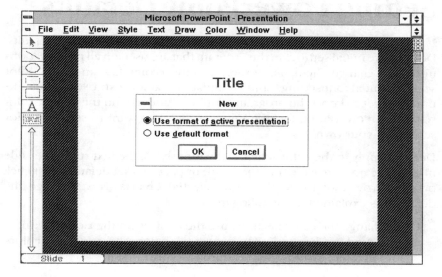

Fig. 3.2. *The New dialog box.*

3. Choose one of the options. Here, choose Use Format of Active Presentation. Click OK.

   PowerPoint puts you into the new, as yet untitled presentation.

4. To name the presentation, choose Save from the File menu.

   You see the Save dialog box.

5. Type a name for the presentation. Use a name that conforms to the requirements for DOS names, as explained later in this chapter in the section "Saving and Exiting." For the example, type *my_pres.ppt*.

6. Choose OK by clicking on the OK button or by pressing Enter.

The presentation screen reappears. Notice that the name you have given the presentation now appears at the top.

You may want to review and change the defaults that are in effect when you start PowerPoint, as explained in the next section.

Setting PowerPoint Defaults

If you have used other software, you are probably familiar with defaults. Defaults are initial settings in the program that are used on all presentations until you change them. For example, PowerPoint has an initial color scheme, initial font settings, and an initial format for text. Use the defaults until you get to know the program. Until you understand the default color scheme in PowerPoint, for example, you may not want to set up a color scheme of your own.

Defaults apply to the color scheme, the font styles, the text ruler, the slide master, the notes master, and the handout page. To set defaults, first click on the arrow tool to deselect any selected objects. Next, change the defaults, as explained in the following steps:

1. To change the color defaults, use the choices on the Color menu, discussed in Chapter 7. You can set the color scheme and set colors for Fill, Line, Shadow, and Pattern Contrast.

2. To set the default fonts, use the Style menu and choose Define Styles, as explained in Chapter 4. Choose Add from the Define Styles dialog box. Next, choose Styles from the Style submenu and select the newly defined format.

3. Select a word processing box (text added with the word processor tool) as explained in Chapter 4. From the Text menu, use Show Text Ruler and Line Spacing to set indents, tabs, and line spacing. From the Text menu, choose Set as Default to make the new settings the defaults.

Whatever you create on a slide master, notes master, or handout page becomes a default. The purpose of a master is to create defaults. See the section "Creating a Slide Master" in this chapter, and the sections "Printing Notes Pages" and "Printing Handouts" in Chapter 9, "Creating Output."

After you begin to change defaults, you may lose track of the initial PowerPoint defaults. If you have not changed the default format, you can restore all the defaults by choosing Use Default Format. Sometimes, however, you may want to restore only some of the initial PowerPoint defaults. For reference, Appendix B summarizes the initial settings in PowerPoint.

After you change any settings, you can use the new settings to replace the original PowerPoint defaults. Follow these steps to assign new defaults to PowerPoint:

1. With the file containing the new settings on the screen, choose Save As from the File menu.

    Be sure that you are in the PowerPoint subdirectory, usually called C:\POWERPNT.

2. In the File Name box, type *default.ppt*.

The newly saved format becomes the PowerPoint default. Whenever you choose Use Default Format from the New dialog box for future presentations, the new presentations will have the format of the presentation that you just saved.

> *Tip:* Microsoft has put much of its collective expertise into designing defaults. The defaults conform to standards of good usage. Until you feel that you have mastered such standards yourself, do not change the default format. To work with a format different from the default, open a file that has the format you want and use the Use Format of Active Presentation option on the New dialog box.

Using Templates

Many busy businesspeople who use PC graphics wish that they could enter the substance of their presentation and have their computerized graphics system do everything necessary to present it well. Often, businesspeople want their presentations to look great, but they do not have time to learn about PowerPoint drawing techniques, color options, and other features covered in this book.

PowerPoint provides templates to meet the needs of these people. PowerPoint templates are more than finished slides for you to plug your thoughts into (as you may have seen in word processing templates): they are finished *presentations.* They are complete collections of slides, put together by the professional artists at Genigraphics Corporation, that work together as a whole. You insert your own ideas into the template.

Thanks in part to the greater memory available for applications programs under Windows 3.0, you can work at your desktop to create the kind of complete professional slide shows you formerly had to commission from professional artists at outside agencies. When you use PowerPoint, the quality of the presentation you create is as high as the quality of the presentation you get from those agencies. (After all, you can copy your formats directly from those created by one of the leading design agencies, Genigraphics.) You do not need to be an expert in graphic arts and you can make changes easily, right up to the last minute.

Reviewing the Elements of a Template

A PowerPoint presentation template consists of several types of slides, as explained in table 3.1.

Table 3.1
Elements of a Presentation Template

Slide Type	Description
Slide master	This type of slide sets up the design of the entire presentation. Text or objects that you put here appear on every slide. See the section "Creating a Slide Master" in this chapter.
Title slide	Like the title page in a written report, the title slide displays the name of the presentation.
Notes master	A notes page for a given slide is a reduced image of the slide and your notes about the slide. The notes master contains elements that appear on every notes page, as discussed in Chapter 9, "Creating Output."
Handout page	You use the handout page to display copies of the slides, as discussed in Chapter 9, "Creating Output." You can have several slides per handout. You set up the format for printed handouts on the handout page.

Slide Type	Description
Color scheme	You can select the color scheme for the entire presentation. See Chapter 7, "Using Basic Color."
Sample slides	The sample slides in a PowerPoint template have various formats you can use for your own slides. If you want to use a sample slide, copy it. See "Creating a Presentation Slide By Slide" in this chapter for information on creating individual slides in a presentation.

You learn about most of these types of slides in this chapter or in later chapters of the book. First, before you learn about the individual slides in the templates, you learn how to find and use the templates themselves.

Selecting a Template

Templates do not appear on the main menu or on a submenu. Although they are not prominent within the program layout, templates have almost everything you need to create professional slide presentations, overhead transparencies, handouts, and notes. They fulfill the requirements for good graphic presentations in their usage of fonts, colors, layout, and all other technical considerations.

Microsoft's advice for using templates in PowerPoint is "browse, choose, and use." Look over the presentations to find one that you like. When you find the presentation that you like, choose it. You then can use it for your own purposes.

The templates are located in the main PowerPoint directory, in the TEM-PLATE subdirectory (usually C:\POWERPNT\TEMPLATE), the COLORSCH subdirectory, and the SAMPLES subdirectory.

In the main directory, the template you can use is the sample presentation, COLUMBUS.PPT, that comes with the program. A listing of the templates in the COLORSCH subdirectory follows:

35MM16.PPT   A template with color schemes selected by Genigraphics Corporation that are particularly suited to 35mm presentations.

35MM256.PPT   A template, based on a 256-color display, with color schemes for 35mm presentations.

DSPLY16.PPT   A template with color schemes suited for video or
                       on-screen presentations.

DSPLY256.PPT   A template, based on a 256-color display, with color
                       schemes for video or on-screen presentations.

OVRHD16.PPT   A template with color schemes particularly suited
                       to overhead transparencies.

OVRHD256.PPT   A template, based on a 256-color display, with
                       color schemes particularly suited to overhead
                       transparencies.

The SAMPLES subdirectory contains another collection of templates, which
are as follows:

PHOTODRP.PPT   The "photo drop-in" is a model of a photo read
                       into a slide, for use on a 256-color display.

PRODUCT.PPT   This sample word chart lists Microsoft products
                       and provides two columns of description.

PRSPP16.PPT   This multiple-slide presentation is an excellent
                       model for a complete color presentation.

PRSPP256.PPT   Like PRSPP16.PPT, this multiple-slide presenta-
                       tion—for 256-color output—is a useful model.

TOKEN.PPT   This one-slide template shows a Windows network.

When you install PowerPoint, you install a number of template files into the
default directory (usually C:\POWERPNT) and into subdirectories directly
beneath the default directory. Each template is a single slide that you can
use as the model for your presentation. The TEMPLATE subdirectory (as its
name suggests) contains templates in four subdirectories, 35MM, GRAPHS,
OVERHEAD, and STRYBRDS. The PowerPoint 35MM subdirectory has
subdirectories especially suited to creating 35mm slides, and the OVER-
HEAD subdirectory has templates suited to preparing black-and-white
overheads. The STRYBRDS subdirectory has two templates—
35MMBORD.PPT and OVHDBORD.PPT. Other subdirectories with templates are COLORSCH and SAMPLES. Two templates in the default directory are PRSNTCLR.PPT and PRSNTB&W.PPT.

The names of the templates suggest their contents, although because they
conform to the requirements of DOS names, they are not always long
enough to be fully descriptive. Slides with 35MM in the name, or slides in
the 35MM subdirectory, have templates with the aspect ratio (2:3) of 35mm

slides. Slides with OVERHD in the name have the aspect ratio of overhead transparencies (3:4). Some slides, such as BLUEGREE.PPT (blue green) and DUALBLUE.PPT, are in color, as their names suggest. Others are in black and white. The color slides may be in 16-color or in 256-color display.

To browse through the presentations, use the File menu, and follow these steps:

1. Start PowerPoint.

   You see the opening, untitled presentation.

2. Open the File menu and choose Open.

   You see the Open dialog box, shown in figure 3.3.

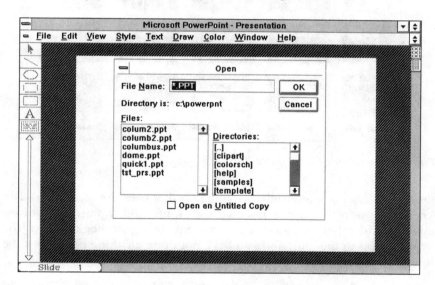

Fig. 3.3. *The Open dialog box, used here to browse through PowerPoint templates.*

3. Click Open an Untitled Copy in the dialog box.

   When you open an untitled copy, the original template remains intact when you make changes to the copy.

4. Browse through the subdirectories by highlighting the subdirectory and file name that you want and clicking the OK button in the dialog box. For the example, choose PRSPP16.PPT from the C:\POWERPNT\SAMPLES subdirectory.

You see the sample template, a collection of slides in miniature form, shown in figure 3.4. The name at the top of the screen is Presentation, which is a copy of the original, leaving the original intact.

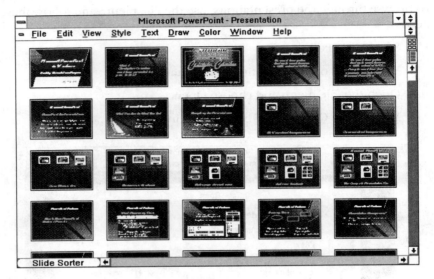

Fig. 3.4. The sample file PRSPP16.PPT.

On-screen is a complete slide presentation that uses the most up-to-date knowledge of color, layout, bulleted lists, fonts, and clip art. The colors, layouts, and other elements are consistent from the beginning of the presentation to the end. And you have not done anything but copy a file into your work space. This simplicity is the beauty of using templates.

After you have the copy of the presentation template, you can supply your own words and pictures to create your own presentation. In later chapters of the book, you learn how to modify text (see Chapter 4, "Adding Text to a Presentation") and graphic objects (see Chapter 5, "Drawing Objects"). You learn to work with clip art and how to import graphics from other presentations into your new presentation (see Chapter 11, "Manipulating Pictures for Special Effects").

The basis of a template is the slide master. As explained in the next section, you can create a slide master yourself.

Creating a Slide Master

If working with presentations instead of individual slides is the key to getting the most out of PowerPoint, working with slide masters is essential to getting the most out of standardized presentations. The basis of creating a consistent presentation is the slide master.

A slide master contains the visual format that you want to appear on every slide: typically a border, a background, perhaps the company logo, sometimes the date of the presentation. You also set the color scheme for the entire presentation with the slide master.

You create a slide master in the same way that you create a slide. In its value to you, however, a slide master is more than just a slide. If you want to change a standardized element (such as the color scheme) in an entire presentation, just change the slide master. You thereby change all the other slides as well.

Consistency is the ideal in any slide presentation. You want all the slides in a presentation to be uniform in certain respects: the color of the background, the color schemes, the fonts used in the titles, the placement of figures and text on the screen, and so on. But consistency can be difficult to maintain.

In the pre-Windows days of constructing one slide at a time, you sometimes had to re-create the background color, the fonts for the title, the placement of the title, the logo in the corner, the color scheme, and so on *each* time you created another slide. You needed a great deal of discipline, a good memory, and, at the very least, a good deal of patience. But when you use a slide master, you create those standard features once, and all the slides in the presentation have the features automatically. You do not have to remember the standard features and re-create them each time.

When you create a presentation with a DOS-based graphics program, you can create a standard format and replicate it again and again for other slides. PowerPoint, however, has the capability to work with multiple slides loaded into memory at one time. In a DOS-based graphics application, if you decide to change the format of a number of slides, you generally have to change the format of every slide individually. With PowerPoint, if you want to change the background color, the color scheme, the title font, or any other standard feature throughout the slide show, you change it on the slide master only. The format of every other slide in the presentation changes automatically. (If, however, you have changed the color scheme or the title attributes—font, typestyle, framing, and so on—of any slides individually, you have to go back and change the format of those slides individually.)

A slide master is powerful. The breakthrough from using DOS-based graphics comes when you understand what a slide master is and how it helps you create powerful presentations. You must *use* the slide master— if you create individual color schemes for each slide, for instance, or create individual title styles or separate frames, you cannot readily standardize with the master.

Creating a New Slide Master

Creating a slide master is no more difficult than creating any slide, such as the one you created in the quick start in Chapter 2. Follow these steps to create a slide master:

1. Start up the presentation for which you want to create a new master. Here, use the presentation titled MY_PRES.PPT that you created earlier in this chapter. You can use the Window menu to switch to this presentation.

2. With the presentation on the screen, choose View and then Slide Master.

   If you are just beginning a presentation, the slide master is almost identical to any other blank slide. Notice that the slide counter in the lower left says Slide Master, as you can see in figure 3.5.

   After you have the slide master on-screen, you can set up your standard elements—the fonts for the title, the frame, the color scheme, the date, and any other text or objects that you want to appear on every slide.

3. Select the title by clicking on it once.

   Two ways to select text are available. You can enclose the text in a selection box, or you can highlight the text. When you double-click on the text, you highlight the text, indicating that you are ready to change the wording in the text. When you use the slide master, you probably want to leave the word Title as it stands, then change it to create a fresh title for each slide. You may want to set the attributes for the title on the slide master.

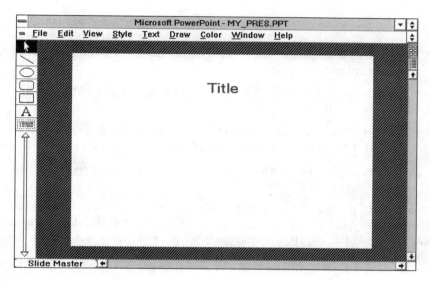

Fig. 3.5. *Blank Slide Master.*

4. From the Style menu, choose Styles, and set a style for the title. You
   can use any of the choices on the Style menu. (See Chapter 4,
   "Adding Text to a Presentation," for more information on setting
   styles.)

Tip: If you do not want a title for a slide, you have to be a little
creative to get rid of it. You can cover the title with an opaque
object, as explained in Chapter 5, or you can use the Backspace key
to delete all the text in the title. If the title is framed, filled, or
shadowed, use the Draw menu to remove those attributes, as
explained in Chapter 5.

In addition to setting the style for the title in each slide, you can set
the color scheme that should appear in each slide. Set the color
scheme as explained in Chapter 7, "Using Basic Color."

5. Choose Color from the menu bar, then choose Color Scheme.

Set the background, foreground, and accent colors, as explained in
Chapter 7.

You also can shade the background, as explained in Chapter 7.

A frame around each slide in a presentation can give a finished look. The frames of all slides in the presentation should be identical. If you set up the frame in the slide master, the frames will be identical in each slide.

6. Add a frame, using the drawing tools as explained in Chapter 5, "Drawing Objects."

7. If you want, add your logo to the slide, using the tools for importing and cropping an image, as explained in Chapter 11.

8. To resume working with slides instead of the slide master, choose Slides from the View menu.

PowerPoint provides special codes that you can place on the slide master that enable you to enter slide numbers, the time, and the date automatically. To number the slide, use the labeler or word processing tool to type the characters ## wherever you want the slide numbers to appear. Use // to put in the date, and type :: to put in the time.

You can change the slide master later by using editing tools such as the Style menu, the Color menu, and so on. If you change the slide master for an existing presentation, all the slides in the presentation will have the elements of the new slide master, with two exceptions. If you have set either the slide title attributes or the color scheme individually for particular slides and want those slides to look the same as the slide master, you have to change the characteristics on those slides individually.

When you create an individual slide, you do not have to use the characteristics of the slide master. When the slide is on-screen, from the Edit menu choose Omit Master to avoid using the slide master for that slide. If you want to restore the slide master format to a slide you have created with Omit Master, display the slide and choose Include Master from the Edit menu.

You do not have to create all the details in a slide master yourself. You can choose a slide master from a template and use it as your own, as explained in the next section.

Copying an Existing Slide Master

You can create a slide master from one of the PowerPoint predesigned templates. That way, you can use the color scheme, title attributes, frame, and other elements created by the Genigraphics artists. To create a slide master from a template, follow these steps:

1. From an existing presentation, such as the one called Presentation copied from the file PRSPP16.PPT, choose the View menu and then choose Slide Master (see fig. 3.6).

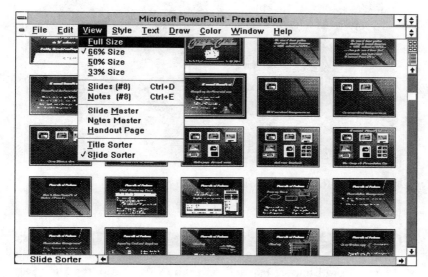

Fig. 3.6. The View Menu, from which you choose Slide Master.

You see a basic slide with the elements that appear on every slide—in this case, the background, the color scheme, and the formatted title (see fig. 3.7). The slide master also specifies the style characteristics that you choose from the Style menu, such as font, size, color, and typestyle of the title.

You can use the slide master to create your own presentation and the individual slides in it, as explained in the section "Creating a Presentation," at the beginning of this chapter.

After you have the master for a presentation, use the Edit menu, the Title Sorter, or Slide Sorter to create new slides. All the new slides have the characteristics of the slide master.

2. Choose New Slide from the Edit menu.

Your new slide master takes on the characteristics of the slide master from the template.

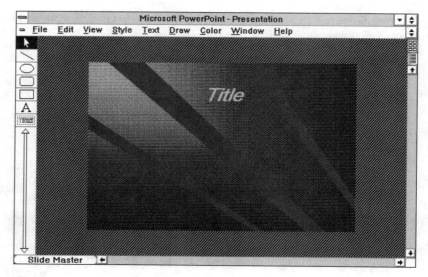

Fig. 3.7. Slide master for the sample presentation.

Viewing the Presentation

As you know from Chapter 1, you can use the View menu, the Slide Sorter, and the Title Sorter buttons to change your views of the presentation. In this section, you see how to create the various views. In the sections that follow, you see how the various views help you manage the presentation.

Viewing an Individual Slide

You now have the Slide Sorter view on-screen. If you want to see any individual slide in the presentation, follow these steps:

1. Move the cursor to the slide that you want and select it.

   A box around the slide shows that you have selected the slide.

2. Double-click or press Enter to choose the selected slide.

   You see the slide on your screen. Figure 3.8 shows slide number 8 from the template used in this chapter.

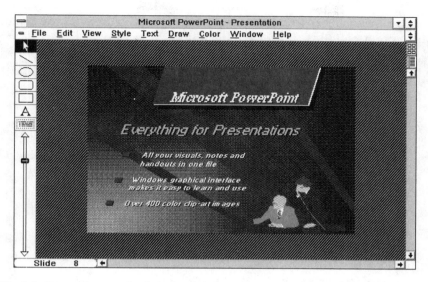

Fig. 3.8. View of a sample slide from the presentation.

3. Choose Slide Sorter from the View menu or click on the Slide Sorter button to return to the view of all the slides.

PowerPoint also provides you with two ways to move through the slides one at a time.

- Click on the up or down arrows on the Slide Changer in the lower left portion of the window to move up or down one slide at a time. (On the keyboard, use the PgUp or PgDn keys.)

- On the Slide Changer, drag the marker up or down. The slide counter tells you the number of the slide in the window.

Viewing Slides by Title

Rather than look at the slides as miniatures, you can look at them by title—a valuable procedure when you want to sort slides or, as you see in Chapter 11, when you want to use clip art. To view slides by title, choose Title Sorter from the View menu or click on the Title Sorter button.

You see the screen shown in figure 3.9. In the template, all the slides already have titles. When you create slides, you begin with the title already selected.

You next add titles of your own. (The more descriptive the titles you create, the more useful those titles are in the title sorter view.)

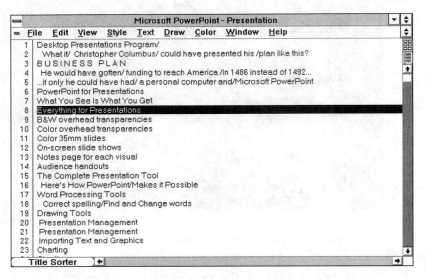

Fig. 3.9. *Title Sorter view of the sample presentation.*

You also choose Slide Sorter from the View menu. To choose any slide from the Slide Sorter or Title Sorter view, double-click on the slide. You also can use the views to rearrange the slides, as explained in the next section.

Rearranging the Presentation

When you work with a complete presentation in a DOS graphics program, you usually work with file names or written descriptions of the slides in the presentation. PowerPoint, however, has enough memory available to display all the slides in a presentation on the screen in miniature form. You can manipulate slides from this view by following these steps:

1. Choose the Slide Sorter view or the Title Sorter view. Choose the Slide Sorter view for this example.

   The Slide Sorter enables you to work visually; you look at the appearance of the slide. The Title Sorter enables you to work verbally, with a written description of the slide. If your written descriptions are detailed enough, you may find the Title Sorter a fast way to work. With the Slide Sorter, though, you can tell what a slide contains by looking at it.

> ***Tip:*** If you want, you can choose the 50% Size view from the View menu so that PowerPoint can display as many slides as possible on the screen in the Slide Sorter view.

2. Select the slide you want to move—slide 8 for this example.

   The selection box appears around the slide.

3. Drag the slide with the mouse to the new position. For the example, drag slide 8 to the right of slide 10. Release the mouse button.

You can move slides in the same way in the Title Sorter view. Click on the number, not on the text, and drag the slide to the position you want.

You can use PowerPoint to rearrange multiple slides, even multiple slides that are not in sequence. To rearrange multiple slides, follow these steps:

1. Select the first slide that you want to move—here, the first slide in the presentation.

2. Hold down the Shift key and select a second slide—in this case, the second slide in the presentation.

3. Release the Shift key.

4. Put the pointer on either of the selected slides and drag them both to the new position. For this example, drag the slides to the end of the presentation.

After you finish dragging them, the slides remain in the new position. To move multiple slides that are not in sequence, follow the same steps that you just completed. After you release the Shift key, you see a small slide image rather than the pointer. Drag the image to wherever you want to put the slides.

> ***Tip:*** If you want to return the slides to their original positions, choose Undo from the Edit menu.

Changing the slide order in PowerPoint is as simple as working with 35mm slides and changing the order by hand—simpler, in fact, because you do not have to hold the slides up to the light to see them or worry about dropping them or try to get them into the slide carousel facing the right way. Like so much else in managing a PowerPoint presentation, rearranging slides is simple. You do not have to know much to be able to do it. Preparing and refining a good presentation often involves arranging and rearranging slides at the last minute. If you are able to arrange and rearrange your slides quickly, you are more likely to prepare better presentations.

Deleting, Copying, and Adding Slides

Deleting, copying, or adding slides is no more difficult than changing their order. You can use either the slide view or the title view (or work with individual slides one at a time).

Follow these steps to delete a slide:

1. Select the slide you want to delete.

2. Choose Cut from the Edit menu or press Shift-Del.

If you want to restore the slide, press Undo, or keep the cursor in the same position and choose Paste from the Edit menu, or hold down Shift and press Insert.

Follow these similar steps to copy a slide:

1. Select the slide that you want to copy.

2. Choose Copy from the Edit menu.

3. In the Title Sorter or Slide Sorter, position the cursor where you want the copy to appear.

4. Choose Paste from the Edit menu.

    The copy of the slide appears at the new position.

You also use the Edit menu to create a new slide in the same format as the other slides in the presentation:

1. Position the cursor where you want the new slide to appear.

2. Choose New Slide from the Edit menu or press Ctrl-N.

If you are in the Slide Sorter or Title Sorter, a new slide appears in the position where you have the cursor. If you are in the slide view, the new slide appears right after the current slide. If you are in a slide master, choosing New Slide creates the first slide in the presentation.

The new slide has the same format as the previous slide. If you are using the template PRSPP16.PPT, for example, you notice right away that the new slide has the same background and frame as the other slides.

Saving and Exiting

At the start of this chapter, you saw how to use the File menu to create a new presentation. You also use the File menu to save your presentation as you go along, to close it when you are finished with the presentation, and to exit PowerPoint.

If you are finished with a presentation but not yet finished with PowerPoint, you can close the presentation without exiting PowerPoint. To close a presentation without exiting PowerPoint, do the following:

1. Be sure that the presentation you want to close is the active presentation. Choose the presentation from the Window menu or click on its window.

2. From the File menu, choose Close.

If you have made any changes since the last time you saved the file, PowerPoint asks whether you want to save the file before closing. Choose Yes, No, or Cancel. If you choose Yes, PowerPoint saves the file with the latest changes and then closes it. If you choose No, PowerPoint closes the file without saving the latest changes. If you choose Cancel, the presentation returns to the screen.

To save the presentation, you can use Save or Save As from the File menu. If you use Save, you save the file under its current name and replace the existing file on the disk with that name. If you choose Save As, you save the presentation under a new name and do not replace the file on-disk with the current name.

Tip: If you have used a template and did not use Open an Untitled Copy when you began, be sure that you use Save As when you save the presentation. Otherwise, you will write over the original template.

To use Save or Save As, follow these steps:

1. Be sure that the presentation you want to save is the active presentation.

2. From the File menu, choose Save or Save As.

   If you choose Save, PowerPoint saves the presentation. If you choose Save As (or if you choose Save and are saving the presentation for the first time), you see the Save As dialog box, shown in figure 3.10.

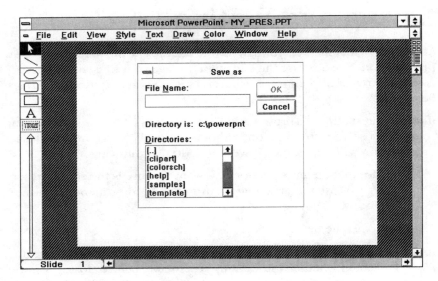

Fig. 3.10. *The Save As dialog box.*

3. For the file name, type a name that satisfies the requirements for DOS names.

4. Choose a directory for the file.

   If you do not want to save the file, choose Cancel.

5. After you type the name and choose the directory, choose OK.

   PowerPoint saves the file.

Although in this chapter you have waited until the end to save your file, it is good practice to save the file often as you go along.

Tip: The shortcut combination for saving a file is Ctrl-S. Get into the habit of pressing Ctrl-S frequently as you work. Saving with the key combination does not take more than a second or two and helps you avoid the frustration and wasted time of accidentally losing your work.

To exit from PowerPoint, choose Exit from the File menu. If you have made changes since the last time you saved any active presentations, PowerPoint asks whether you want to save the changes. Choose Yes, No, or Cancel. Unless you choose Cancel, you exit from the program.

Chapter Summary

In this chapter, you saw how you use PowerPoint to work with a complete, multiple-slide presentation. You learned how to start PowerPoint, review defaults, and create a presentation. You saw how to use templates to begin with a finished presentation and how to create a slide master to set standard elements for every slide. You became familiar with the various ways you can look at your overall presentation: the Slide Sorter view, the Title Sorter view, or the view of an individual slide. You found out how to add, copy, and delete slides. Finally, you learned how to save slides and exit PowerPoint.

This chapter is, in a sense, an opening wedge into the rest of the book, because you start thinking about the whole presentation rather than just the parts. You probably cannot use PowerPoint to its full potential unless you break the DOS habit of thinking about "slides" and develop the Windows habit of thinking about "presentations." In the rest of the book, you learn about tools for developing individual slides. The next chapter tells you how to work with text.

Adding Text to a Presentation

Adding text to a page in a graphics application used to be much different from adding text in a word processor. When you used a graphics application, you typed in the text and positioned it on the page. You may have changed fonts or sizes, but you probably did not have word processing features such as word wrapping or spell checking available to you.

Word processing in the graphics program PowerPoint is almost as powerful as word processing in an actual word processing program. You can do a great deal with the PowerPoint word processor.

In this chapter, you use the simple labeler tool and the full-fledged word processor tool to create text. You find out how to select words and titles—selecting is often the first step in formatting and making other changes. Next you learn to make changes, such as in the typeface and style of your selected text. Because knowing *how* to change styles isn't much use if you don't know *when* to change them, this chapter provides some basic guidelines for using different text styles. You also discover how to format your text by having it appear on the screen the way you want it to appear on the page (centered, for instance, or justified). Finally, you learn to use two word processor tools that are now becoming available for the first time in graphics packages: the search and change feature and the spelling checker.

Creating Text

People sometimes confuse the labeler and the word processor tools in PowerPoint. You can use both tools to create text on your PowerPoint slides and to change the text font, size, and position, but you use them in different ways and for different features. The labeler tool does not wrap words or enable you to access the text ruler (discussed in Chapter 11, "Manipulating Pictures for Special Effects"), whereas the word processor does both.

Each tool is appropriate for different situations. Use the labeler to enter short explanatory text, such as a label for a drawn object or an imported picture. Use the word processor tool to enter larger blocks of text, such as whole paragraphs or a series of bulleted items.

The following two sections show you how to use the labeler and word processor tools for writing text.

> *Tip:* Chapter 5 introduces a third way to insert text into your presentation. Select an object, such as a circle or rectangle, and start typing. The text goes inside the object and is part of that object. When you move or delete the object, the text goes with it.

Creating Text with the Labeler Tool

When you create text with the labeler rather than the word processor tool, you don't have to draw a text box. The labeler is easier to use for small labeling jobs. Suppose that you are designing a slide show to illustrate a lecture on Ireland. You have on your slide a picture of the Irish flag and a map of Ireland, imported from the file INTERNAT.PPT in the clip art subdirectory (see fig. 4.1). You want to identify the flag.

Use the following steps to label your slides:

1. Click on the labeler tool to select it.

   The labeler tool, the button or box containing the letter A, is located in the column of tools on the left side of your PowerPoint screen.

2. Place the mouse cursor, now in the shape of a vertical line, where you want to begin typing. In the example, place the mouse cursor to the right of the flag.

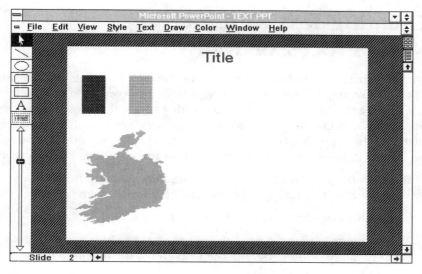

Fig. 4.1. *A slide with imported pictures.*

3. Click your mouse button and begin typing your text. Here, type *The Irish flag*.

4. After you finish typing, click anywhere away from the text to revert to the default arrow tool.

Your screen should now look like figure 4.2.

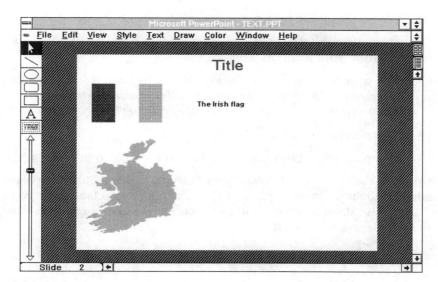

Fig. 4.2. *Text drawn with the labeler.*

Creating Text with the Word Processor Tool

Use the word processor tool when you want to create a substantial amount of text—anything longer than a few words. Before you begin to type your text, draw a text box, a rectangular shape that covers the approximate area in which you want your words to fit. If necessary, you can change the size of the text box later. Suppose that you want to add a few introductory words on Ireland to the slide in the example. Follow these steps to insert the text:

1. Select the word processor tool, located underneath the A and above the Slide Changer on the left side of the screen.

    Use the word processor tool to draw the text box.

2. Position the cursor, now in the shape of a crosshair, on your slide. Here, place it to the right of the map and at the height of the northern tip of Ireland.

    A text box is rectangular, so you can start to draw it from any one of its four corners. In this example, start from the upper left corner.

3. Hold down the mouse button and drag the rectangular text box to fill the required area. Here, drag the box down to the right until you almost reach the right corner of the slide.

    Like any other drawn object, a text box can be resized later, if necessary.

4. Release the mouse button.

    A line cursor blinks in the upper left portion of your text box. You can insert your text now.

5. Type your text. Here, type *The Republic of Ireland: a land of bliss and greenery. Explore its pleasures in this presentation and explore your own hidden capacity for enjoying life.*

6. Click outside the text to deselect the box.

You have created a text box similar to the text box shown in figure 4.3.

If you are using the initial PowerPoint defaults, all lines but the first are indented slightly. The examples in this chapter use the default settings. In Chapter 11, "Manipulating Pictures for Special Effects," you learn how to set the indentation yourself.

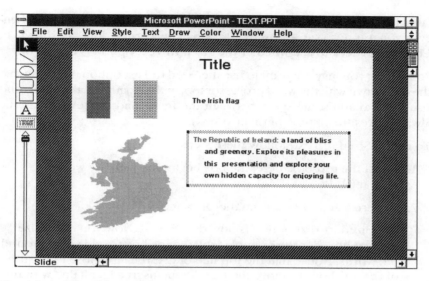

Fig. 4.3. *A slide with a text box.*

You also created a text box when you added text to your slide in the section "Creating Text with the Labeler Tool." The labeler, however, draws the box automatically. You can resize or move a text box made by either tool.

Manipulating Text

Chapter 5, "Drawing Objects," discusses how to select and manipulate objects. Text boxes are objects and you can change them the same way that you can change all other drawn objects—you can make them opaque, frame them, fill them, add shadow, add a pattern, and apply a line style to them. The following sections briefly show you how to manipulate text boxes.

Resizing a Text Box

By default, PowerPoint applies the Sized to Text option in the Draw menu to text boxes. The box shrinks or expands to fit precisely around the words you type. This resizing occurred when you drew the text box in the preceding section. If the box you draw with the word processor tool is too large for the text, the box automatically shrinks to the correct size. Whenever you cannot size a box by dragging the corner dots, as shown in Chapter 5, check to see whether the Sized to Text option is turned on.

Sometimes you may not want to use the Sized to Text option. Suppose that the text drawn with the word processor tool in the example has a frame, and you want to add some space between the frame and the text (the frame always traces the outline of the text box).

To cancel Sized to Text, follow these steps:

1. Select the text box; here, the box beginning with the words
   `The Republic of Ireland`.

2. Choose Sized to Text from the Draw menu.

   The Sized to Text option is now deactivated. Now you can resize the text box. For the example, enlarge the box to add space around the words. Notice that the top line of text remains close to the top of the text box. To move the text down, insert a blank line with the Enter key. You end up with something similar to figure 4.4.

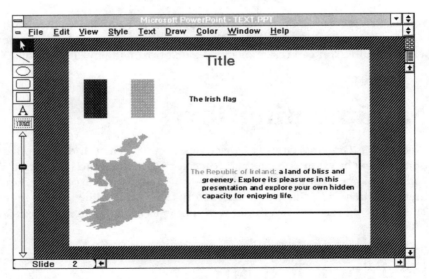

Fig. 4.4. *A framed text box with the Sized to Text option turned off.*

Moving a Text Box

You learn how to move a drawn object in Chapter 5, "Drawing Objects." You move a text block in the same way. In the example, the text box is positioned a little too high on the page. Follow these steps to reposition the box:

1. Use the arrow tool to select the text box you want to move by placing the mouse pointer over it and clicking once. Here, click over the text box beginning with the words `The Republic of Ireland`.

   You can use the left or right mouse button to move the box.

2. To use the right mouse button, place the mouse pointer over the text box, hold down the right button, and drag the box. Here, move the text box down lower on the slide.

3. Release the mouse button when the text box is where you want it.

4. To use the left mouse button, place the mouse pointer directly over the lines that outline the text box, then drag the box and release the button.

Using Draw Options on Text Boxes

Using Draw options such as frame, fill, shadow, and line style can add greatly to the appearance of your text boxes. Chapter 5 discusses the use of Draw options in detail. You can apply any Draw option to a text box simply by clicking it, as shown in the steps below. Suppose that you want to frame the text box in the example. To do so, follow these steps:

1. Click over the text box to select it.

2. Display the Draw menu by clicking the word Draw in the menu bar or pressing Alt-D.

   You see the options shown in figure 4.5. Notice that Sized to Text is active.

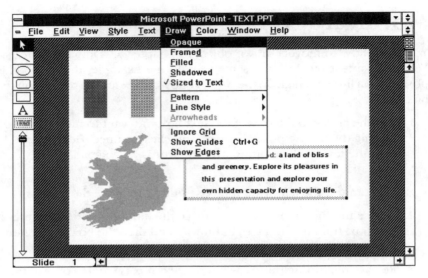

Fig. 4.5. *The Draw menu.*

3. Choose any of the first seven options by clicking them (because the Sized to Text option is active, you switch it off if you click it now). Here, choose Framed.

4. A line frame appears around your text box.

Selecting Text

Selecting text inside a text box is different from selecting the text box itself. You select the box by clicking over it once as you do over any object (see Chapter 5). When you select the text box, you can change the font and size and color of all the text as well as move and resize the box itself.

In addition to selecting the box, you can select the words in the box directly. In the example, suppose that you want to change the title of the slide. The title box is just another text box in all ways but one: you cannot delete the actual box. If you delete the title words and do not replace them, the box still remains. Follow these steps to select and change the title:

1. Click twice over the word Title.

   The word Title, as distinct from the title box, is now selected, as indicated by the dark rectangle surrounding the word Title. Double-click to select individual words in text boxes.

2. Type your new text. Here, type *Discover Ireland*.

Suppose that you want to select two or more words in a text block. Use the following steps to select the desired words:

1. Select the text box.

2. Place the mouse pointer to the left of the first word that you want to select. Here, place it to the left of the first word in the text box: `The`.

3. Click and hold the mouse button and drag the cursor over the words that you want to select. Here, select the words `The Republic of Ireland`.

   The words receive a dark background.

4. Release the mouse button when all the words have the dark background.

Now you can change the words that you have selected. Only selected words will change.

Changing Text Style and Color

Two menus—Style and Text—on the menu bar refer specifically to text on your slides. The Text menu, covered in a later section, mainly affects the positioning of text. The Style menu affects how the text looks: whether the text is plain, bold, italic, or underlined; what font and size you use; and the overall style (a combination of the style options just mentioned plus color).

You apply all options in Style in the same way. Select the text that you want to change. Choose the option from the Style menu. PowerPoint applies the option to the selected text. When you use some options, however, you also need to choose from a submenu.

Create a second slide in the presentation about Ireland. Copy the map of Ireland and resize it to fit in the upper left corner of the slide or put it on the slide master as a basic motif for this presentation. Next, create some bulleted text items and a headline. You can create the text yourself as shown later in this chapter in the section "Indenting Text." An easier way to create a bulleted list, however, is to copy one of the PowerPoint templates.

The presentation ARROW.PPT, located in the subdirectory OVERHEAD within the directory TEMPLATE, has bulleted charts. Go to the second slide in that presentation and copy the two text boxes, one containing a headline, the other containing bulleted text. Paste the text boxes into slide 2 of the sample presentation. If you need help, please refer to Chapter 3, "Creating a Presentation," and Chapter 5, "Drawing Objects." (If you prefer, create your own text samples directly on the slide and work with them.) The text boxes remain selected. Move them down, as shown in the section "Moving a Text Box," so that they don't overlap with the map. You end up with slide 2 looking like figure 4.6.

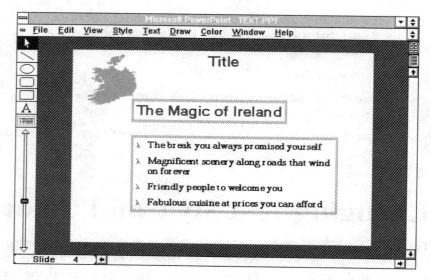

Fig. 4.6. The pasted bulleted text.

In the following sections, you learn to apply the options in the Style menu to text.

Applying a Style to Text

To change the appearance of text, you can use the individual options, such as italic, size, font, and color, or you can apply a preset combination of all the options.

The Styles option on the Style menu offers five combinations of options: Helv 18 B, Helv 24 B, Helv 36 B, Zapf Dingbats 18, and Zapf Dingbats 24, with keyboard equivalents Ctrl-1, Ctrl-2, Ctrl-3, Ctrl-4, and Ctrl-5, respectively. Helv indicates the font Helvetica. The numeral represents the size of the type. The B stands for bold type, as distinct from plain typeface. Zapf Dingbats is a special kind of font that produces symbols rather than letters. The Keyboard option under Help, discussed in Chapter 1, contains the full listing of symbols produced by Zapf Dingbats. Chapter 12, "Using Advanced Features of Text," shows you how to use Define Styles to make up your own styles and add them to the list.

In the example, suppose that the imported text style in the lower box isn't right for your purposes and you decide to change it to Helv 24 B. Follow these steps.

1. Select the text that you want to change. Here, select the lower text box, which begins with `The break`.

2. Choose Styles from the Style menu.

    You see the menu shown in figure 4.7. Note that none of the styles has a check mark.

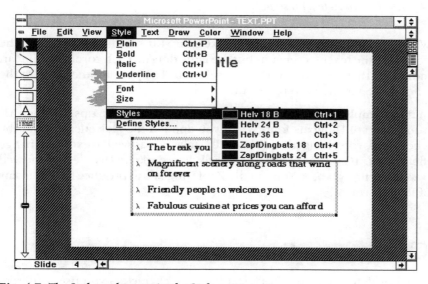

Fig. 4.7. *The Styles submenu in the Style menu.*

3. Choose Helv 24 B.

You also can press Ctrl-2 after step 1 rather than go through steps 2 and 3. The keyboard shortcut appears in the menu, as shown in figure 4.7. Your text changes as shown in figure 4.8.

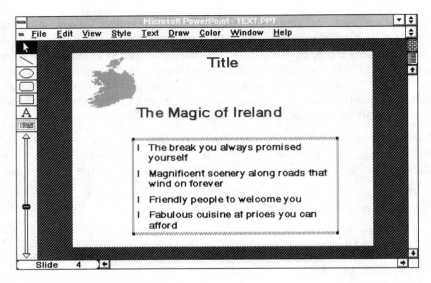

Fig. 4.8. *Text in Helv 24 B style.*

When you click inside a selected text box, you see the line cursor. The outline of the text box remains but the large dots on each corner disappear, indicating that the box is no longer selected. To apply another style to the whole box, you need to reselect the box.

In the example, you changed the bullets, which look like upside-down Ys, from the Zapf Dingbats font. When you applied the Helvetica style to the whole box, you changed the bullets to Helvetica as well. Next, you change them back. (Conventional bullets look like darkened circles, shadowed boxes, or empty boxes. You can use Zapf Dingbats to produce bullets in any of these forms.)

Changing a Font

The font determines the basic shape of the characters you use. Different fonts work best in different circumstances. Helvetica, a good font for headlines and large type, is a basic style font in PowerPoint because slide shows often consist of nothing but headlines and large type. In contrast, Zapf Chancery is an informal font that looks like handwriting. Its occasional use can enhance your slides. The fonts you have available depend on your target printer, as explained in Chapter 9, "Creating Output." To see the list of fonts available with your current setup, choose Font from the Style menu (see fig. 4.9).

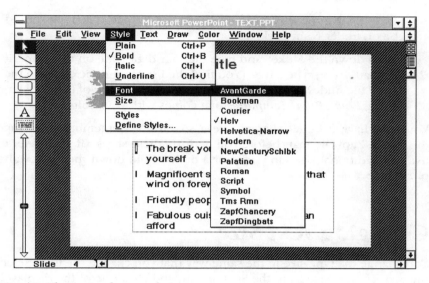

***Fig. 4.9.** The Font submenu choices.*

The Zapf Dingbats font produces symbols. In the example, the bullet shaped like an upside-down Y changed to Helvetica when you applied the new style. You can select each individual bullet and change the font back to Zapf Dingbats, as shown in the following steps:

1. Select the text that you want to change. Here, select a bullet in the lower text box.

2. Choose Font from the Style menu.

    You see the submenu shown in figure 4.9.

3. Click a font to choose it. Here, choose Zapf Dingbats.

    Your letter changes to the new font, back to the upside-down Y in this case.

You can access additional Zapf Dingbats characters through the numeric keypad. Suppose that you want to change the bullets in the example to shamrocks. (You also can produce the classic bullet shape, a filled-in circle. See the Keyboard option under Help for a list of available symbols.) Follow these steps to use the numeric keypad method to produce bullets in the shape of shamrocks:

1. Select the text.

2. Select a bullet.

3. Press the Num Lock key on your numeric keypad. The light should be on under Num Lock.

4. Hold down the Alt key and type the four-digit code on the numeric keypad. Here, type 0168. (You find the list of numeric codes in the Help file under Keyboard and inside the back cover of the booklet *Using PowerPoint Templates* that comes with your software.)

You now have a bullet shaped like a shamrock. Remember to change the font to Zapf Dingbats before you perform these steps. (If you prefer to use the traditional filled-in circle for a bullet, hold down the Alt key and press 0183.)

Changing Text Size

You change the type size in the same way that you change the font. Select the text, choose Size from the Style menu, and click one of the displayed sizes. Sizes range from 8 to 96 points. For a slide show, you rarely use anything smaller than 18 points. You can use the Other dialog box to type in any size you want. Choose Style from the menu bar, choose Size, and then choose Other.

Changing Text Styles

The four basic text styles are plain, bold, italic, and underline. Suppose that you want to italicize your headline, The Magic of Ireland.

1. Select the text The Magic of Ireland.

2. Choose Italic from the Style menu by clicking it or by pressing Ctrl-I on the keyboard.

The selected text becomes italicized. You can apply more than one style option at a time. For example, you can have text that is bold and italic, italic and underlined, and so on. You cannot have text, however, that is plain and anything else at the same time. The text in this example remains in boldface. Figure 4.10 shows the final state of slide 2 in the sample presentation.

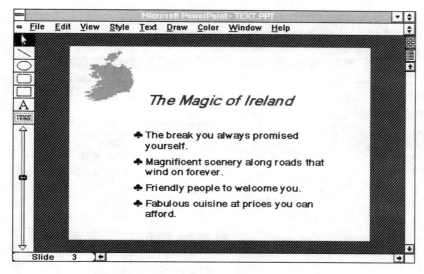

***Fig. 4.10.** The restyled text in the example.*

Table 4.1 lists all the styles and their keyboard shortcuts.

Table 4.1
Text Styles and their Keyboard Shortcuts

Text Style	*Keyboard Shortcut*
Plain	Ctrl-P
Bold	Ctrl-B
Italic	Ctrl-I
Underline	Ctrl-U

Do not apply styles randomly. Follow the standard guidelines on the use of styles, discussed in the section "Following Style Guidelines."

Changing Text Color

To change the text color, select the text, choose Text from the Color menu, and select a new color. See Chapter 7, "Using Basic Color," for more information on changing a color. The Color menu is shown below in figure 4.11.

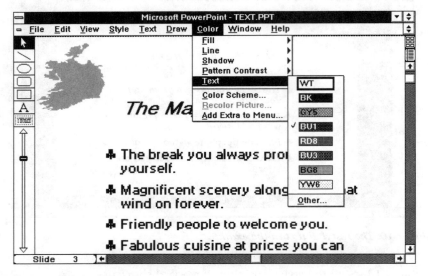

Fig. 4.11. The Color menu options.

Tip: If you want to change the color of a few selected words, use the Color menu rather than the Style menu. Every time you change a color with Style, you define a new style that remains on the menu.

Following Style Guidelines

When you make a presentation, you must select styles, fonts, and sizes appropriate for your audience and the occasion. The following are a few general guidelines:

- Serif fonts are much easier to read in a body of text than sans serif fonts. *Serif* fonts have small notches at the ends of letters. *Sans* (French for "without") *serif* is a plainer type without notches. Times and New Century Schoolbook are examples of serif fonts; Helvetica is a sans serif font.

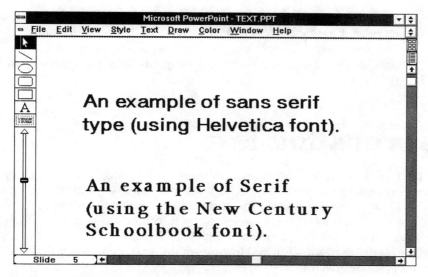

Fig. 4.12. *Serif and sans serif fonts.*

Serif fonts work well for smaller-point text sizes and sans serif fonts are best for headlines and subheads. Compare the page layout in a good newspaper with the layout of a supermarket tabloid and the ads inside the tabloid. See how the tabloid layout and ads are hard on the eyes?

- All-uppercase headlines and subheads are hard to read and should be used sparingly. Use larger type and bold to emphasize headlines.

- In most presentations, three fonts and three sizes will suffice for headlines. Select one standard size for subheads and put most or all of your text in a single font and point size.

- Use underline sparingly—too much is hard on the eyes—and limit it to text rather than headlines. Underlined headlines, especially in larger point sizes, are difficult to read.

- Be cautious about mixing italic with regular text for emphasis. Bold or even underlining is easier to read. In general, reserve italic in text for foreign or specialized words.

- Italic headlines create contrast and variety, especially when surrounded by nonitalic headlines. A 24- or 36-point italic headline is easy to read and produces contrast without clutter.

- When you use color in text, always compare it with the background color of the slide. Yellow text on a white background does not stand out very well, for example, whereas yellow on a black background is fine. Use bright colors against dark backgrounds and dark colors against light backgrounds.

Formatting Text

The term "formatting" covers many things, including aligning and positioning text, setting the spacing between lines, and indenting and tabbing text. This section discusses basic formatting features available on PowerPoint's Text menu: aligning text on the left or right, centering, justifying left and right margins, indenting, and tabbing. See Chapter 12, "Using Advanced Features of Text," for advanced features of the Text menu, such as the text ruler and line spacing.

Specifying Text Alignment

Word processors align text along the left margin by default. PowerPoint's Text menu gives you four options for aligning text: Left, Right, Center, and Justify. Using the Left option aligns text along the left margin, leaving any extra space at the end of the line. Right alignment aligns text along the right margin, leaving extra space at the beginning of the line. Choosing the Center option aligns text along the center point of each line, leaving equal space to the left and right. Use the Justify option to align text along both the left and right margins, so that the words on a line cover the full width of a text box.

Most of the time you use Left, but occasionally the other alignment options are useful. Use the Left option for ordinary entry of text. The uses of Right are less standard. You can use Right for visual effect. If your text box is close to an illustration, you can use Right to move one or more paragraphs away from the illustration. Center is a good choice when you want to put titles over a set of paragraphs. Justify is often used with text in columns next to one another. Text in columns without justified margins is sometimes hard to read. In PowerPoint, you can use the Justify option only on word processing objects, not labels. (You can use Left, Center, and Right with labels.) Apply all four options in the same way: select the text and choose the option from the Text menu. Suppose that you have a situation like that in figure 4.13.

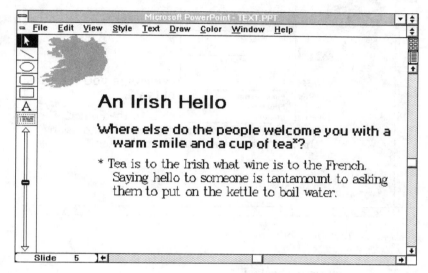

Fig. 4.13. *Unformatted text.*

Now suppose that you want to center the headline, `An Irish Hello`, over the text. You can use the space bar to bring the headline toward the center, but the following steps show you an easier way to center the headline:

1. Position the line cursor on the text that you want to align.

   To position the cursor, select the text box and click once over the text.

> **Tip:** In PowerPoint, the alignment options (Left, Right, Center, and Justify) always apply to whole paragraphs rather than to individual words, so you can position your cursor anywhere within a paragraph to change alignment. A paragraph is the text between Enter keystrokes. The slide in figure 4.13 contains three paragraphs because the Enter key was used three times—after "Hello", after "tea*?", and after "water." Indenting and tabbing also work on whole paragraphs.

2. Choose the Text menu.

   The menu drops down, as shown in figure 4.14.

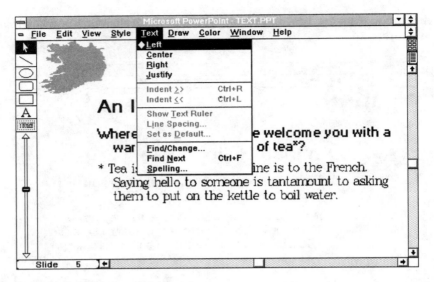

Fig. 4.14. The Text menu options.

The Left option is checked.

3. Choose your new option: Left, Center, Right, or Justify. Here, choose Center.

Your headline becomes centered, as shown in figure 4.15.

Fig. 4.15. A centered headline.

As explained in the next section, you indent and tab in the same way as you align text.

Indenting Text

PowerPoint has five levels of indentation. When you typed text in the section "Creating Text with the Word Processor Tool," you automatically entered the first indentation level in PowerPoint. You access the other four levels through the Text menu or the keyboard. When you go to another level, your text starts farther to the right in the text block, as explained in Chapter 12, "Using Advanced Features of Text."

An indent is the space between the left margin and the text. In most books, the first line of a paragraph is indented. In the first indentation level in PowerPoint, the reverse is true (as illustrated in figure 4.3). The first line starts at the margin and all subsequent lines in a paragraph start farther to the right. This creates a "hanging indent" effect that places emphasis on the first words in a paragraph. You can change this default situation, as shown in Chapter 12.

Each of the five indentation levels has two positions where text begins, the indentation point and the tab stop. The indentation point is farther to the left than the tab stop. In figure 4.3, the first line of the paragraph starts at the indentation point; all subsequent lines start at the tab stop. You also can reach the tab stop by pressing the Tab key.

PowerPoint provides default indentations and tabs. To change the defaults, see Chapter 12.

Suppose that you want to produce a slide like the one shown in figure 4.16.

Follow these steps to indent and tab your text to produce bullet charts:

1. Draw your text block.

   As mentioned previously, in the default setting, the tab at each indentation level is farther to the right than the indentation point. Chapter 12 explains how to set the indents and tabs at the same place. When you begin typing in a text block, PowerPoint automatically puts you in the first indentation level.

2. Type the text for the first indentation level. For this example, type *This series of indented text will show you how to produce bullet charts. This is the first level of indentation.*

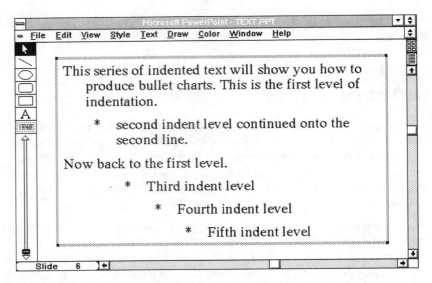

Fig. 4.16. Indented and tabbed text inside a selected text box.

When the text wraps (after the word "to" in figure 4.16), all subsequent lines begin at the tab stop. If you want the first line to begin at the tab too, press Tab before you type to get to the tab point for this level. In this example, you would put the cursor before "This" and press Tab. To continue with the example, suppose that you want to create the second indent level.

3. Press Enter.

4. Choose Indent >> from the Text menu to reach the next indentation level. Here, you go to the second level.

   Alternatively, press Ctrl-R (for right) from the keyboard to move to the next indentation level. Ctrl-L (for left) moves you back up a level (or to the left, which is the same thing).

Tip: You also can indent text that you typed previously. Select the text and choose the indent that you want from the menu.

5. Make a bullet.

   You can use Zapf Dingbats to make a bullet, or press the asterisk (*) key on your keyboard. The second indent is to the right of the tab point of the first indent level, although this difference may not be obvious on-screen.

6. Press the Tab key and type your text. For the example, type *second indent level continued onto the second line.*

   The words that wrap to the second line start from the tab point of the second indent level. When you press Enter within any indent level, the next paragraph begins at the same level. Now suppose that you want to go back a level.

7. Choose Indent << from the Text menu or press Ctrl-L.

   The cursor returns to the beginning of the line.

8. Continue choosing Indent >> to reach lower levels of indentation. Use Tab when necessary and type your bulleted text.

Chapter 12 shows you how to tab from the right, from the center, and with decimal-point alignment.

Finding and Changing Text

The Find/Change option on the Text menu enables you to make individual and global changes in your text. Suppose that you discover that you have misspelled a proper name in your presentation. Rather than hunt through your entire presentation and change each occurrence of the name, you can use Find/Change to make the changes for you.

The Find function searches through all the text in your presentation, including your notes pages. Here, take as an example the text you typed in the preceding section. Position the cursor at the start of the first paragraph, that is, before the T in This in figure 4.16.

To use the Find/Change function, follow these steps:

1. Choose Find/Change from the Text Menu.

   A dialog box appears, as shown in figure 4.17.

2. In the Find Text box, type the word you want to find and change. Here, type *first*.

3. In the Change To box, type the word you now prefer. Here, type *top*.

   Notice the two small boxes at the bottom, labeled Match Only Whole Words and Match Case. Activate Match Only Whole Words if you want to locate a whole word, not the same series of letters in some other word. For example, use this option to find "car" and not "carpet," "cartoon," "career," and so on. Choose Match Case if you want to find only words that match in upper- and lowercase characters. For instance, if you have a client named Steve Grey and you spelled his name "Gray," you don't want the program to stop on every occurrence of the word "gray" with a lowercase g.

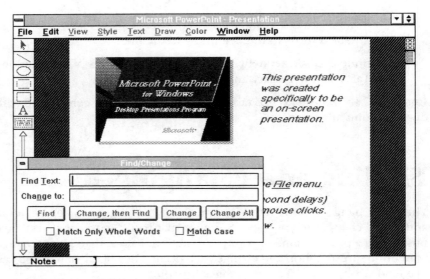

Fig. 4.17. *The Find/Change dialog box.*

You have four options: Find, Change, Change then Find, and Change All. This first time you search in the example, Change and Change then Find are not available because nothing is found (highlighted) yet. You can change something only after you have found it.

4. Choose your method for finding and changing. For this example, choose Find.

   The word first is highlighted. After a word is highlighted, you can use all four options.

   Use Find if you simply want to find the text typed in the box. PowerPoint searches for and highlights the text, but does not change it.

   Use Change then Find if you want to change the characters typed in the Find Text box and then find the next occurrence of the characters, without automatically changing them.

Use Change when you want to change a single occurrence of the text without continuing the search. You must click another button to restart the search.

Use Change All when you want to change all occurrences in your presentation of the text in the Find Text box. Using Change All searches the slide master and notes master as well as the body of the presentation.

5. Select the Change option.

   The word `first` changes to `top`.

> **Tip:** If the Find/Change dialog box gets in your way, move it to another part of the screen with the usual Windows methods for moving a selection box. Place the mouse pointer over the title line of the box (`Find/Change`, in this case) and drag it to another position. Alternatively, click on the presentation to send the box "behind" the window. If you will be using the box repeatedly, you can drag it to the edge of your presentation and just leave a small part visible.

6. Continue to search. Try the other two options, Change and Change All. The word `first` occurs once more in this slide. To create an example to use in the next section, "Using the Spelling Checker," deliberately misspell "top" as "topp" and then save the presentation as SPELL.PPT.

7. To exit the dialog box, close it or click the presentation.

The Find Next option enables you to find the next occurrence of a word or phrase in your text. You can find the word or phrase by selecting it from the Text menu or by using the key combination Ctrl-F. If the Find/Change dialog box has no character in the Find Text box, you see the dialog box the first time you choose Find Next. If the Find/Change dialog box does contain a character, you do not see the dialog box. PowerPoint just finds the next occurrence.

With the PowerPoint word processor, you can find and change text just as you can in a word processor. Note, however, that you cannot use the Undo command on the Edit menu to change the text back to its original form. You must use Find/Change again. You also can use a spelling checker, as explained in the next section.

Using the Spelling Checker

The Spelling option, the last option on the Text Menu, finds misspelled words and typographical errors. You have to determine the correct spelling and the correct context.

> *Tip:* The spelling checker will check the spelling of all labels, text, and objects. It will not check spelling, however, in items that have been pasted onto your presentation as a picture.

Open SPELL.PPT, the presentation file you created in the section "Finding and Changing Text."

Follow these steps to use the spelling checker:

1. Choose Spelling from the Text Menu.

   The Spelling dialog box opens on the screen.

   Like the Find/Change dialog box, you can move the Spelling dialog box to another part of the screen if it is in your way. The spelling checker has six options: Check Spelling, Change, Ignore, Suggest, and Add, with the Added Words option at the bottom. You learn about the last two (used with custom dictionaries) in Chapter 12.

2. Select Check Spelling to start the spelling checker.

   The dialog box registers the first misspelled word, as shown in figure 4.18.

   An hourglass icon appears on-screen while the spelling checker runs through your presentation. When the spelling checker finds a misspelled word, *topp* in this example, that word appears in the central bar of the box where the cursor is blinking. The borders around the other five boxes darken, indicating that you can click them.

3. Choose Suggest to make the spelling checker suggest an alternative spelling.

   A list of words appears in the scroll box. In this example, the first word, top, is correct.

> *Tip:* If the word isn't on the Suggest list, consult your dictionary.

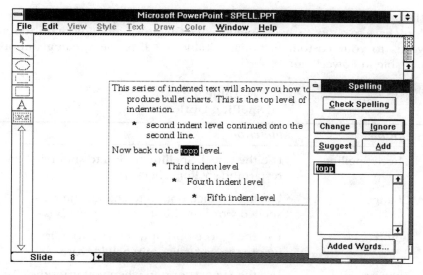

Fig. 4.18. *The Spelling dialog box with a misspelled word highlighted.*

4. Scroll down the suggestion list and choose the correct word. In this case, click on `top` in the scroll box.

   The word that you select replaces the misspelled word in the central bar. Now replace `topp` in the slide.

5. Choose the Change option.

   The word in the presentation changes.

Alternatively, you can type the new spelling directly, as follows:

1. Type the correct spelling into the central bar where the misspelled word appears. Here, you type *top* into the central bar.

   To avoid retyping the whole word, click over the letter you want to change. Here, click before the *p* and delete the incorrect letter.

2. Choose Change to change the word in the presentation.

3. Choose Check Spelling to restart.

Sometimes the spelling checker stops on a slang expression or a contraction that isn't in the PowerPoint dictionary. To ignore a word found by the spelling checker, choose Ignore.

The spelling checker automatically restarts when you choose Ignore: you don't have to choose Check Spelling. See Chapter 12 for advice on adding words to your custom dictionary. Table 4.2 lists the spelling options available in PowerPoint.

Table 4.2
Spelling Options

Option	Function
Check Spelling	Use the Check Spelling option to start or restart the spelling checker.
Change	Use the Change option to change the misspelled word on the slide in the text box.
Ignore	Use the Ignore option when you want to ignore the particular misspelled word.
Suggest	Use the Suggest option when you want the PowerPoint spelling checker to suggest an alternative spelling for the misspelled word.
Add	Use the Add option to add the word to the custom dictionary file.
Added Words	Use the Added Words option when you want PowerPoint to show the list of words added to the custom dictionary.

To exit the spelling checker, close the dialog box by double-clicking the Control menu box in the extreme upper left corner of the Spelling dialog box.

Chapter Summary

This chapter introduced you to the two basic tools for creating text, the labeler and the word processor tools. You learned about sizing to text and selecting words. You saw how to apply the different styles, fonts, and sizes, and you got a quick lesson on using and mixing styles. You then learned about formatting—using Left, Right, and so on, as well as indenting and tabbing. You saw how to find and change a word and how to use the spelling checker to find and change misspelled words.

You probably will add text to your charts more often than you will add other items. To enhance your text, however, you may want to add graphics—pictures, geometric shapes, or other objects—to your slides. To appreciate the full power of your graphics package, you must know how to create and manipulate objects, as explained in the next chapter.

5

Drawing Objects

If you know how to work with Windows, you already know much about working with objects in PowerPoint. You are familiar with techniques for selecting, resizing, and moving objects. You probably know a good bit about changing or deleting them. This chapter teaches you the basics of manipulating objects.

In this chapter, you learn to draw the many varieties of shapes possible in PowerPoint—lines, squares, ovals, rectangles, and circles. Next you learn how to manipulate them. You can move your drawings around on your slide and change their size, often in specific and refined ways, such as outward from a central point or, for a line, from one end or from both ends simultaneously.

Drawing objects can be confusing if you are not familiar with the basics. If you draw an unfilled object without a frame, you cannot see the object on the screen. If you have one object stacked beneath another, you cannot see the bottom object and may not be able to work with it. If you have Snap to Grid turned on, your objects automatically snap to invisible lines as you move them—a powerful capability, as long as you know that you are using it.

You learn how to fill shapes that enclose space, such as ovals, with color and how to change the fill pattern using the Color menu choices. You discover how to give patterns to shapes in a variety of ways. You also learn to cast shadows on shapes to produce a three-dimensional effect and to apply different line styles to a frame. PowerPoint provides refined tools, such as guides and grids, to help you align objects precisely, and you learn about those as well.

This chapter focuses on the line, oval, rectangle, and rounded-corner rectangle tools. Most of the techniques covered in this chapter, such as

121

moving, filling, and framing, also apply to the labeler and word processor tools and work in exactly the same way.

Drawing Lines and Shapes

With PowerPoint you can draw straight lines, ovals, circles, rectangles and squares with rounded corners, and rectangles and squares with right-angled corners. The tools to draw lines and shapes are located on the top half of the left edge of your PowerPoint screen, below the (default) arrow tool and above the Slide Changer, as shown in figure 5.1.

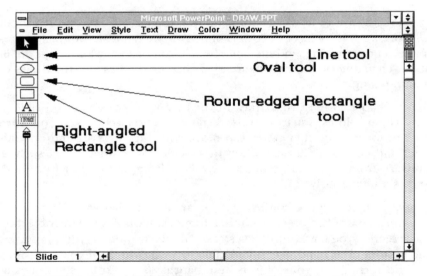

Fig. 5.1. The basic PowerPoint screen, with drawing tools on the left.

You need only follow a few simple steps to draw any of these shapes. In general, you create any shape by clicking on the shape you want from the menu, putting the pointer at the place on the slide where you want the object to appear, and dragging with the mouse until the object is the size you want.

Suppose that you have a slide with the words Using our landscaping services and you want to emphasize the text by framing it with an oval shape. To add the oval, follow these steps:

1. Click the shape button to select the shape you want. For the example, click the oval tool.

   The background of the button changes to black, indicating that the tool is now selected.

2. Move the mouse pointer to wherever you want the shape to appear. For the example, place the pointer to the left of the text you want to enclose.

   The pointer changes from an arrow to a crosshair. You see this effect with whatever drawing tool you select. You can begin drawing immediately.

3. Select the starting position on the slide and then press the left mouse button. Keeping the mouse button down, you can drag the mouse pointer in any direction. Here, drag to the right and down.

   As you drag the mouse, PowerPoint shows you what the potential drawing looks like by shrinking and elongating the figure as you move back and forth. You know exactly what you will get when you decide to make the drawing permanent.

4. Release the mouse button to make the shape permanent.

   In this example, the oval shape draws attention to the enclosed text. The line or shape remains selected after you release the mouse button, as indicated by the dotted line surrounding the shape (see fig. 5.2).

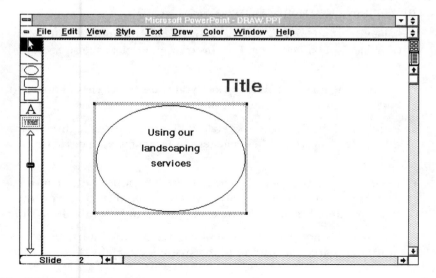

Fig. 5.2. *A selected oval shape.*

When a shape is selected, you can manipulate it in many ways, including changing its size, color, and location on the slide. Later sections in this chapter discuss these activities.

5. To deselect the shape, click anywhere outside the dotted lines that surround the object or shape.

> *Tip:* If you want to deselect an object without accidentally selecting another one from the screen, click the arrow tool (the top tool on the left of the screen).

Wherever you click to deselect the shape, the black background moves to the arrow tool in the upper left and the arrow tool is selected. Follow the steps you used in this section for all drawing tools—the line tool, the oval tool, the rounded-corner rectangle tool, and the right-angled rectangle tool. You can use these same tools to draw refinements of these shapes. The next section discusses drawing circles and squares.

Drawing Circles and Squares

You draw a circle or square by pressing the Shift key while you perform the basic steps for drawing an oval or rectangle and dragging diagonally. For the landscaping example, suppose that you want to draw a square representing a house, with a circle representing a lawn in front. To draw this picture, follow these simple steps:

1. Select the drawing tool you need by placing the mouse pointer over the tool and clicking. For this example, select the right-angled rectangle tool.

2. Position the mouse pointer where you want the circle or square to begin, in this case, to the right of the center of the slide.

3. Hold down the Shift key and keep it down until you begin to draw the shape. PowerPoint has registered that you want a circle or square.

4. Begin drawing the shape by clicking the left mouse button and dragging the mouse diagonally in the required direction. For the example, draw a square that takes up about one-eighth of the slide.

   This shape is not permanent until you release the mouse button, so move the pointer around until the shape looks right.

5. Release the mouse button.

   Next, select the oval tool. Follow the same steps to draw a circle to the left of the rectangle. You end up with something similar to figure 5.3.

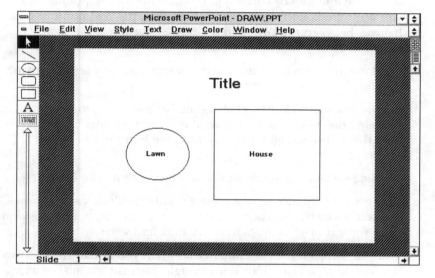

Fig. 5.3. *A square and a circle drawn using the Shift key.*

6. Click outside the selection box (the dotted line surrounding the shape) to deselect the shape.

You use a similar technique to draw lines with specific properties, as shown in the next section.

Drawing Vertical, Horizontal, and 45-Degree Angle Lines

You draw vertical, horizontal, and 45-degree angle lines in almost the same way that you draw any line, as shown in the following steps. To draw a vertical line, hold down the Shift key and drag vertically. To draw a horizontal line, hold down the Shift key and drag horizontally. To draw a line at a 45-degree angle to another line, hold down the Shift key and move the mouse clockwise or counterclockwise. (If you do not hold down the

Shift key, the line or shape is "free form"—that is, not necessarily square, horizontal, or vertical.) To continue the example, suppose that the company wants to draw a vertical line between the lawn and the house shown in figure 5.3. To add the vertical line, do the following:

1. Select the line tool by clicking it. Position the mouse pointer where you want the line to begin. For the example, put the mouse pointer halfway between the lawn and the house, starting at the same height as the top line of the house.

2. Hold down the Shift key and keep it down until you begin drawing the line.

3. Begin drawing the line by clicking the left mouse button and dragging the mouse in the required direction. For the example, drag the mouse straight down as far as the bottom side of the house.

   The line is not permanent until you release the mouse button.

4. Experiment with moving the mouse pointer in a clockwise or counterclockwise direction. Notice that the line "flips" into position from vertical to 45 degrees to horizontal, and so on.

   You can see from the experiment that when you initially hold down the Shift key, you can draw lines in eight basic directions—at 45, 90, 135, 180, 225, 270, 315, and 360 degrees from a starting point. Returning to the landscaping example, you can draw the vertical line, and then, using the Shift key, draw another line starting from the same point to mark off the landscape at 45 degrees to the original (see fig. 5.4).

5. Release the mouse button to make the line permanent, then click outside the selection box (the dotted line surrounding the line) to deselect the line.

In certain situations, you may want to keep an object in the same position relative to other objects on the slide. In these cases, you can draw the object from the center outward, as explained in the next section.

Drawing Objects and Lines from the Center Out

You have seen how to draw lines and other shapes by starting at one of the corners (or ends in the case of lines) of the shape. Sometimes, however, you

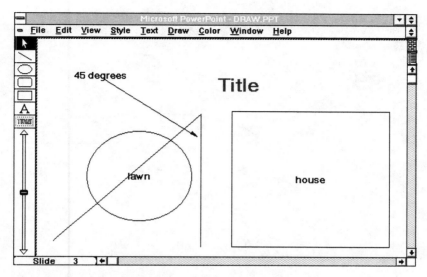

Fig. 5.4. *Two lines at 45 degrees to each other.*

may want the center of the rectangle or circle or line to be located in a particular position. For example, you may want the center of a line to begin at the end of another line. In our landscaping example, suppose that you want to draw two concentric ovals with their centers located at the intersection of the two lines drawn previously. Hold down the Ctrl key as you draw the object.

1. Select the drawing tool that you want by clicking it. Here, select the oval tool.

2. Position the mouse pointer where you want the center of the line or shape to be, in this case at the intersection point of the two lines at 45-degree angles.

3. Hold down the Ctrl key and keep it down until you begin drawing the line or shape.

4. Draw the shape by clicking the left mouse button and dragging the mouse away from the starting point. Release the button when the drawing looks correct.

   Repeat the process using the same oval and the same center point. You end up with concentric ovals drawn from the same point, like those in figure 5.5.

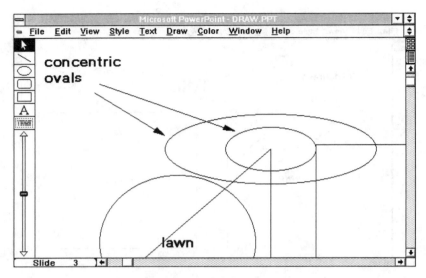

Fig. 5.5. Concentric ovals drawn using the Ctrl key.

5. Click outside the selection box (the dotted line surrounding the line) to deselect the line.

> ***Tip:*** If you need to use the same center point more than once, mark the point beforehand by drawing two lines, one horizontal, one vertical, that intersect at the point. If you draw the lines horizontally and vertically, you can better place the crosshair drawing pointer directly over the point. You later can remove the lines from the picture by selecting them and choosing Cut from the Edit menu.

To draw circles and squares or to draw lines at an angle, hold down the Shift key when you begin drawing. Hold down the Ctrl key to draw shapes from the center out. Hold down the Shift and Ctrl keys at the same time to do both together. For example, you can draw a circle or square from the center out or lines at certain angles from the center out by following these steps:

1. Select the drawing tool by placing the mouse pointer over the drawing tool and clicking, and then position the mouse pointer where you want the center of the line or shape to be.

2. Hold down the Shift and Ctrl keys together and keep them down until you begin drawing the line or shape.

3. Begin drawing the shape by clicking the left mouse button and dragging the mouse away from the center point. Release the mouse button when you have drawn the shape or line to your satisfaction (see fig. 5.6).

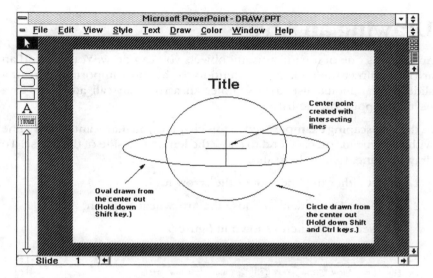

Fig. 5.6. *Hold down the Shift key to draw a shape from the center out. Hold down Shift and Ctrl together to draw a symmetrical shape from the center out.*

Table 5.1 summarizes how you use Shift and Ctrl in drawing.

Table 5.1
Using the Shift and Ctrl Keys in Drawing

Use	With Line Tool	With Other Drawing Tools
Shift	To draw vertical, horizontal and 45-degree lines	To draw circles and squares
Ctrl	To draw from the center out	To draw from the center out
Shift-Ctrl	To draw vertical, horizontal and 45-degree lines from the center out	To draw circles and squares from the center out

In this section, you have seen how to use the drawing tools to draw a number of special shapes. A particularly useful shape is the arrow, explained in the next section.

Drawing an Arrow

An arrow is one of the most useful objects you can draw. You can add an arrow to direct the audience's attention to the most important part of a slide. In a bulleted list, for example, an arrow can call attention to a particular point on the list.

In the landscaping example used in this chapter, you may want to add a line with arrowheads on each end to show the length of a side of the house. To draw the line, follow these steps:

1. Select either the line tool or the arrow tool.

2. From the Draw menu, choose the Arrowheads option.

   You see the submenu shown in figure 5.7.

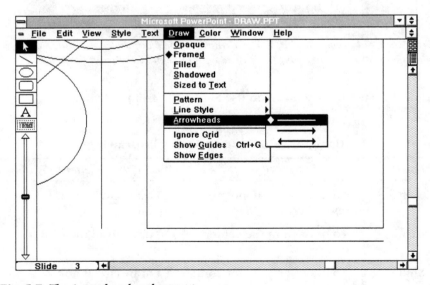

Fig. 5.7. The Arrowheads submenu.

If you select any tool other than the arrow tool or the line tool, the Arrowheads option is not available from the menu. The word

`Arrowheads` **appears in gray, not black, and nothing happens when you click it.**

The first choice in the Arrowheads menu is a line with no arrowhead. This line is the default choice and, unless you have changed it, is the choice currently selected (as indicated by the diamond to the left of the line). The second choice is a line with one arrowhead. This arrowhead automatically points in the direction you draw the line, with the arrowhead on the end of the line you draw last. The third choice enables you to draw a line with arrowheads at both ends.

> *Tip:* In PowerPoint, you see two kinds of check marks next to menu items. The diamond is the default. When you see a mark of a different shape, whatever is currently selected on the slide has the characteristics of the checked item, which is not a PowerPoint default.

3. Select one of the bottom two options by clicking it. Here, select the line with arrowheads at each end.

   You exit the submenu automatically.

4. Select the line tool, if it isn't already selected, and draw a line. For the example, draw a horizontal line parallel to the bottom side of the house.

The arrowheads appear at the ends of the line. Now add the length, 60 feet, with the labeler tool (as described in Chapter 4, "Adding Text to a Presentation"). You end up with the diagram shown in figure 5.8.

You can add an arrowhead to a line you already have drawn. Select the line (as shown in the next section), then pick one of the arrowhead options from the Arrowheads menu. PowerPoint always "remembers" in which direction the line was drawn and puts a single arrowhead (if chosen) at the proper end. If you want to put the arrowhead at the other end of the line, you need to draw the line again, beginning at the correct end.

Editing Lines and Shapes

As you revise your diagrams, you may want to change or delete lines and shapes. This section shows you how to delete a selected object with the Del key. You also learn how to move and copy an object.

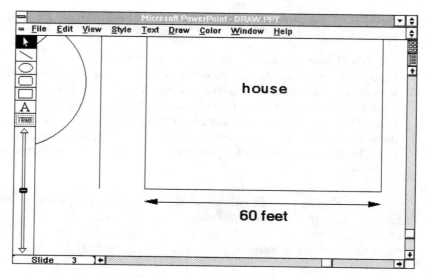

Fig. 5.8. A line with double arrowheads.

> *Tip:* Remember that after you have drawn an object, you must use the arrow tool to manipulate the object further. You cannot use the tool you originally used to draw the object.

Selecting an Object

Suppose that you want to delete the words concentric ovals and the two lines pointing to the ovals, shown in figure 5.5. Follow these steps to select an object.

1. Select the arrow tool, if it is not already selected.

2. Place the mouse pointer over the object you want to select and click. Here, click over the words concentric ovals.

   A dotted line encloses the object or line, indicating that it is selected.

   By following step 3, you now can select as many drawn objects as you want. The first object remains selected as well.

3. While holding down the Shift key, place the mouse pointer over a second shape and click. Here, click over each straight line in the landscaping slide while you hold down the Shift key.

All three objects become selected, as shown in figure 5.9.

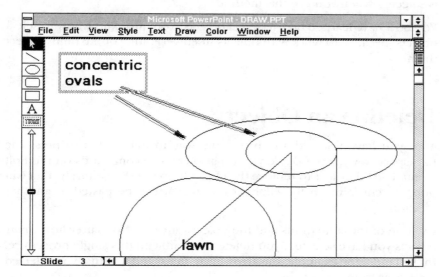

Fig. 5.9. *Selected objects on a screen.*

You also can select groups of objects by dragging with the mouse. To do so, follow these steps:

1. Place the mouse pointer above and to the left of the left-most object of those you want to select (the text, in the landscaping example).

2. Hold down the mouse button and drag the mouse pointer toward the other objects to be selected—the lines with arrowheads.

   You see a broken rectangle delineated as you drag the mouse.

3. Completely enclose the objects to be selected with the broken rectangle and then release the mouse button.

The rectangle disappears and the objects become selected, as shown in figure 5.9.

When you dragged the mouse, the broken rectangle partly enclosed the ovals. You did not select the ovals, however, because the rectangle did not completely enclose them.

To select all objects on the current slide—text blocks and pictures as well as drawn objects—pull down the Edit menu and then choose Select All. Alternatively, press Ctrl-A.

All objects on the slide become selected. It doesn't matter which object tool is selected when you use this method.

You now have learned how to select objects. You must know how to select objects, because to work with objects in PowerPoint, you first must select them.

Deleting an Object

After you have selected an object, one way to delete it is to press the Backspace key (or the Del key). You also can use commands on the Edit menu. Use Edit Clear to remove the object from the slide entirely; Edit Cut puts the cut item on the clipboard so that it can be pasted to another location.

Use one of these methods and the object vanishes. No matter how many objects you have selected, you delete them all with this single procedure. In the landscape example, the arrowhead, lines, and text that you selected disappear from the screen.

If you delete an object by mistake, you can undo the deletion. Undo works only when you have done nothing else on the screen after the delete action. If you draw another line or type words following the deletion, you cannot bring back the deleted object. To undo a deletion, do the following:

Choose Undo from the Edit menu.

The deleted object returns. Deleting and undeleting objects are operations you will use often in PowerPoint. Often, too, you will want to change and move objects, as explained in the next section.

Copying and Pasting Objects

In the preceding section, you learned that you can cut an object to the clipboard as one method of deleting it. You use a similar capability to make a copy of an object—that is, you cut the object to the clipboard while leaving the original in place. You then can paste the copy into another location in the drawing.

For instance, suppose that you want to copy the rectangle shown in figure 5.10.

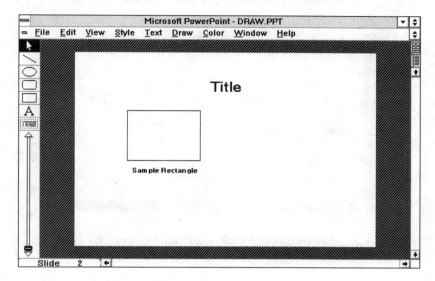

Fig. 5.10. *A rectangle to be copied.*

Follow these steps to make your copy:

1. Select the rectangle by clicking it with the arrow tool.

   You see the selection box around the rectangle.

2. From the Edit menu, choose Copy.

   The rectangle on the screen does not change. By choosing Copy, though, you copied the object onto the clipboard, where the copy stays until you copy another object into the clipboard. (***Be careful.*** Remember that after you do copy a new object to the clipboard, you lose whatever was on the clipboard before.) Now you can create as many copies of the original as you want.

3. Place the cursor where you want the copy to appear, and choose Paste from the Edit menu.

   Figure 5.11 shows the drawing with both the original rectangle and the copy. You can make as many copies as you like as long as the original remains on the clipboard: just choose Paste for each copy. You can even copy into other Windows applications, such as Microsoft Word.

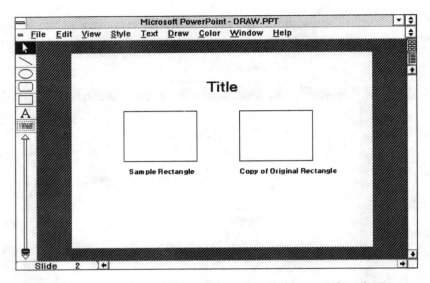

Fig. 5.11. The original rectangle and the copy made by using the Edit Copy command.

Chances are that you are familiar with copying and pasting from word processing applications. In the next section you learn about another process that may be familiar from elsewhere—moving objects.

Moving Objects

In PowerPoint, you can move drawn objects with the left or right button of your mouse. If you use the left button, you first select the object, then drag it. If you use the right button, you do not have to select the object. Place the cursor anywhere inside the object, click the right button, and drag to the new position. Examples of each method follow here.

Use the slide shown in figure 5.12 as an example. Suppose that the lawn is too close to the house.

Follow these steps to move the lawn:

1. Select the arrow tool, if it is not already selected. Next, select the shape or line to be moved by placing the mouse pointer over the shape and clicking once. Here, click the circular lawn.

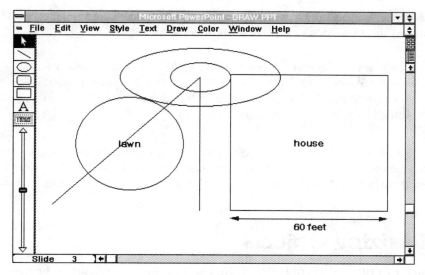

Fig. 5.12. *The sample slide before you move the lawn.*

Now you can choose which mouse button to use.

2. To use the right mouse button, place the mouse pointer anywhere over the object. (You do not have to select it first.) Hold down the right button. The pointer changes to a crosshair with arrowheads on the ends.

3. Hold down the button and move the mouse. The object moves around the screen, but as a "shadow" version (with dotted lines) of the original. In the landscape example, drag the circle labeled 1awn to the left. Release the button when the object is in the desired position.

4. To use the left mouse button, place the mouse pointer directly over one of the selection lines that encloses the shape (anywhere except on the black dots on each corner). While holding down the button, move the mouse to drag the shape in any direction. Again, the object moves as a "shadow" until you release the mouse button. Release the button when the shape is where you want it to be.

The choice of buttons is up to you. Try both to see which you prefer.

The procedure for moving more than one selected object is exactly the same. Use the left mouse button. Position the mouse pointer over a selection line and drag the line. You then move all selected objects, which stay in the same position relative to one another.

> *Tip:* You can force an object to move only horizontally or vertically, a useful feature when you want to keep a series of objects in alignment (such as keeping text bullets in left alignment). Hold down the Shift key while you drag the object.

You now know how to move objects without changing their shape. The next section shows how you use the resizing handles—the black dots in each corner of the selection box—to change the shape of objects.

Resizing Objects

Moving objects does not change their size or shape. Sometimes, however, you need to change the size or shape of an object you already have drawn. Suppose that you want to enlarge the outer concentric oval in the landscape example so that the oval reaches the lawn. To resize an object without deleting it and starting from scratch, follow these steps:

1. Select the drawn object by placing the mouse pointer over it and clicking. For this exercise, select the outer concentric oval.

   The usual broken lines with the black dots in each corner surround the object: two dots for lines, four for all other shapes. The black boxes at the corners are *resizing handles.*

2. Place the mouse pointer on one of the resizing handles and, holding the button down, drag the object in the desired direction. In the landscaping example, the outer oval is concentric with the inner oval and you want to keep the center where it is. Hold down the Ctrl key (as explained in table 5.2) and drag one of the dots to elongate the oval until it reaches the lawn.

   The shape expands in the direction toward which you drag. The example now looks like figure 5.13.

The Shift and Ctrl keys have special uses in drawing objects. They have similar special uses in resizing objects. The many combinations that are possible are worth investigating. Hold either or both keys down while dragging the resizing handles. Use table 5.2 as a guide. Any gaps in the table (for instance, no move direction given in the table for the Ctrl key) mean the keys have no effect.

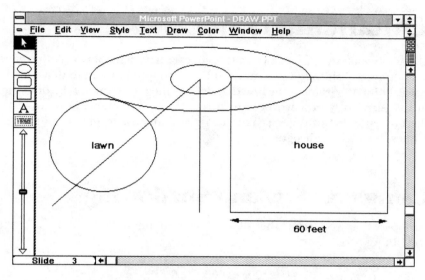

Fig. 5.13. Oval elongated by using the resizing handle.

Table 5.2
Resizing and Moving Guide

Use	With Line Tool	With Oval/Rectangle Tools
Shift	To resize with no change in the angle	To resize vertically, horizontally, and diagonally
	To move only vertically or horizontally	To move only vertically or horizontally
Ctrl	To resize length and angle while keeping the center fixed	To resize while keeping the center fixed
Ctrl-Shift	To resize length from both ends, keeping the center fixed	To resize vertically, horizontally, and diagonally, keeping the center fixed

You now have seen how to move objects. In the following sections, you learn ways to improve or manipulate objects by changing the frame or shadowing around them, the fill inside them, and so on.

Enhancing Objects

All the objects you have drawn in this chapter have what PowerPoint refers to as "frames," although you may not have thought of them in that way. In PowerPoint, the frame is the line that defines the outer limit of the drawing. In this section, you learn how to turn off this frame and how to add a shadowing effect to objects. You also discover how to give the lines (or frames) a different design.

Using Framing and Shadowing

Suppose that you have the slide shown in figure 5.14, with a circle containing text.

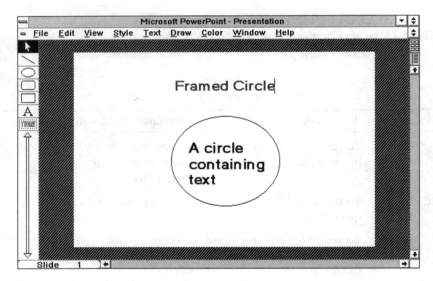

Fig. 5.14. *A framed circle.*

To get rid of the frame around the circle, follow these steps:

1. Select a drawn object or draw a new shape and keep the shape selected. Here, select the circle.

2. Choose Draw from the menu.

Notice that Framed in the Draw menu has a diamond or a check to the left, indicating that this feature is active or selected. You want to make it inactive.

3. Choose Framed.

    You return to the slide. Your shape disappears, although in the example, the text remains.

If a slide has no text and you click outside the selection box at this stage, you are left with nothing on the screen, although the shape is still there. What is the purpose of this unframed feature? You do not necessarily need a frame around the edges of a shape with a color or pattern in order to see the shape. This unframed feature is discussed in the section "Filling Objects and Adding Patterns."

To reframe a selected shape, again choose Framed from the Draw menu. The frame returns to the selected objects.

You switch on and off all choices in the Draw menu except Pattern, Line Style, and Arrowheads. On the menu, these choices have arrow-shaped pointers to their right, indicating a range of choices. You learn about these choices later in this chapter in the section "Changing Line Styles."

You can shadow your shapes in the same way that you frame them, except that shadowing is not a default option—you have to switch it on. Shadows are a form of special effect. If you do not use them to excess, shadows make objects look finished and attractive. You can, of course, draw shadows yourself for objects you have created, but this method is time-consuming and you can make errors. Because shadows are a popular feature, PowerPoint enables you to choose them from the menu rather than draw them yourself. If you want to place a shadow on the unframed circle above, follow these steps:

1. Draw an object (not a line) or select an object you have already drawn. Here, select the circle.

2. Choose Draw from the menu and then choose Shadowed.

When you return to the slide, your shape "casts" a shadow similar to the one shown in figure 5.15. If the shape overlaps another shape, you will notice that the shadowed shape is no longer transparent; it is solid and covers part of the shape beneath it.

You cannot apply framing and shadowing to individual lines (as distinct from lines that are part of a rectangle). You can style the lines, however, to achieve a similar effect, as explained in the next section.

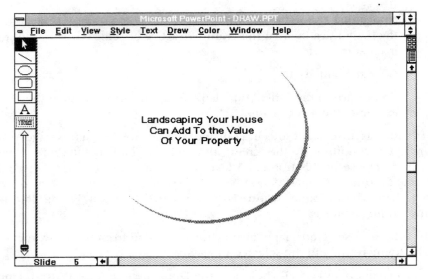

Fig. 5.15. A shadowed circle.

Changing Line Styles

You can restyle all frames and lines in PowerPoint to double lines, thicker lines, and so on. Styling is often a useful way to draw attention to certain parts of your slide or to distinguish between different objects. Continuing with the "shadowed circle" example, add two horizontal lines above and below the text. Then make them double lines, as shown in these steps:

1. Draw a new shape or shapes or select one or more shapes that you already have drawn. Here, select the two horizontal lines.

2. Choose Line Style from the Draw menu (see fig. 5.16).

   The check next to the top option indicates that this style is active.

3. Click the line style of your choice.

PowerPoint applies the style to your lines. Figure 5.17 shows the result in the current example.

Use different line styles for different emphasis. A heavy line, for example, makes an object stand out.

You saw earlier in the chapter that you can remove the frame from an object, making that object invisible. This capability does not make much sense unless you are dealing with filled objects that remain visible without the frame. The next section explains how to change the colors and patterns inside your objects.

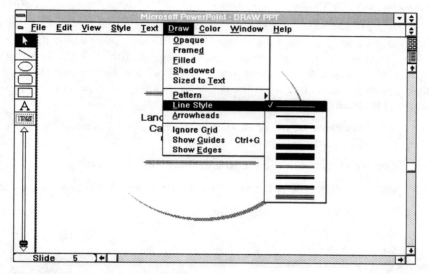

Fig. 5.16. *The Line Style menu options.*

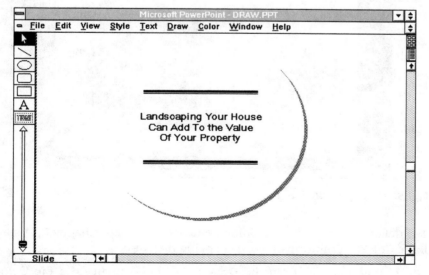

Fig. 5.17. *Restyled lines.*

Filling Objects and Adding Patterns

This section discusses the many varieties of colors and patterns you can apply to your drawn objects and shows you how to make an object opaque. These techniques do not apply to lines.

To add fill and patterns to objects, follow the same steps you followed in the section "Using Framing and Shadowing." In the example shown in figure 5.13, suppose that you want to fill in the house and lawn to distinguish these shapes from the other shapes on the slide. Follow these steps to fill them in:

1. Select a drawn object or draw a new shape. For this example, select the house and lawn shapes.

2. Choose Draw from the menu and then choose Filled.

Your selected objects fill with the default color. Figure 5.18 shows the filled shapes.

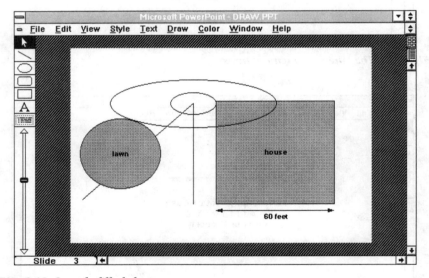

Fig. 5.18. *Sample filled shapes.*

The default color is set in the Color menu. Please refer to Chapter 7, "Using Basic Color," for information on changing the color.

You change patterns from the Draw menu rather than from the Color menu. For this example, keep selected the object you have just filled. Continue with these steps:

1. Choose Pattern from the Draw menu.

   Figure 5.19 shows the Pattern submenu.

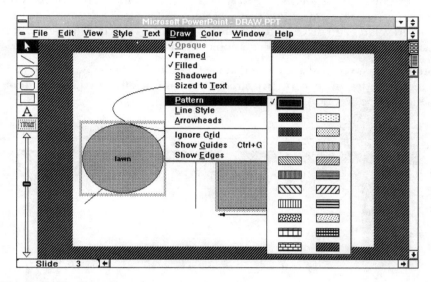

Fig. 5.19. *The Pattern options.*

2. Choose a new pattern by clicking one of the choices with the mouse pointer. Try one of the striped patterns.

On the slide, you see the object displayed with the new pattern. See Chapter 7, "Using Basic Color," for more information on using colors and patterns.

You do not have to choose Filled if you choose a pattern, because a patterned object is also a filled object. If you draw an unfilled shape and then choose a pattern, the Filled option in the Draw menu automatically registers active for that shape.

Use these simple steps to fill and pattern your objects. All filled objects are opaque. Opaque objects don't look opaque unless you place them on top of other objects. Choose Edit and then Bring to Front to put an object on top of another object; choose Edit and then Send to Back to put an object under another object, as explained in this chapter in the section "Changing the Stacking Order of Objects." In the next section, you see how to make an unfilled object opaque.

Making an Object Opaque

An opaque object is impossible to see through and blocks anything behind it. In PowerPoint, any object that you draw is "behind" other objects that you draw later and place on top of the first object. In practice, however, you can see all the objects, unless an object on top is filled or made opaque.

Suppose that you had a slide similar to the slide shown in figure 5.20, with a rectangle drawn on top of two circles. You cannot tell from this slide alone which shape is "on top."

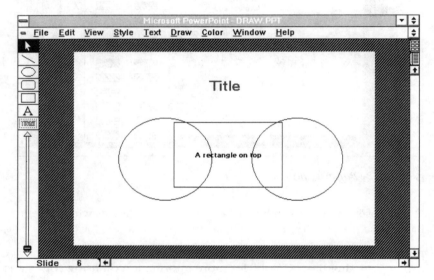

Fig. 5.20. *A rectangle overlaying two circles.*

Follow these steps to make the rectangle opaque:

1. Select the object that you want to make opaque. Here, select the rectangle.

2. From the Draw menu, choose Opaque.

The sections of the circles that are directly underneath the rectangle disappear from view. If you now make the rectangle unframed, you have the slide shown in figure 5.21.

An opaque object can have several useful applications in a drawing. For example, you can create a "build chart" in much the same way that you might create it on an overhead projector. For the first slide in the series, use an opaque rectangle that matches the background color to cover all but one bullet in a five-bullet chart. For the second slide, use the opaque rectangle to cover all but two bullets, and so on. As noted in Chapter 2, you can use an opaque object to cover the title on a slide, because in PowerPoint you cannot delete the title.

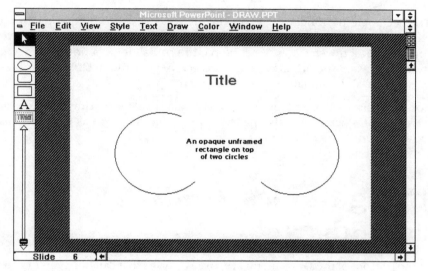

Fig. 5.21. *An opaque unframed rectangle partly obscuring two circles.*

If you want to have one object cover another one, the first object has to be "on top of" the second. To make sure that you have an object on top, you can change the stacking order of objects, as explained in the next section.

Changing the Stacking Order of Objects

In PowerPoint, you can place one object on top of another. Unless you change the order of the objects, the last object you draw is the top object (just as it would be if you were stacking physical objects). Knowing how to change the stacking order of objects can be particularly important if you want one opaque object to cover another opaque object that you drew after you drew the first object. For example, suppose that you draw an opaque circle and want it covered by an opaque rectangle that you drew earlier. You must change the stacking order.

Follow these steps to change the stacking order of objects:

1. Select the object whose order you want to change, for example, the opaque unframed rectangle from the preceding section.

2. From the Edit menu, choose Bring to Front or Send to Back. For the example, choose Send to Back.

The rectangle no longer obscures the circles. In PowerPoint, you cannot change the stacking order of certain objects. A slide title always remains at the bottom of the stack, as does the picture of a slide on a notes page. On the slide master, the title always remains at the top of the stack. On the notes master, the slide miniature always stays on top.

You now have seen the drawing tools that you use to draw objects in PowerPoint. PowerPoint also provides tools that help you as you draw, as explained in the next section.

Using Guides, Grids, and Edges

At the bottom of the Draw menu are three options that can help you in your drawing: Snap to Grid, Show Guides, and Show Edges. Each option also has another name on the menu: Ignore Grid, Hide Guides, and Hide Edges, respectively. When you choose an option, its name on the menu automatically changes to its opposite. If, for example, you choose Show Guides, the guides appear on-screen and the menu option changes to Hide Guides.

You can use these three options to help you align, move, and display objects, as explained in the following sections.

Using the Guides To Align Objects

Sometimes you need to align objects to make your slide look neater or easier to understand. The guide lines available through the Draw menu help you align objects along the vertical or horizontal axis. Suppose that you have an oval in the upper left portion of your screen, representing an area to plant, and a rectangle on the right, representing a garden shed. You must have the shapes aligned exactly to illustrate a particular example of landscaping. Follow these steps to align them:

1. Choose Draw and then choose Show Guides.

   You see a pair of dotted lines, one vertical, one horizontal, as shown in figure 5.22.

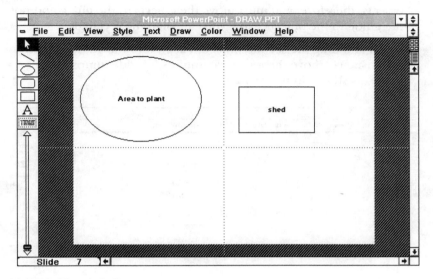

Fig. 5.22. The guide lines.

PowerPoint places the lines in the center of the screen. Suppose that you want to align the shed vertically with the point at the farthest right of the planting area.

2. Place your mouse pointer over the vertical guide line. Press and hold down the mouse button. Now drag the line to the left.

   As you drag the line, a number, 0.00, appears at the center when you first hold down the button, and then rises in increments as you drag the line. This number represents inches (or centimeters, if you chose centimeters as the default unit when you installed PowerPoint) from the center of the slide, as measured on the printed output, not on the screen slide.

   Stop dragging when you reach the point where you want to align the objects. In the example, stop to the right of the oval.

3. Move the drawn object to the guide line. Here, move the oval until its right side touches the guide.

PowerPoint makes aligning easy by giving the guide a sort of "magnetic" attraction to objects. Objects "jump" to a guide line when you move them close to the line. When you move the guide line, however, objects do not jump to it. If you want to align objects, therefore, you must move the objects to the guide and not the guide to the objects. Now you can align the rectangle.

4. Select and drag the second object to align it to the guide line. In this instance, move the rectangle until its left side jumps to the guide, as shown in figure 5.23.

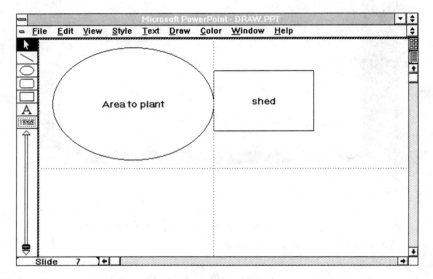

Fig. 5.23. *An oval and rectangle vertically aligned.*

If the guides are no longer necessary, you can hide them by following the instructions in the next step.

5. Choose Hide Guides from the Draw menu.

The lines disappear from the slide.

Tip: If you have trouble seeing clearly when aligning objects, use the View menu to switch from the 50% Size default to Full Size.

You can use the guides with the Ctrl and Shift keys to align objects. You can, for example, draw a square centered on a specific point. First, move the guide lines so that they intersect on the point you have chosen to be the center point of the square. Next, position the cursor on the point of intersection and draw the square while holding down the Ctrl and Shift keys.

Use the guide lines as shown in the preceding steps to place objects with precision. You can use an additional tool—the grid—to help you place objects exactly where you want them.

Using the Grid

The grid is a series of invisible lines that run vertically and horizontally across the slide screen. You can switch grid lines on and off. When on, grid lines, like guide lines, attract objects that are nearby. The grid is useful if you want to align objects automatically as you draw. (If you have the grid lines switched on and do not know it, you may wonder why your objects keep "snapping to" a position slightly different from where you place them. After you are familiar with the grid, you understand what is happening.)

Don't confuse the grid with grid lines, which you only use with the PowerPoint graph screen (see Chapter 8, "Creating Basic Graphs").

To see how the grid works, continue with the guide lines example from the preceding section. Suppose that the oval and rectangle (representing an area to plant and a shed) are not aligned in their exact positions, one inch from the left side of the slide. First, place the vertical guide line one inch from the left side of the slide, and then align the objects, as follows:

1. Change the view to Full Size through the View menu and switch on the guides, as shown in the preceding section.

    When you use Full Size and the guides, you can see better what happens when you use the grid.

2. Select the Draw menu.

    If the grid option (third from bottom) says Ignore Grid, the grid is switched on. If the option says Snap to Grid, click it to make the "snap to" feature functional. The default setting is *on*; the grid snaps to unless you previously set it to *off*.

3. Move any object on the slide and notice that the movement is jerky.

    When the Snap to Grid option is on, all objects move by jumping from (invisible) grid line to grid line. This movement is illustrated with the guides.

4. Move one of the guides and watch the numbers change. For example, move the vertical line to the left until the number reads 1.00.

The numbers always increase or decrease in units of 0.08 or 0.09, the distance between each grid line.

For the example, move the oval and rectangle to the new guide line position to realign them.

Now see how moving works without the grids by following these steps:

1. Go back into the Draw menu and choose Ignore Grid.

2. Move a guide line and notice that the increments can be as low as 0.01.

PowerPoint leaves the grid turned on by default. You can turn off the grid if you need to position objects with greater precision.

Showing the Edges of Objects

In the section "Using Framing and Shadowing," you saw that you can make unfilled objects invisible by turning off the Framed option. The shapes remain and can be manipulated and filled as usual, but you cannot see them. If you have many such objects on your slide, you may want to make them visible (so that you can decide to keep the objects you want or get rid of any objects you do not want). Suppose that you drew many objects without a frame, and you now want to see their positions. To make them visible, choose Show Edges from the Draw menu.

When you return to the slide, all invisible objects are surrounded by a broken line. A slide with many unframed objects and a few framed objects might look something like figure 5.24.

The line produced by the Show Edges option, unlike the selection outline, follows the exact shape of the object (oval, for example). Notice that you can see the outline of the Title box, as well.

Go back into the Draw menu and choose Hide Edges to turn off the Show Edges option.

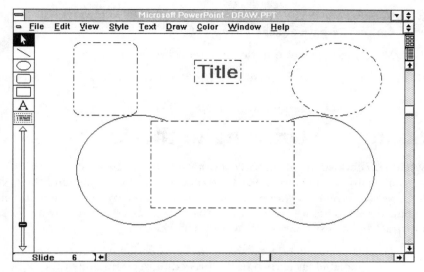

Fig. 5.24. *The edges of unframed objects.*

Labeling Objects

Often you will want to add a brief description to identify your object. You can use the word processor, the labeler, or an attached label to add a label to an object. This section describes the attached label and discusses the text sizing option in Draw. See Chapter 4, "Adding Text to a Presentation," for information on using the word processor and the labeler.

Attaching a Label to an Object

If you use the attached label method to label an object, whenever you move the object, the label moves, too. If you create the label with the labeler tool or with the word processor, the label will not move when you move the object. Many examples shown in the figures in this chapter have attached labels. Follow these steps to create an attached label:

1. Select a drawn object other than a line.

2. Begin typing whatever you want.

The text goes inside the object. The rectangle and oval in figure 5.22 have attached text.

3. Move the object and notice that the label moves, too.

If you delete the object, you also delete the text.

Sizing the Drawing to the Text

When you choose the Sized to Text option in the Draw menu, PowerPoint automatically changes the size of the object to fit exactly around the text. Suppose that you now want to change the size of the oval and the rectangle in figure 5.23 to fit the size of the text that they enclose. The following steps illustrate how to size an object to its attached text:

1. Draw a shape or select a shape that is already on your screen. Attach a label, as shown in the preceding section. For example, select the oval and rectangle shown in figure 5.23.

2. Choose Sized to Text from the Draw menu.

   (The default position is off for the Sized to Text option. The usual check mark appears to the left if the option is switched on. The example assumes that you began with the Sized to Text option off. If not, the objects automatically shrink to the size of the text, as illustrated in figure 5.25.)

When you return to the slide screen, the object has shrunk to fit around the text, no matter how big the object was when you began. Figure 5.25 shows the effect of the Sized to Text option on the oval and rectangle from figure 5.23.

If you add more words, the object elongates as necessary to surround the additional text. The object remains sized to text until you turn off the Sized to Text option for that particular object. To turn off the option, select the object, go into Draw, and click Sized to Text.

If an object is sized to text, you cannot resize the object in the usual way—the object snaps back to fit the text. As mentioned earlier, the default position for Sized to Text is off for all objects except the Title box. Try it: select the Title box and try to make it bigger. You cannot do it..

The Sized to Text option is most useful if you have selected it intentionally. If you don't know that you have the option switched on, you may wonder why you cannot resize your objects.

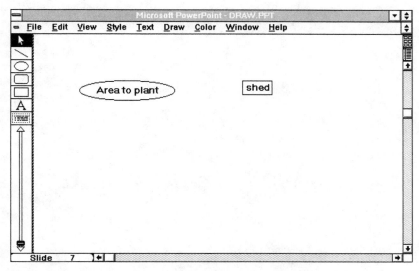

Fig. 5.25. *An oval and rectangle sized to text.*

Chapter Summary

In this chapter, you learned to draw lines, ovals, circles, rectangles, and squares. You saw how to move objects around your screen and how to change their size. You also learned how to fill objects with colors and patterns, and how to frame, shadow, and change the line styling. Finally, you discovered how to use guides, grids, and edges with your drawings, and how to attach labels to your objects.

PowerPoint puts at your disposal many drawing tools so that you can create professional, finished drawings. When you create slides, however, color is at least as important as the objects on the slide. In the next chapters, you learn how to use color.

6

Quick Start: Choosing Color Schemes

C olor is more difficult to use than any other graphics tool. The number of possibilities is infinite. PowerPoint enables you to create any color allowed by your computer and put this color together with any other color. Though the possibilities are endless (and the possibilities for error, or at least bad taste, are just as great), you can use PowerPoint's color capabilities effectively.

In this quick start, you find out how to choose an existing color scheme and apply it to your own presentation. You then go into the Graph window of PowerPoint, which is the window you use to produce charts and graphs, and you enter data. You choose the kind of chart that suits you best and then place it on the slide in your presentation. Afterward, you recolor the chart to make it stand out on the slide.

Transferring a Color Scheme

Using the professionally designed color schemes available with the PowerPoint software enables you to use colors well without being a professional artist. A color scheme is a range of colors available through the Color menu. The scheme covers the background color, the text, the fill color in objects, and so on. In this section, you transfer a color scheme from one of the PowerPoint sample color scheme presentations to your own presentation.

Suppose that you want to create a new slide presentation with strong background colors. You are in the default PowerPoint presentation that appears when you first enter PowerPoint. Follow these steps to transfer a color scheme from another presentation:

1. Choose Open from the File menu.

2. Double-click over the line that says [COLORSCH] in the box titled Directories.

   You move to the COLORSCH subdirectory.

   COLORSCH is short for "color scheme." This subdirectory contains the presentation files with different color schemes from which to choose. You see six files listed in this subdirectory. Some files are good for slides, some for screen displays, and some for overhead projections. The numbers 16 and 256 that you see in every file title refer to the number of possible colors on your particular screen display. As an example, assume that your screen falls in the 256 category and you are producing slides.

3. Click in the box to the left of the words Open an Untitled Copy. Using this option prevents you from damaging the original template.

4. Double-click on 35MM256.PPT to open that presentation.

   You see Slide 1 on the bottom left corner of your screen. For this example, you want to go to slide 18.

5. Place the mouse pointer over the thick-framed oval shape under the upward-pointing arrow in the Slide Changer, which is above the words Slide 1.

6. Hold down the left mouse button and drag downward until the slide number indicator says Slide 18.

   You see the slide shown in figure 6.1.

   Every slide in the color scheme presentations has a different set of colors. This slide has a strong black background with white text. Now, transfer this scheme to your own presentation.

7. Choose Color Scheme from the Color menu.

   The Color Scheme dialog box comes on-screen, as shown in figure 6.2. Chapter 7 shows you how to use the functions in this box.

Fig. 6.1. Slide 18 of a color scheme presentation.

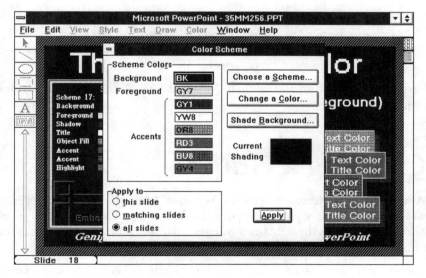

Fig. 6.2. The Color Scheme dialog box.

8. Choose Presentation from the Window menu.

   The Window menu should contain three available windows at this stage: Presentation, Presentation2, and Color Scheme.

   The Color Scheme dialog box disappears from the screen as the presentation changes behind.

9. Choose Color Scheme from the Window menu.

   In the bottom left portion of the dialog box you see three options in the Apply To box. The three options are This Slide, Matching Slides, and All Slides. In other words, you can apply this color scheme to the present slide only, to this slide and all other slides with the same color scheme as the present slide, or to all slides in the presentation.

10. Select the All Slides option.

11. Click on Apply or press A.

    You see the slide color change to black from white.

12. Exit the dialog box.

    You can exit by double-clicking the Control menu box (in the extreme upper left corner of the dialog box, on the same line as `Color Scheme`) or by opening the menu from that box and selecting Close. Your screen now looks like figure 6.3.

Save this presentation and name it QSTART2.PPT. Next, you create a graph to put on this slide.

Creating a Graph

PowerPoint Graph has a window separate from the main PowerPoint window. With Graph, you insert your raw data and play around with a graph or chart to express the data until you get what you want. You then put your finished graph or chart on the slide.

Assume that you want to create a graph for a major client. You planted trees for this client and now the client wants to see a breakdown of the cost among the various types of trees. Rather than present the information in numbers alone, you decide a graph will convey the information better.

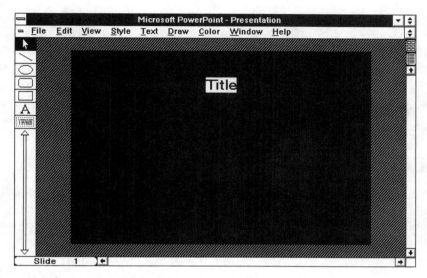

Fig. 6.3. *The applied color scheme.*

To get into Graph and prepare to enter your data, choose Insert Graph from the File menu.

You see the screen shown in figure 6.4.

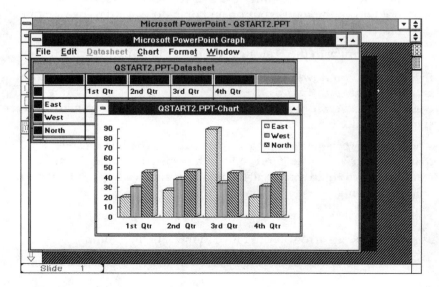

Fig. 6.4. *The PowerPoint Graph screen.*

Graph displays a sample graph to give you an idea of what can be done. Graph has two subsidiary windows called Datasheet and Chart. The Chart window is the active window when you enter Graph. (A note on terminology: This book uses the word "graph" in many cases where the PowerPoint documentation uses the word "chart.")

Your first task is to enter your numbers, as shown in the next section.

Entering Data

You enter data through the Datasheet window. The other Graph window, the Chart window, gives you the graphic representation of these numbers. Follow these steps to make Datasheet the active window and to insert your data:

1. Switch to the Datasheet window by clicking any visible portion of the window or by pressing Ctrl-T or Ctrl-F6 from the keyboard.

   You see the numbers that produced the sample graph visible in the Chart window. You now need to make the Datasheet window bigger to accommodate an extra row of numbers.

2. Place the mouse pointer over the bottom edge of the Datasheet window. When the pointer changes to the double-arrow shape, hold down the mouse button and drag downward to expose one more row in the window.

   You are now in the Datasheet window within the Graph window.

If you use the windows Maximize button (the arrow pointing upward that is to the right of the words `Microsoft PowerPoint Graph`) in the top corner of the Graph (not Datasheet) window, you end up with a screen similar to figure 6.5.

A heavy black rectangle outlines the particular cell in the Datasheet window that is active, which in figure 6.5 is the cell containing `20.4`. For this example, you want to change all the numbers and headings. Start at the first column heading.

Follow these steps to insert your numbers and headings:

1. Press the up-arrow key to move to the 1st Qtr column.

   Using the arrow keys is the easiest way to move from cell to cell.

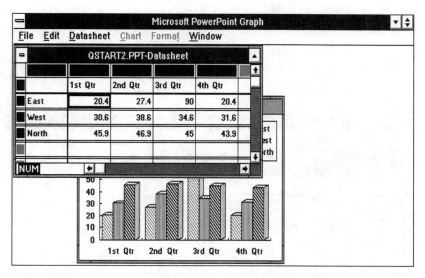

Fig. 6.5. The Datasheet window within the Graph window.

2. Type your first column heading. Type *May* and press the right-arrow key or the Tab key to move to the cell on the right.

    The current cell contents are overwritten.

3. Type *June* and *July* in the next two cells, respectively, then move to the first cell on the next row, titled East, by using the down- and left-arrow keys.

    Later you see how to delete the 4th Qtr column. Next, you type in the row titles and the actual numbers.

4. Type *Cedars* to replace East and press the right-arrow key once.

    This next cell, the first number cell, has one unique feature: Using a symbol in this cell (dollars, here) means that you don't have to use it in all the other cells.

5. Type *$500* and then *800* and *700* in the other cells, respectively, on this row.

6. Fill in the other three rows in the same way using these titles and number:

Junipers	1200	1670	1840
Sycamores	2100	0	0
Oaks	600	360	240

Your Datasheet window now looks like figure 6.6.

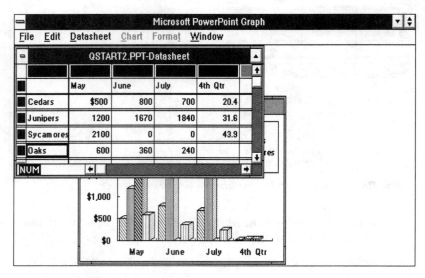

Fig. 6.6. *The filled-in Datasheet window.*

You need to do one more thing in the Datasheet window before switching to Chart to look at your result—delete the unused fourth column. You probably noticed that the graph changes each time you enter or delete a cell in Datasheet even though the Chart window is not the active window.

Follow these steps to select and delete the column:

1. Click the black rectangle above the words 4th Qtr.

   The whole column goes black, meaning it is selected.

2. Choose Delete Row/Col from the Edit menu.

   A small box appears asking you to confirm your choice. In this case, the Delete Columns option in the box is active.

3. Click OK to delete the column.

The column disappears. In the next section, you see and manipulate the graph produced by these figures.

Changing a Graph

After creating your graph through the Datasheet window cells, you can manipulate the resulting graph through the Chart window and its options. First, go back to the Chart window. Switch to the Chart window by clicking on it or by pressing Ctrl-T or Ctrl-F6. You see the graph shown in figure 6.7.

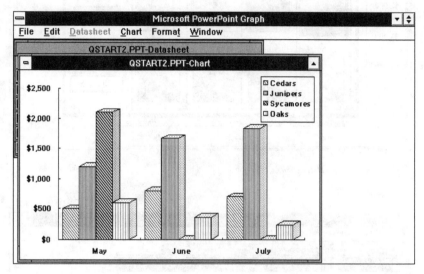

Fig. 6.7. *A column graph.*

This type of graph, called a column graph, is the default type. For the presentation to your client, however, you decide that an area-type graph would better suit your purposes. Follow these steps to change to an area type of graph:

1. Choose Area from the Chart menu.

    You see the dialog box shown in figure 6.8.

    You can choose between many different kinds of area graphs. Choose the most common type, the one labeled 1.

2. Choose 1 by double-clicking over the box containing this type.

    The Chart window and your graph now look like figure 6.9.

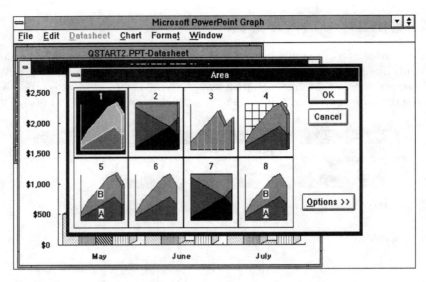

Fig. 6.8. The Area dialog box.

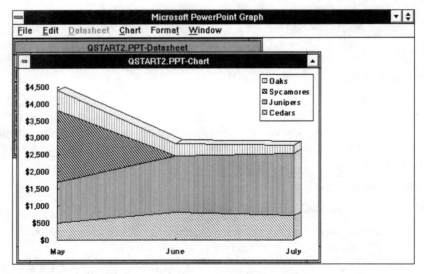

Fig. 6.9. An area graph.

Adding a Label

The box in the upper right part of the screen, called the legend box, identifies the patterns. Suppose that you decide you no longer need the legend box, because you added the labels. To remove the legend box, do the following:

1. Select the legend box by clicking on it.

2. Press the Del key to delete the legend box.

The area graph shown in figure 6.9 gives a good overall impression of the totals involved. Suppose that you want some stronger way to identify the different trees on the graph. Follow these steps to put the names directly on the graph:

1. Choose Data Labels from the Format menu.

   You see a small dialog box with three choices: None, Show Value, and Show Label. The default is None.

2. Select Show Label and then click OK.

   Your graph now looks like the one shown in figure 6.10.

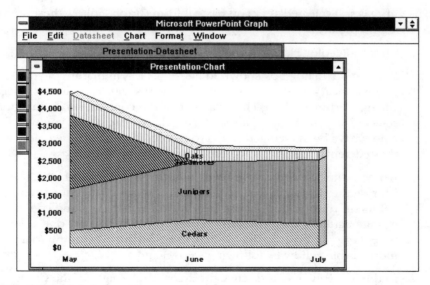

Fig. 6.10. *A labeled graph.*

Adding the Graph to the Slide

You decide to put this version of the graph on the slide. Remember, you always can go back and change the graph later, which will change the image on your slide as well. To exit Graph, choose Exit and then Return from the File menu.

PowerPoint pastes your graph onto the current slide. Unfortunately, the colors clash with the dark background in this case. You can recolor the graph as shown in the next section.

Recoloring a Graph

PowerPoint regards any graph as a picture, not an object. You therefore can use the Recolor Picture option to change all the colors and the patterns of your graph. In the example, the black type on the graph doesn't show against the black slide background, so you want to change the background. Also, perhaps you feel the patterns don't stand out strongly enough and you want to replace them with more basic colors.

The graph is still selected after you paste it from Graph. Follow these steps to recolor a picture:

1. Choose Recolor Picture from the Color menu.

   You see the dialog box shown in figure 6.11. A miniature of your graph appears on the left. On the right you see three columns titled Change, From, and To. The Change column contains boxes that are selected as you change colors. This marking system tells you which colors have been changed. The From column contains the colors as they currently are; the To column shows the new colors.

   Beneath these columns you see two buttons: Colors and Fills. Choose the default choice, Colors, and you can change the basic colors on your graph. Choose Fills, meaning patterns, and you can change patterns also. You can do these procedures only one at a time. For your project, first change the black on your graph to a more visible yellow by following steps 3 and 4.

2. In the first row of colors, click the arrow to the right of the Color box under the To column.

   A box containing eight colors (the colors of the color scheme) drops down. You can choose any of these colors to replace the black. You also can select the Other option in this drop-down box (as shown in the section "Using the Other Color Dialog Box") and choose from a much greater range of colors.

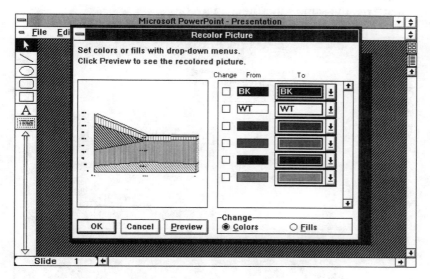

Fig. 6.11. *The Recolor Picture dialog box.*

3. Click YW8, a strong yellow color.

   The drop-down box disappears. When you return to the main dialog box, the yellow is displayed in the To column. The box in the Change column now has an X. All the other changes you want to make are fills or patterns. To make the change from black to yellow permanent, you need to exit before changing the patterns.

4. Click OK.

   On the slide, your text is visible in the yellow color. Reenter the dialog box to change the patterns.

Changing the Patterns

You change patterns the same way you change colors. Follow these steps to change the patterns:

1. Choose the Recolor Picture option from the Color menu.

   The dialog box comes on-screen.

2. Select Fills to make it the active option instead of Colors.

   The From row choices change to display the patterns, diagonal and vertical lines, and so on, as shown in figure 6.12. You change these patterns the same way you change colors.

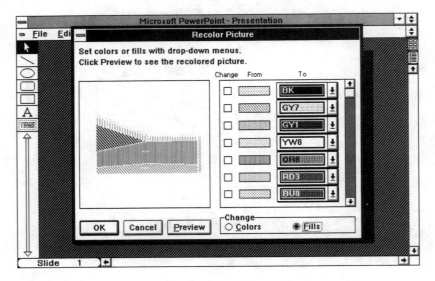

Fig. 6.12. The Recolor Picture dialog box with the Fills option active.

3. Click on the desired color in the To column—in this case, choose BU8.

   You decide that the To color option OR8 in the fifth row looks good, so you do not need to open the drop-down box to select another color.

4. Click over the Change box in the fifth row to accept OR8 as the new color.

   The two other patterns in the graph are out of sight—"underneath" the visible patterns.

5. Scroll down using the long scroll bar on the extreme right of the dialog box until a color labeled GY4 in the To column comes into view.

To change this color, use the Other option in the drop-down color box.

Using the Other Color Dialog Box

The Other Color dialog box gives you a large range of colors from which to choose. To access this box, you perform an additional step after you open the drop-down menus of eight choices seen above. Follow these steps to change a color through the Other option:

1. Click the arrow to the right of GY4 and then click Other.

    The Other Color dialog box replaces the Recolor Picture box on-screen, as shown in figure 6.13.

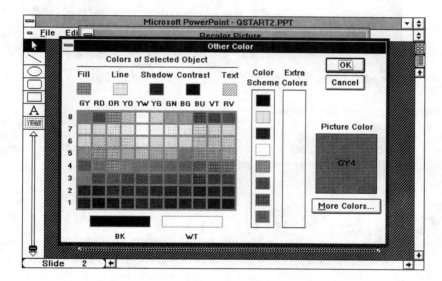

Fig. 6.13. *The Other Color dialog box.*

Any of the palette of colors displayed here is available for use by simply selecting the one you want.

2. Select GN1, the color in the GN column and the number 1 row.

3. Choose OK to exit the dialog box.

You return to the Recolor Picture box with GN1 in the To column. Continue with the normal pattern color changes. Change GY1 to RD3 and then select OK to exit this dialog box. You end up back on the slide with your graph looking like the one in figure 6.14.

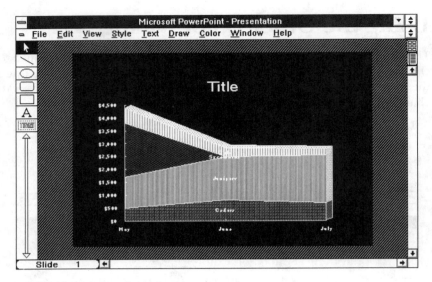

Fig. 6.14. *The recolored graph.*

Use the steps you learned in this chapter whenever you want to change the colors and patterns of any picture on your slides.

Chapter Summary

In this chapter, you learned some basics for using color and creating a graph. First, you saw how to transfer a color scheme from another presentation to use with your own presentation. You then entered PowerPoint Graph and entered data through the Datasheet window of Graph. You moved to the Chart window in Graph and made changes there, including changing the type of the graph, moving the legend box, and adding labels to the graph. You then pasted the new graph onto the slide. Finally, you changed the colors and patterns in the graph using both the Recolor Picture dialog box and the Other Color dialog box.

Already having used PowerPoint's flexible tools for using colors and creating graphs, you can learn about them in detail next. Chapter 7 explains how to use colors in PowerPoint, and Chapter 8 discusses creating graphs.

Using Basic Color

For graphics such as handouts or overheads, color is not always available or essential. You can be reasonably effective at desktop graphics and know little or nothing about color. Color is important, however, when you create slides.

Coloring your slides can make the difference between an attractive presentation and a dull one. As with almost everything in PowerPoint, you do not have to go into the details of the color features available to use color well. PowerPoint sets up default colors for you to use. All you need to do is start drawing and typing to use these default colors.

Even better, you can use advanced color schemes without knowing how to design advanced color schemes. As you see in Chapter 3, you can copy the templates prepared by Genigraphics artists and have well-developed color schemes in your slide shows without knowing about the art and science of using colors together.

Nevertheless, knowing the basics explained in this chapter will help you better understand the coloring potential in PowerPoint. Many people will not want to go beyond basics in color, certainly not at the start, so two separate chapters in this book cover the full range of PowerPoint coloring. This chapter deals with the basics, and Chapter 14 deals with advanced features.

The chapter starts by showing you how to browse through the sample templates, choose one, and use it for your own presentation. You can use this approach to create good-looking slide shows even without becoming an expert using color.

From there, the chapter goes back to the basics and starts by explaining the Color Scheme dialog box, a box offering features that refine and expand the basic eight-color choice. You also learn how to color individual objects and text, and how to change the default colors in certain capabilities, such as filling and shadowing an object.

Finally, because using colors in patterns creates a number of combinations, a special section explains using colors in patterns.

Some Color Guidelines

Because color has endless possibilities, the color feature is often thought of as the most advanced capability in any graphics program. Unfortunately, most people do not have the background and knowledge to take full advantage of software's color capabilities. Most people have nothing more than an elementary sense of good taste in colors.

A few basic guidelines for using color may prove helpful:

• Limit the number of colors you use.

You can, of course, use PowerPoint default color schemes. Designed by professional artists, the color schemes apply established rules about which colors look good together, which background colors look good with which foreground colors, and so on. If you begin to create color schemes of your own, tread lightly at first. Use just a few colors.

• Use bright colors for slides.

For printed handouts, limit your use of bright colors. For slides, though, bright colors work well. Use bright colors for large objects on slides and subdued colors to highlight thin lines on the slides.

• Choose color combinations carefully.

Using primary colors together is acceptable: red, yellow, and blue, as well as green. Also, the cool colors go well together (green, blue, and violet). The warm colors also complement each other well: red, orange, and yellow.

Using the Color Scheme from Another Presentation

The templates prepared by Genigraphics artists have well-developed color schemes. You can use the default color scheme, or you can copy the color scheme from a template.

Follow these steps to copy the color scheme from a template:

1. Choose Open from the File menu.

   You see the open dialog box, shown in figure 7.1. One of the directories is called [colorsch]. In this directory, you can find a repository of outstanding professionally prepared color schemes. Browse through the presentations to see what the color schemes are like.

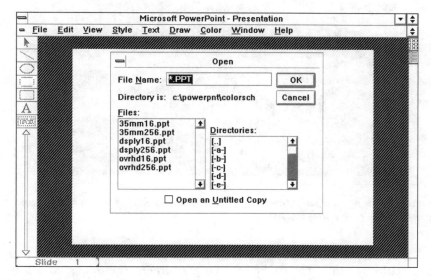

Fig. 7.1. The Open dialog box used for choosing a color template.

2. Choose a template from COLORSCH. The template DSPLY16.PPT is a good choice for showing a slide show on your color monitor.

   PowerPoint conveniently provides a description of "How To Use These Schemes in Your Presentations"—essentially, the instructions in the next steps here.

3. Look at the slides, perhaps beginning with the Slide Sorter view, so that you can quickly look over all the color schemes offered.

4. Choose the slide with the color scheme that you want.

When you see the slide in a form big enough to read the text, you see that the slide contains the words `This is the Title Color`, `This is the text color`, and so on, as shown in figure 7.2. You could hardly do better than hiring a professional color consultant from Genigraphics. Check again to be sure that the color scheme is the one you want. If so, you can apply the color scheme to a new or existing presentation with a few more steps.

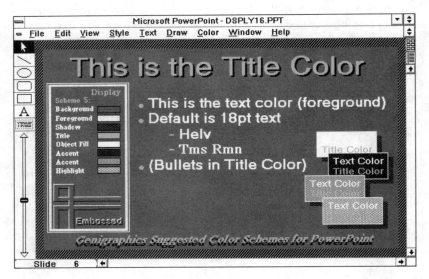

Fig. 7.2. Sample slide designed by Genigraphics explicitly for you to copy and use for your own color schemes.

In slide 6, shown in figure 7.2, the title color is yellow and the text color is white. The background is gray/green. The full list of colors for the color scheme is in the box on the left and includes purple and sky blue.

5. From the Color menu, choose Color Scheme.

You see the Color Scheme dialog box, shown in figure 7.3. Check the Scheme Colors on the left side of the box to be sure the color scheme is the one you want. Keep the dialog box open.

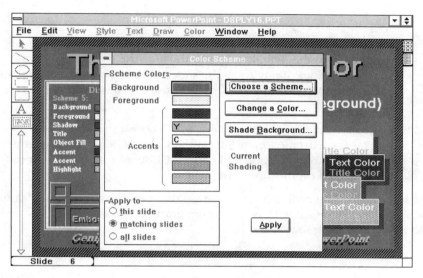

Fig. 7.3. The Color Scheme dialog box.

6. Now you have two choices. From the File menu, choose New to use the color scheme in a new presentation or choose Open to use the color scheme in an existing presentation. Use New for the example.

   You see the dialog box prompting you to choose between Use Format of Active Presentation and Use Default Format.

7. Choose one. Here, choose Use Default Format and click OK.

   The new presentation opens. You now are ready to use the color scheme of the previous slide.

8. Click the Color Scheme dialog box, or choose it from the Window menu. (Do not choose it from the Color menu or you will choose the default color scheme instead of the one from the template.)

9. Choose one of the Apply To options—This Slide, Matching Slides, or All Slides. For the example, select All Slides.

   The This Slide option applies to the current slide only. The Matching Slides option applies to all slides in the presentation with the same color scheme as the slide in the slide view. The All Slides option applies to all slides in the presentation.

10. Choose Apply.

    The initial slide on display behind the Color Scheme window now changes from the default colors to those of the template. You now apply the color scheme to all the slides in the new presentation (or to the existing presentation if you choose Open instead of New in step 6).

11. To close the Color Scheme dialog box, choose the Control menu box (at the extreme upper left on the Color Scheme line) for the Color Scheme dialog box and choose Close. Alternatively, you can press Ctrl-F4 on the keyboard.

At some point, you probably will want to create your own colors and color schemes instead of using those from Genigraphics. You find out how to do so in the following sections.

Using the Color Scheme Dialog Box

In PowerPoint, the basic colors you use the most make up the color scheme. The color scheme consists of eight colors, each of which is used automatically for specific tasks when you draw, fill, write, and so on, on your slide. Mostly you have one color scheme for the presentation, but you are not limited to one. You can have color schemes for individual slides and for a group of slides. In complicated slide shows, you may use these multiple color schemes.

> *Tip:* You can change a color scheme at any time, even after you have completed the presentation. You can even change black-and-white slide shows to color (and vice versa). You also can have one color scheme for the slides and another (often black and white) for your handouts and notes pages. PowerPoint gives you a great deal of flexibility in coloring.

Suppose that you have a slide like the one shown in figure 7.4. The figure is black and white. On a color screen, the background is white, the text is black, the oval is filled with a red color, and the shadow color around the oval is a dark gray. Refer to the chapter on drawing objects, Chapter 5, if you don't understand about filling and shadowing. These colors are the default PowerPoint colors for these uses.

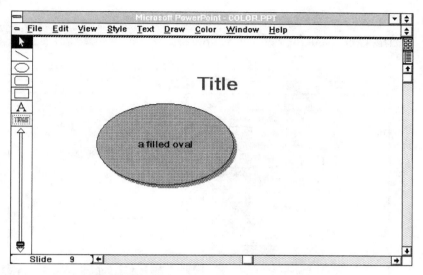

***Fig.* 7.4.** *A slide with the default color scheme.*

Now, assume that you want to change these default colors. The following steps show you how to change a color scheme to suit your needs and how to apply this scheme to one or more slides:

1. Choose Color from the menu bar. A drop-down menu appears (see fig. 7.5).

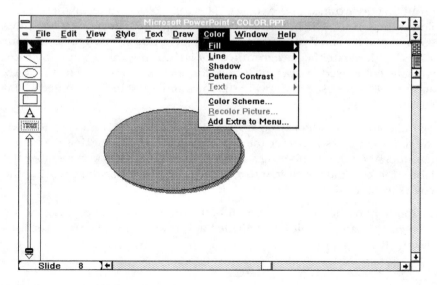

***Fig.* 7.5.** *The Color menu options.*

2. Choose Color Scheme.

The Color Scheme dialog box appears (see fig. 7.6).

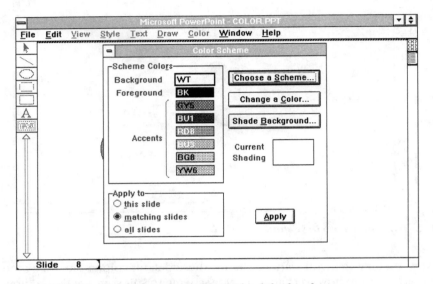

Fig. 7.6. *The Color Scheme dialog box with the default colors .*

On the left of the box is a list of colors—the eight basic default colors. Identifying labels to the left of the default colors divide them into Background, Foreground, and Accents. The top color, white in the default PowerPoint color scheme, is the background color. In other words, this color would remain if you wiped out all objects, titles, and so on, from your slides. Underneath the background color is the foreground color, the basic working color used in drawing frames for objects and writing text. The six accent colors are used in drawing shadows and titles, in filling objects, and so on.

All the colors have identifying labels—WT for white, BK for black, RD8 for the red color, and so on. (See the section "Changing a Color" in this chapter to understand the numbering system for the colors.) If you remember the labels for key colors that you use, you can be accurate when reusing the colors in other slides and presentations.

To the right of the dialog box you find the three available options: Choose a Scheme, Change a Color, and Shade Background. The next three sections discuss their use.

Choosing a New Color Scheme

Use the Choose a Scheme option in the Color Scheme dialog box when you want an entirely new set of basic colors for a slide, group of slides, or the presentation. To change just one color, the Change a Color option is easier to use. Follow these steps to change your scheme:

1. Click Choose a Scheme in the Color Scheme dialog box.

   Refer to the preceding section to find how to get to the Color Scheme dialog box, if necessary. PowerPoint then takes you to the Choose a Scheme dialog box shown in figure 7.7.

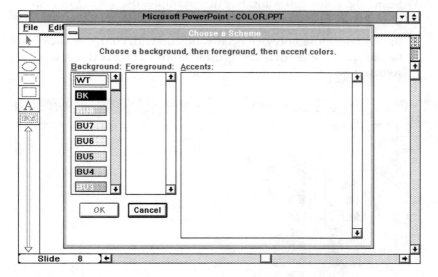

Fig. *7.7. The Choose a Scheme dialog box.*

The Choose a Scheme dialog box has three scroll boxes: Background, Foreground, and Accents. The instruction line along the top of the box says: `Choose a background, then foreground, then accent colors.` When you first open the Choose a Scheme dialog box, only the colors in the Background scroll box to the left are displayed. The foreground and accent boxes are empty.

You can see all the available background colors by scrolling through the box.

2. Place your mouse pointer on the white square under the arrow in the scroll bar in the Background color box.

3. Press your left mouse button and, without releasing it, drag the white square down.

   As with usual Windows scrolling, the top of the box (the top colors in this case) disappears, and other colors come into view from the bottom. In this way you can scroll through the entire list of colors and back up again. You might find scrolling in this way goes too fast. You can scroll more precisely by clicking the arrows at the top and bottom of the slide.

4. Select the color you want. For this example, use OR2, a kind of orange/brown.

   Immediately, the Foreground box fills up with colors. A thick black line around the chosen background color indicates that it has been selected (see fig. 7.8).

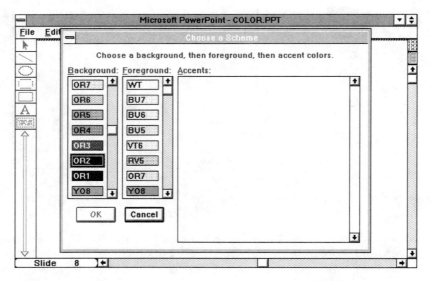

Fig. 7.8. The foreground colors appear after you choose a background color.

The foreground color determines the color of your text and the outlines of your drawn objects. You have far fewer foreground colors than background colors from which to choose. In this case, you have 10 colors—eight are visible on-screen and two are not.

The number varies according to which background color you choose. PowerPoint displays different foreground (and accent) colors according to the background color you choose. This variation occurs because certain background, foreground, and accent colors have been found to work better together. Sometimes you do not have to do any scrolling to see all the foreground colors.

5. Choose your foreground color by clicking the desired color. Here, use WT (for white).

   The accent colors appear in the large space on the right of the box, as shown in figure 7.9.

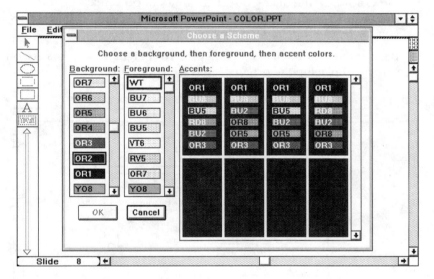

Fig. *7.9. The accent colors in the Choose a Scheme dialog box.*

Accents appear in groups of six colors, and you choose one batch of six, not individual colors. As mentioned previously, you use accent colors for fills and shadows and for changing the color of particular words or objects.

The previously chosen background color is displayed behind the boxes containing the accent colors to help you make your choice of accent colors. Also, the borders between each accent combination show the foreground color you chose.

6. Select one of the accent boxes containing six colors by clicking it. For the example, use the box on the far right.

   You have finished selecting your color scheme. At this stage you could go back and change the background color or the foreground color. Experiment to get the best color scheme for this particular slide or presentation—some text may not be visible against a certain background. If you do change the background, PowerPoint makes you choose the foreground and accents again, and the choices offered in both cases are different.

7. When you're satisfied with the color scheme, click OK to go back to the Color Scheme dialog box. (Clicking Cancel cancels all the choices you made in the Choose a Scheme dialog box and returns you to the Color Scheme dialog box.)

   Back at the Color Scheme dialog box, your eight new colors are on display, replacing the original eight (see fig. 7.10).

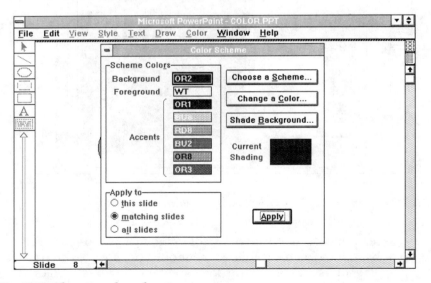

Fig. 7.10. The new color scheme.

At this stage you have set up the new scheme but not actually applied it to the presentation. To put the scheme to use in the presentation, use the Apply button in the lower right part of the Color Scheme dialog box. Before you apply the presentation, however, take a preliminary step.

As shown in figure 7.10, the Color Scheme dialog box contains three buttons in the lower left portion of the box: This Slide, Matching Slides, and All Slides. Choose one of these options before applying a new color scheme to your slides. The This Slide option means that the color scheme will be applied to the current slide only. Using the option Matching Slides means that the color scheme will be applied to all slides in the presentation with the same color scheme. The default option is a presentation with only one color scheme in All Slides. When a presentation has more than one color scheme, the default option is Matching Slides.

8. Choose one of the three options, This Slide, Matching Slides, or All Slides, by clicking the circle to the left of the option you want or by clicking the option itself.

Tip: Always check which option is chosen before using the Apply button. You could ruin your slide show if you have been intentionally using separate color schemes for certain slides and accidentally apply one scheme to all slides.

9. Click the Apply button, and the new scheme takes effect.

   If you already have drawn and written on slides, the colors change to the equivalent new colors. For example, if the fill color was red previously and has been changed to blue, all objects using the red fill in the relevant slides (This Slide, Matching Slides, or All Slides) change to a blue fill.

10. Close the dialog box by double-clicking the Control menu box in the extreme upper left corner of the dialog box (or press Alt-F4).

Alternatively, if you want to keep the dialog box open but want to see the slide, click the portion of the slide that is visible. The dialog box disappears behind the PowerPoint window but remains open. Refer to the Window menu, and you see that Color Scheme is one of the menu choices. Choose this menu item when you want to see the Color Scheme dialog box again. The slide example has changed, as shown in figure 7.11.

The background color is dark brown; the fill color in this case remained the same red color; the text changed to white. The frame of the rectangle is now also white. Finally, the shadow color is a brown very similar to the background color.

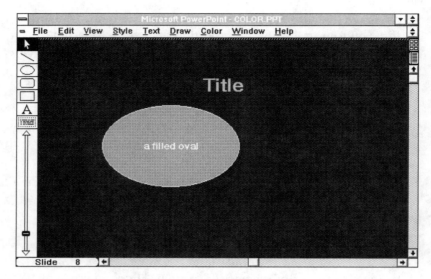

Fig. 7.11. The new color scheme applied to the slide.

One important point to note is that the color scheme does not apply to the title of your slide. The text in the title is always different from your foreground color. In this case, the title text is in blue and the other text has changed to white. You can change the title to the foreground color if you want, but you have to select and change it individually.

Sometimes you may be satisfied with a particular color scheme except for one color. The next section discusses changing an individual color.

Changing a Color

You can change individual colors in your color scheme, and you also can change the position of colors in your scheme. Changing or rearranging colors in a scheme means that you change everything already drawn or written from the original color to the new color. Follow these steps to change a color:

1. Bring up the Color Scheme dialog box by opening the Color menu and then choosing Color Scheme. You also can call up the Color Scheme dialog box through the Window menu.

You can choose the individual color to change in two ways, as shown in step 2. If you don't choose a color yourself, PowerPoint uses the default color for background, the top color in the list. Suppose that you don't like the fill color, RD8, and want to change it.

2. Select the color to change and then choose Change a Color, or double-click the color. Either way, you see the Change a Color dialog box shown in figure 7.12.

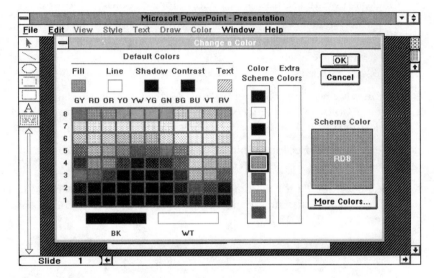

Fig. 7.12. The Change a Color dialog box.

This screen looks more complicated than it is. The colors showing in the Color Scheme column toward the right are the eight colors of your current scheme. The color you previously selected to change is marked with a thick black rectangle. Beside this column is another column titled Extra Colors. This column is blank unless you have added some extra colors yourself already. Add extra colors when you need more than the basic eight from the color scheme. See Chapter 14 for information on adding extra colors and on using the More Colors option (located in the lower right portion of the Change a Color box.)

The large rectangle on the right titled Scheme Color contains the color you chose to change. Its label—RD8 in figure 7.12—is displayed in the center of the rectangle. You can understand the origin of this labeling system by referring to the large block of different colors on display to the left of this Change a Color box. Across the top of this block are double letters—GY, RD, and so on—and along the side are numbers—going from 8 to 1, top to bottom. You can denote the position of any color by using this chart. For RD8, the color used in the example, you locate RD along the top of the block and locate line number 8, which is the top line.

Black and white are under this main block of colors. Over the block, your color scheme's colors for Fill, Line, and so on are displayed for reference purposes.

3. Click any color to choose it as the new color. For the example, choose RD3.

   The newly chosen color immediately is displayed in the large Scheme Color rectangle to enable you to see the color more clearly. Click different colors to see which is best suited to your purposes.

4. When you find a color that looks good to you, click OK, or click Cancel to revert to the old color.

   Either way, the Color Scheme dialog box returns to the screen. If you clicked OK, the new color replaces the old color in the Color Scheme (see fig. 7.13).

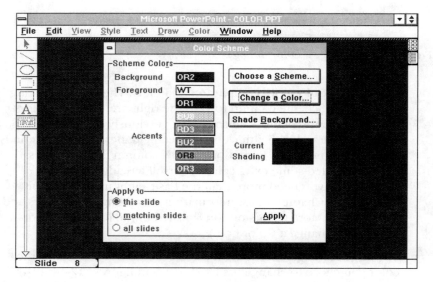

Fig. 7.13. *The new color has replaced the previous color in the color scheme.*

5. Choose between This Slide, Matching Slides, and All Slides by clicking one of them.

6. Click Apply to apply the new color to your slides.

   Elements that previously had the old color now change to the new one. In the example, the fill color changes.

Another way of changing your color scheme is to rearrange the existing colors, which is described in the next section.

Rearranging Colors

You can change the order of the colors in your color scheme any time you want. As with changing colors, changing the order also can change the colors of the background, objects, or text in your slides. For instance, you can replace the shadow color (number three in the list) with a lighter color. To rearrange a color, follow these steps:

1. In the Color Scheme dialog box, place the mouse pointer over the color you want to move. Use OR8 for the example.

2. Click and hold down the left mouse button and drag the color to the new position. For the example, choose OR1.

3. Release the mouse button, and the colors change places.

4. Click This Slide, Matching Slides, or All Slides.

5. Click Apply to apply the new color to your slides.

Everything that previously had the old color now changes to the new one and vice versa. OR8 becomes the new shadow color in this case.

Changing and rearranging colors in the color scheme is as easy as the previously outlined steps. The last option of the three in the dialog box is Shade Background. The next section explains how to use this feature.

Shading the Background

Shading is making part of the background slide color lighter and other parts darker. Below the Shade Background option on the Color Scheme dialog box is the Current Shading dialog box. Unless you already have used the

Shade Background option, the box shows an even color, meaning that you have applied no shading. You can choose from several shadings by following these steps:

1. In the Color Scheme dialog box, click Shade Background. The Shade Background dialog box appears, as shown in figure 7.14.

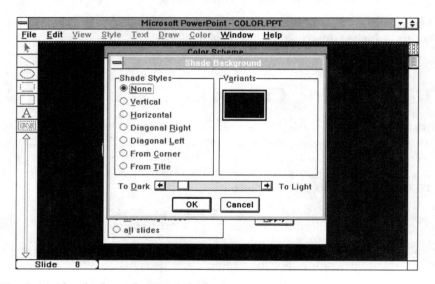

Fig. 7.14. *The Shade Background dialog box.*

On the left, a column titled Shade Styles lists the titles of the various styles: None, Vertical, Horizontal, Diagonal Right, Diagonal Left, From Corner, and From Title. None, the first style listed, is the default, as indicated by the black circle to the left of the word. Because no variation of the current choice (no shading) exists, the Variants section of the Shade Background box shows only one choice (one rectangle). Other styles have up to four variants, as you see in the following paragraphs.

2. Click any of the Shade Styles to see the variants possible with that style. For instance, click From Corner, and you see something similar to figure 7.15.

From Corner has four variants, each shown in differently shaded rectangles. Each variant shows the color becoming lighter as it spreads out from one of the four corners of the rectangle, hence the title From Corner.

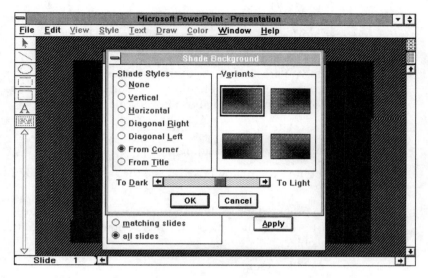

Fig. 7.15. *The From Corner style in the Shade Background dialog box.*

From Title has two variants: one showing the color lightest around the slide title, another showing the color darkest around the slide title.

Choosing Vertical puts a lighter band of shading across the screen—the shading moves vertically in the different variations. Using the Horizontal option puts a band of shading running up and down, and moves horizontally across and back in the different variations. Choosing the Diagonal Right and Diagonal Left options moves the band diagonally across the screen, from the right and the left, respectively.

All shade styles have interesting effects. Click each in turn to see their variants, then decide which one suits your purposes best.

3. Click one of the variants to choose it. As an example, use the From Corner option.

   One more feature of this box remains to be investigated. At the bottom, above OK and Cancel, you see a horizontal scroll bar with the words To Dark and To Light at either end. Use this bar to lighten or darken the shading on whichever variant you choose.

4. Click the left arrow to darken the color or the right arrow to lighten the color.

One example of when you might use this feature is when you want to make text more visible against the background. The Dark/Light scroll bar has no effect on the None shade style.

5. Click OK when you are satisfied with the overall shading, or click Cancel to revert to the original shading. The Current Shading box back in the Color Scheme dialog box shows your changes.

6. Click This Slide, Matching Slides, or All Slides.

7. Click Apply to apply the new shading.

On the slide behind the dialog box you see the new shading take effect.

8. Exit the dialog box by double-clicking the Control menu box in upper left corner. Keep the box open by clicking the portion of the slide that is visible.

Your slide now looks like figure 7.16.

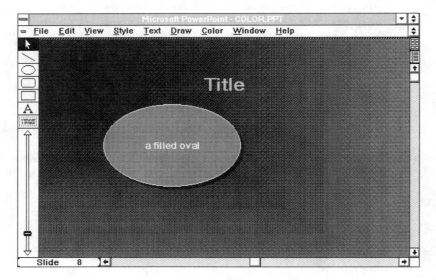

Fig. 7.16. *The slide after shading the background.*

See Chapter 14 for a discussion of advanced features that can multiply your color variations and combinations into the millions. The next section of this chapter deals with the remaining choices on the Color menu.

Coloring Individual Objects

The first five options in the Color menu are Fill, Line, Shadow, Pattern Contrast, and Text, as shown in figure 7.5. These terms may be familiar from the previous chapters of this book and the preceding sections. Table 7.1 summarizes their usage.

Table 7.1
Using Color Menu Options

Feature	Use
Fill	The color selected here is used to fill the inside of objects such as ovals, text blocks, and so on.
Line	The color selected here is used to frame ovals, rectangles, and so on, and to draw straight lines.
Shadow	The color selected here is used to shadow objects.
Pattern Contrast	This option sets the secondary color in a pattern with two colors.
Text	The color selected here becomes the color of selected text.

All of these features have default colors set up when you enter a presentation—either the PowerPoint defaults or your own defaults. You can change any of these defaults when you like. You also can change the color of an individual object or text without changing the default color.

Changing Object Color

Changing the color of an object is similar for all the Color menu choices. The example uses a line, but the steps are the same for all the menu choices of Fill, Line, Shadow, Pattern Contrast, and Text. Change the color of an individual object when you want to use a particular color in a particular situation. Change the default color, as shown in the next section, when you want to use the new color in the future.

Follow these steps to change a color:

1. Draw an object—a line, for example—on a PowerPoint slide. See Chapter 5 if you're not sure how to use the drawing tools to draw a line.

   The line has a color—black if you are using the PowerPoint default, white if you're using the new color scheme discussed in this chapter. The line is still selected after being drawn, as indicated by the two black dots at either end of the line (see fig. 7.17). For this example, use the default because figures show up better against the white background.

2. Choose Line from the Color menu.

   You see the drop-down menu shown in figure 7.17.

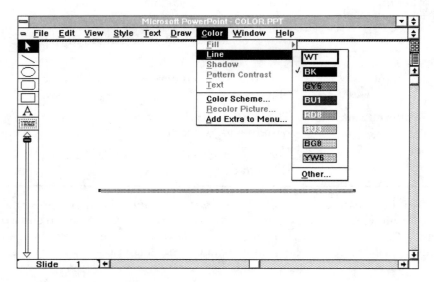

Fig. 7.17. *The Line menu and a selected line.*

You see the color scheme of eight colors. At the bottom is the Other option, giving you access to the whole multitude of PowerPoint colors, as explained in Chapter 14.

When no object is selected, the default color is marked with a diamond—on BK (for black) in the Line menu in the original PowerPoint color scheme. (If something is selected, however, such as the line in figure 7.17, the default color has a check mark.) Any line or frame of an oval or rectangle will be drawn in black.

Don't be confused if you pull down the Line drop-down menu (or Fill, Shadow, Pattern Contrast, or Text) showing the list of colors and no diamond is visible. For example, if you have a line selected and another object on the slide has a different line color, then the selected line color shows on the menu as a check mark, not a diamond. Also, if everything on the slide is selected and a line and an oval, for example, have different line or frame colors, neither a check mark nor a diamond shows on the drop-down menu. If nothing is selected, the Line menu always shows the default color.

3. Click the desired color of the eight shown. For this example, use blue, BU3.

You return to the slide, and the line color has changed. Any new lines (or frames of ovals and rectangles), however, are still drawn with the default color. Changing the color of the individual line does not change the default color.

Changing the Default Object Color

When you change the color scheme, as discussed earlier in this chapter, you change your basic palette of eight colors that are directly available through the Color menu option. Each color automatically is marked as the default for various functions, such as shadowing, drawing lines, and so on, but you can use any of the eight as your default.

To change your default color, follow the steps below. The procedure is the same for all options. This example changes a default line color.

1. Click the arrow tool with the mouse pointer to deselect any objects or lines.

2. Choose Line from the Color menu.

3. Click the desired color to make it the default.

After you return to the slide, any lines or frames you draw in the future will be the color of the new default. Also, this default applies to all slides, not just the current one.

Changing Text Color

As mentioned, the steps are similar for changing individual or default colors in the other menu options—with one exception: Text. Text works a little differently in that you cannot change the default color through the Color menu but only through the Style menu. See Chapter 4 for information on changing the default color of text. You can, however, change the color of *selected* text through the Color menu (not the Style menu). The steps are the same as those outlined (except that you choose Text rather than Line on the Color menu.)

In this section, then, you have seen how to work with colors. In the next section, you learn about a related topic—patterns.

Working with Patterns

Chapter 5, "Drawing Objects," discusses Filled and Pattern on the Draw menu. On the Draw menu, you create filled objects and assign their patterns. On the Color menu, you determine the color of the fill and the color of the pattern.

When you work with the color of a pattern, you are working with the pattern itself (such as a brick pattern, selected from the Draw menu), the color of the fill (such as the default of red), and the nature of the Pattern Contrast, as set up from the Color menu. Balancing the three ingredients in your mind can become rather complicated. Probably the best way to work with the colors of patterns is to see what happens as you change the various possibilities—the Pattern, the Fill, and the Pattern Contrast.

Defaults exist for Pattern in the Draw menu and for Pattern Contrast in the Color menu. In the default PowerPoint color scheme, the defaults are black for Pattern and white for Pattern Contrast. The Pattern Contrast feature (having two colors—one primary, one secondary) is not being used. The following example illustrates this situation:

1. Go back to the original PowerPoint color scheme. Open a new presentation with the default template, if necessary.

2. Draw an oval and then choose Filled from the Draw menu (as explained in Chapter 5).

   The oval fills with the default red color of Fill in the Color menu.

3. Choose Pattern from the Draw menu.

   You see the menu shown in figure 7.18.

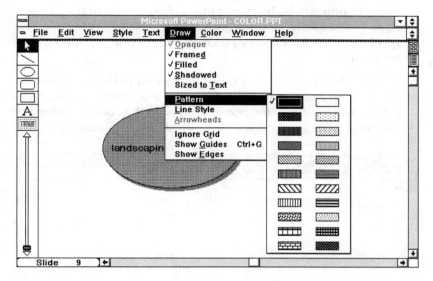

Fig. 7.18. The Pattern menu appears below the Draw menu.

The all-black rectangle in the upper left corner of the Pattern menu has a check mark, indicating that it is active. When the all-black pattern is active, your secondary color doesn't matter (as set by the Pattern Contrast option in Color). This color never shows on the slide. In contrast, the all-white option in Pattern does the opposite: it blanks out the primary (or foreground) color, as demonstrated in the steps that follow.

4. Click the all-white rectangle to choose it as the new pattern for this object.

   On the slide, the red fill in the oval disappears. The oval is still filled, but the secondary color is totally dominant and the secondary color (set in Pattern Contrast) is white, the same color as the background color on the slide as a whole.

5. You can prove this is the case by keeping the oval selected, going into Pattern Contrast, and changing the color from white to blue. Choose Pattern Contrast from the Color menu and then choose the blue (BU3).

The oval turns blue inside. The key to this situation is in the Pattern menu in Draw, shown in figure 7.18. Within the rectangles showing different patterns, any white represents the secondary color (set in Pattern Contrast); all black and blue colors represent the primary color (set in Fill in the Color menu). Any rectangle other than the all-white or all-black shows a combination of primary and secondary colors.

6. Try choosing a striped or dotted rectangle from the Pattern drop-down menu and seeing the result in the oval. For example, choose the brick-like pattern, the bottom choice in the column headed by the black rectangle. You get the result shown in figure 7.19.

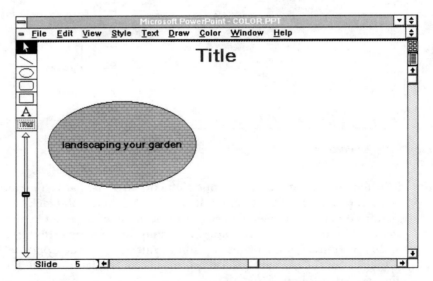

Fig. 7.19. *An oval with two colors, set in Fill and Pattern Contrast in the Color menu.*

Combining Fill, Pattern, and Pattern Contrast enables you to create quite a number of colored patterns that you may want to use in your objects. Initially, use the defaults. As you become comfortable with using the varying combinations, PowerPoint has the power to enable you to create many colored patterns.

Such possibilities with the patterns begin to give you a taste of the advanced possibilities for using color in PowerPoint. In Chapter 14, you see these advanced possibilities in depth.

Chapter Summary

You began this chapter by finding out how you could perform like an expert immediately by using PowerPoint templates to create color schemes. You then explored the basics of creating such color schemes yourself.

You saw how to change your eight-color color scheme, how to change an individual color within that scheme, and how to reposition colors in the scheme. Next, you saw how to shade your background color so that different parts of the screen would be lightened and darkened. You then saw how to change the colors of individual items on your slide, such as text, lines, or objects, and also learned how to change default colors for the Fill, Line, Shadow, Pattern Contrast, and Text features. Finally, you learned how to color and use patterns.

You now know how to manipulate color in PowerPoint. Later, in Chapter 14, you learn to use advanced capabilities of color. In the next chapter, you become familiar with the basics of another PowerPoint capability—creating graphs.

8

Creating
Basic Graphs

As spreadsheet users know, a graph consists of two components: data, which you enter into the spreadsheet, and the graph itself, which you select as a way to display the data. PowerPoint reduces graphing to its two lowest terms—data and graph forms—to enable you to combine them in just about any way you want. (Note that this book uses the term "graph" where PowerPoint documentation often uses the term "chart.")

In PowerPoint graphing, you have on-screen a set of rows and columns to hold data and—simultaneously in another window—a collection of chart and graph forms you can use to display the data. You can devote most of your energy to the content of what you want to say—to the data itself. To express the data, you click the graph you want. The two windows are interrelated. When you change the data in one window, the data changes on the graph in the other window.

PowerPoint differs from many spreadsheet graphics programs in that it does not keep the graphs in files separate from the slides. After you have produced a graph, PowerPoint transfers it onto the slide and saves the graph with the presentation.

In this chapter, you learn how to access the Graph menu from the main PowerPoint menu and how to enter data into datasheets. Using a sample datasheet, you insert data into the datasheet cells; organize the data (or series) into rows or columns; select, cut, copy, paste, and clear; and manipulate columns and rows. You learn to work within a datasheet to change the appearance of your data and labels by formatting numbers, altering text, and changing column widths. (Importing data is covered in Chapter 13.)

201

After you have entered data into a datasheet, you learn to work with graphs (or "charts," in PowerPoint terminology). You see how to open the Chart window, where you see the graph that actually goes onto your slide. Six kinds of graphs are available in Graph, so you learn to display and choose the right graph for your data. You then learn to change line styles, fonts, and fill attributes and to move objects around your graph. Finally, you find out how to return to the current slide and take the graph with you.

Accessing the Graph Menu

PowerPoint Graph has its own menu bar. When you are in Graph, you cannot access the regular PowerPoint menu bar options. Follow these steps to access the Graph function in PowerPoint:

1. Create a new slide or go to the slide that you want to receive the graph.

   When you exit the Graph function, PowerPoint always places the graph in the current slide.

2. Choose File from the menu bar.

3. Choose Insert Graph.

You see the screen shown in figure 8.1.

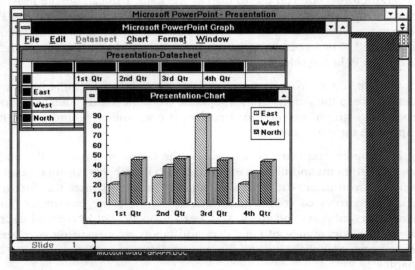

Fig. 8.1. *The initial Graph screen.*

Three new windows appear: the main window, Microsoft PowerPoint Graph; the Datasheet window; and the Chart window. The title of the current presentation (here, the default name), Presentation, appears along the tops of the Datasheet and Chart windows. The sample graph appearing in the Chart window is the current graph form for the current data, which is sample data provided by PowerPoint. You can use the Chart menu to change the graph form, as you see in a later section, "Choosing a Graph Type." But first, you learn to move between the two components of your graph—datasheets and graph forms.

Moving between Datasheet and Chart Windows

Enter the data you want to appear in a graph when you are in the Datasheet window. PowerPoint converts the data into a graph, which is displayed in the Chart window. That graph appears on your slide when you exit the graph program (though the proportions may be slightly different). You cannot put the Datasheet window data directly onto your slide.

When you first enter Graph, the Chart window is active and is on top of the Datasheet window on-screen. To switch between the Chart and Datasheet windows, click on any visible portion of the Datasheet window to make it the active window.

After you select the Datasheet window, it overlaps the Chart window. If you have many datasheet entries, you may need to enlarge the window to see as many numbers as possible at one time. You can make either window larger or smaller by clicking on the edges and dragging. You also can enlarge a window by clicking on the Maximize button. You may prefer the following alternative method to move between windows:

1. Choose Window from the menu bar.

   You see two options—Chart and Datasheet.

2. Click on the option to open the desired window.

You also can switch windows through the keyboard by pressing Ctrl-T or Ctrl-F6. The key combination switches you to whatever window you are not currently in.

Using Datasheets

Like a spreadsheet, the datasheet arranges your data into cells in rows and columns. Each rectangle in the datasheet is a cell. Some cells have text; most have numbers. You can enter only numbers and text into a PowerPoint datasheet; you cannot enter formulas as you can with a spreadsheet. Before you enter data, you must decide if you want to use your rows or columns as a series, which is discussed in the next section.

Putting Series in Rows or in Columns

A series is a group of related numbers. When you change to the Chart window, each series becomes a row of columns, a line, a pie slice, and so on, depending on what kind of graph you use. You determine whether a group of numbers is grouped meaningfully in series. PowerPoint accepts whatever you enter. Usually series will be time periods, places, people, dollar amounts, and so on. In the example PowerPoint gives you when you enter Graph, the data is grouped in two ways: by region (East, West, North) and by quarter (1st, 2nd, 3rd, and 4th). You can display this data in a graph by putting the series—regions or quarters in this example—in rows or in columns. Rows is the default. When the series is in rows, your graph measures the columns grouping. When the series is in columns, your graph measures the rows grouping. In the example (which has its series in rows), then, the graph shows the column labels (1st Qtr, 2nd Qtr, and so on), along the baseline. In the pie graph (discussed in the section "Choosing a Graph Type"), the pie is sliced into quarters when the series is in rows. Use series in rows when you want to measure the column headings in your datasheet, and use series in columns when you want to measure the row headings.

Suppose that you want to change from series in rows to series in columns in order to get a better visual reading of the regions East, West, and North. Follow these steps to make the change:

1. Choose Datasheet from the menu bar.

   At the bottom of the Datasheet window, you see two options: Series in Rows and Series in Columns. The Series in Rows option is checked, meaning that it is the active option.

2. Choose the Series in Columns option.

In this example, the baseline labels in the graph change to East, West, and North, as shown in figure 8.2.

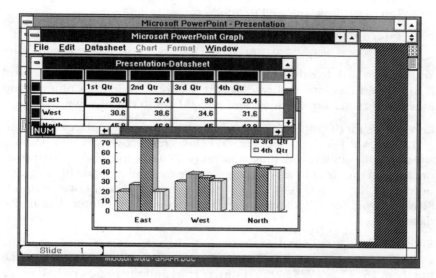

Fig. 8.2. *The graph after changing to Series in Columns from Series in Rows.*

Choose Series in Rows from the Datasheet menu, and the column headings—the quarters here—are measured in the Chart window again.

Next you learn how to insert data into the datasheet.

Inserting Data

In the following steps, you use an example to learn to add data representing the numbers of different types of trees planted over a three-month period. You overwrite the existing data as you insert the new. To insert the data, follow these steps:

1. Click on the label you want to change, here the label 1st Qtr in the first row.

    The cell (rectangle) containing the label now has a thicker frame, indicating that it is selected.

2. Type the new label, *May*.

3. Press the right-arrow key once, or press Tab.

   The cell to the right is now the active cell. Use the arrow keys or Tab to get from one cell to another.

4. Type the second label, *June*, and press the right-arrow key. Repeat the process as often as you need. Here, type *July* as the third label.

You see how to delete the fourth column (now unused in this example) and learn to add columns and rows in the sections "Deleting Columns and Rows" and "Inserting Columns and Rows" later in this chapter.

Enter labels for the rows the same way. In this example, replace *East*, *West*, and *North*, with *Cedars*, *Junipers*, and *Oaks*, respectively. If your graph is still on display underneath the datasheet (which it is unless you have moved or changed the size of the windows), notice that the baseline of the graph now reads May, June, July (and 4th Qtr if the Series in Rows option is active). PowerPoint updates the graph as soon as you enter data in the datasheet.

Enter numbers in cells in the same way as labels. For this example, type the numbers *5*, *8*, and *7* (representing trees planted) in the Cedars row; the numbers *15*, *19*, and *23* in the Junipers row; and the numbers *5*, *3*, and *2* in the Oaks row.

When you enter the numbers in the third row, the top row may disappear because the window is too small. You can use the scroll bar or the arrow keys to bring a row back into view, or you can enlarge the whole window so that all rows and columns appear simultaneously. You enlarge the window in the standard way for Windows, by moving the mouse pointer to the edge of the window and, when the pointer changes to a double-arrowhead, dragging the pointer in the required direction.

Another way to edit a cell is as follows:

1. Place the mouse pointer over the cell you want to edit and double-click.

   A pop-up box labeled Cell Data appears, as shown in figure 8.3.

2. Change letters and digits of the cell contents as needed and click on the OK button to exit the box.

Use the Cell Data dialog box when you want to make minor changes in a cell. When you change an entry by typing directly into a cell, you must retype the entire entry. In this dialog box, you can make those minor changes to the entry without retyping it.

The next section shows you how to select a group of cells to work with rather than just one individual cell.

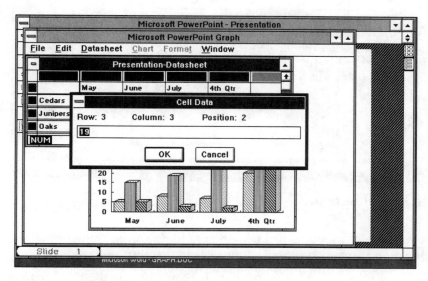

Fig. 8.3. The Cell Data dialog box.

Selecting Cells, Columns, and Rows

Cells can be formatted individually or in groups (see the section "Formatting Data" for a discussion of formatting). One reason you might want to select a group of cells is to format them together. You also might want to delete, cut, or copy a group of cells together. Selecting a group of cells to make them active is similar to selecting one cell.

Place the mouse pointer over the first cell you want to select, then click and hold the mouse button down while you drag the pointer over the cells to be selected. Here, start with the cell containing the number 5 and also select the cells containing the numbers 8 and 7.

The first cell retains the thick border; all the others turn black, as shown in figure 8.4.

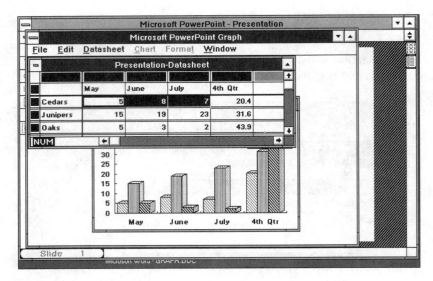

Fig. 8.4. *Selected cells.*

Alternatively, select the first cell, then hold down the Shift key and press one of the arrow keys to select the cells in that direction.

You can select all the cells in a datasheet by opening the Edit menu and choosing Select All. All the cells in the datasheet turn black, indicating that they are all selected.

You also can select columns and rows in Graph in another way. Above the column labels and to the left of the row labels, you see rectangles colored black in active rows and columns and colored gray in inactive rows and columns. You can use these rectangles to select columns and rows. To select the entire column or row, click on the black rectangle above the column or the black rectangle to the left of the row. In this example, click on the rectangle above the label 4th Qtr to select that column.

In the next section, you find how to edit the items you have selected.

Editing Cells

After you have selected the cells, columns, or rows, you can manipulate them in the same way that you can manipulate items in spreadsheets and word processors. The Edit menu in the menu bar includes the following commands: Cut, Copy, Paste, Clear. This section discusses each of these options.

Clearing Cells

When you clear rows and cells, you do not delete them. Clearing empties the cells but leaves them in place. Use the Clear option if you want to delete the numbers but retain the formatting of the cells. Alternatively, you might want to delete the formatting but retain the numbers. To delete information from the cells, do the following:

1. Select the cells, columns, or rows you want to clear. In this instance, select the fourth column.

2. Choose Clear from the Edit menu. Alternatively, press the Del key without clicking on Edit.

   You see the dialog box shown in figure 8.5.

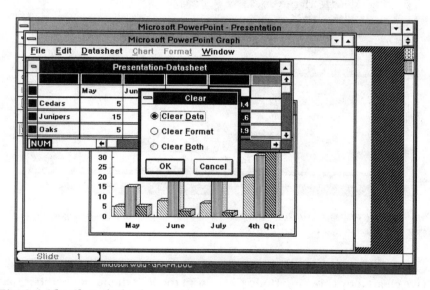

Fig. 8.5. *The Clear dialog box.*

The Clear dialog box contains three options: Clear Data, Clear Format, and Clear Both. The format is the physical arrangement and style of data in a cell. For example, you can format a cell so that all whole numbers will be followed by a decimal point and two zeros. Clear Data clears the data from the selected cells but retains the format for future use. Clear Format leaves the data but clears any formatting in the cells. Clear Both clears both data and formatting.

3. Select one of the options and then click on OK to exit the box. Here, choose Clear Both.

PowerPoint Graph clears your selected cells as requested. In this case, PowerPoint Graph clears the column of all data and formatting but does not delete the column itself. A cleared but undeleted row or column produces blank spaces in a graph, as you can see in figure 8.6. You learn to delete a column in the section "Deleting Columns and Rows."

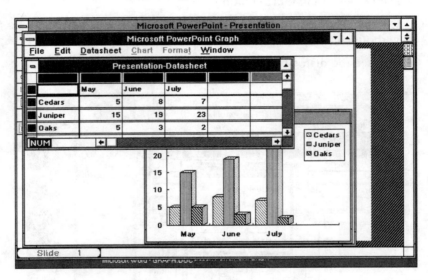

Fig. 8.6. A graph containing a cleared but active column, producing a blank on the right of each group of columns.

As elsewhere in PowerPoint, you can retrieve data or formatting that you have cleared by choosing Undo Clear from the Edit menu. Remember that if you perform some intermediate function after clearing, you cannot use Undo Clear.

Cutting and Copying Cells

When you cut or copy, the data that you select is put into a clipboard (or buffer). The Cut option removes data from a selected cell and puts it in the clipboard. After you cut data, you can paste it into any cell or cells that you want. The Copy option copies the data in a selected cell into the clipboard but does not delete the data from the original cell. From the clipboard, you can paste the data to other cells.

Cut and Copy work in the same way as Clear, but without a dialog box. To cut or copy, select the cells and click on the option. To Paste, select a starting cell and click on the Paste option. Anything in the clipboard is pasted onto the datasheet. To copy cell contents, follow these steps:

1. Select the cells you want to clear. Here, select the active cells in column 4, starting with the heading July, and also the cells 7, 23, and 2. Do not select the whole column.

2. Choose Copy or Cut from the Edit menu. Here, choose Copy.

3. Select the starting cells to which you want to paste. Here, select the cells to the right of July.

4. Choose Paste from the Edit menu.

When you paste to cells that already contain numbers or letters, you overwrite that data. To maintain consistency with the examples shown in the figures, clear this column after pasting it.

Inserting Columns and Rows

Sometimes you need to insert a row or column between two other rows and columns. Graph enables you to insert a blank row or column by pushing aside the other rows or columns. In the example, suppose that you want to insert a line of data about sycamores between the rows of data about junipers and oaks. Proceed as follows:

1. Select the row or column you want to push over one column or down one row. In this case, select the row beginning with Oaks.

2. Choose Insert Row/Column from the Edit menu.

   The Insert Row/Col dialog box appears, as shown in figure 8.7.

   Because you have selected a row, the Insert Rows option is active. Insert Columns would be active if you had selected a column in your datasheet.

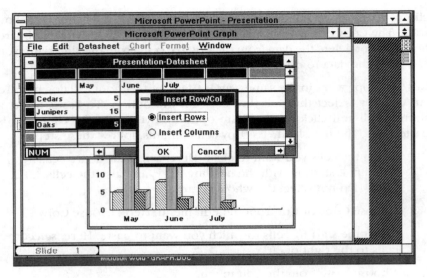

Fig. 8.7. *The Insert Row/Col dialog box.*

3. Click on OK (or press Enter) and a blank row is inserted between Junipers and Oaks.

Now you can add your label and data to the blank row. Type *Sycamores, 15, 0, 5.* Follow similar steps to insert a column.

Because the Insert Row/Col dialog box gives you two choices, Insert Rows and Insert Columns, you can insert a new row or column by selecting a single cell instead of an entire row or column. Follow these steps to insert three columns into the example:

1. Click on several cells, for instance three cells in a row, as shown in figure 8.8.

2. Choose Insert Row/Col from the Edit menu.

   You see the Insert Row/Col dialog box with the Insert Columns option active. Clicking on OK at this point inserts three blank columns in front of your selected cells. If you click Insert Rows and then OK, you insert one blank row, because the selected cells are horizontal. If they were vertical, you would insert three blank rows.

3. Accept the Insert Columns option by clicking on OK or pressing Enter.

Figure 8.9 shows the result.

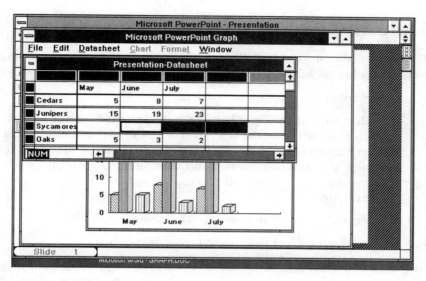

Fig. 8.8. *Three selected cells.*

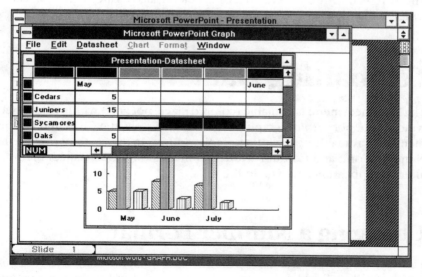

Fig. 8.9. *Three new columns.*

The gray rectangles at the top of the new columns indicate that the columns are inactive.

Deleting Columns and Rows

To delete a column or row, follow the same procedures as for inserting rows and columns, but choose Delete Row/Col instead of Insert Row/Col.

1. Select any rows or columns to delete.

   To select more than one column or row, click on the black or gray rectangle at the top or the side, then drag with the mouse to select other columns or rows. For the example, you might want to delete the three columns just inserted and also the former 4th Qtr column, which is empty but still active, as shown by the black rectangle on top.

2. Choose Delete Row/Col from the Edit menu.

PowerPoint Graph deletes the selected rows or columns.

Including and excluding rows and columns is an advanced topic. Chapter 13 tells you how to include and exclude rows and columns, as well as how to carry out other advanced procedures.

The next section discusses the Datasheet menu, also located in the Datasheet window.

Formatting Data

The Datasheet menu is available (colored black, not gray) within a datasheet window but not within a graph window. Conversely, the Chart and Format menus are available only within a graph window. In this section, you use the Number, Font, and Column Width commands on the Datasheet menu to alter the appearance of data in the cells.

Changing a Number Format

You can display the numbers in your cells in many ways. PowerPoint automatically will add dollar signs, decimal points and zeros, percentages, and much more. To use number formatting, select what you want to format and then apply the number format through the Datasheet menu. For example, suppose that you want the date label in the first row of the inserted data (May, June, July) to include years. Use the Number function, as follows:

1. Select the cells to format. For the example, select the first row—May, June, July—by clicking on the black rectangle to the left of the first blank cell in the row.

2. Choose Number from the Datasheet menu.

   Figure 8.10 shows the menu choices for Number.

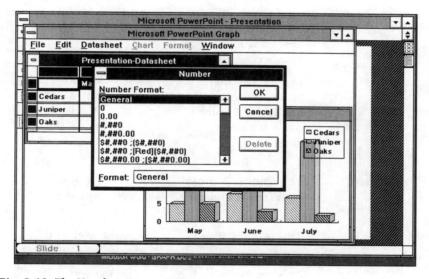

Fig. 8.10. *The Number menu options.*

Table 8.1 explains the options. The first choice, General, is the default, as the dark background indicates.

3. Scroll down to see the full range of menu choices. For the example, scroll until you see MMM-YY.

4. Click on your choice to apply it to the selected cells; here, click on MMM-YY, and click OK.

Back on the datasheet, the cells reformat your numbers. In the example, nothing has changed because the labels do not contain numbers yet. Type *May90, June90,* and *July90* over the current entries and you end up with `May-90, Jun-90,` and `Jul-90`.

Table 8.1
Number Formats on the Datasheet Menu

Symbol	Use	Examples
0 and #	These two symbols hold digits and place them where you indicate. 0 adds zeros. When used alone, it rounds to the nearest whole number.	9 typed in a cell formatted with 00 appears as 09; 9.7 typed in a cell formatted with 0 appears as 10.
. (period)	Use the decimal point symbol to add the decimal point when it's not entered.	Use #.#, and 9 displays as 9.; use #.0, and 9 displays as 9.0; use 0.00, and .9 displays as 0.90.
, (comma)	The comma is useful with large numbers.	Use #,##0, and 9999 displays as 9,999.
$	This symbol adds a dollar sign.	Use $#0.00, and 99 displays as $99.00.
%	This symbol adds the percentage symbol, and the number typed in the cell is multiplied by 100. Type decimal points in the cell, not fractions (not 2/4, for example).	Use 0%, and .25 displays as 25%; use 0%, and 8 displays as 800%.
E	This symbol activates the scientific format. The menu choice is 0.00E+00.	Type 7 in the cell and you get 7.00E+00; type .4 and you get 4.00E-01; type 6666 and you get 6.67E+03.

Symbol	Use	Examples
y m d h s AM/PM	Use these with date formatting. They indicate year, month, day, hour, second, and AM and PM.	Use h:mm AM/PM and 7 displays as `7:00 AM.`

Chapter 13, "Using Advanced Features of Graph," shows you how to create and delete your own formats.

Formatting Tick Marks

Tick marks are the lines that intersect the axes of a graph at regular intervals; tick mark labels identify the intervals. In figure 8.1, you see the numbers 10, 20, 30, and so on, along the vertical axis of the graph. The numbers are the tick mark labels; the small lines on the axis are the tick marks.

You can alter the formatting of tick mark labels through the Number menu option on the Datasheet menu by altering a special cell. The steps for altering tick-mark formatting are as follows:

1. Select the cell two down and two across—always use this cell. In the example, this cell contains the number 5.

   When you change the format for the cell two down and two across, the format applies to the numeric values next to the tick marks along the entire vertical axis.

2. Choose Number from the Datasheet menu.

3. Choose a formatting option from the Number menu, 0.00 for example, by clicking on it.

When you return to the datasheet, the number in the cell has the decimal point and two zeros attached. Switch to the chart window and all the tick mark labels also have this decimal point and zeros. The next section covers changing your text.

Changing the Font

You can use the Font option in the Datasheet menu to change the appearance of the cell entries in your datasheet. You use the Font option in the same way that you use the Number option, except that if you change the font in any one cell in the datasheet (not just the top left cell, two down and two across), then you change the font in all the cells. The Font option does not affect the formatting of text and numbers in the graph. Use the Font option as shown here:

1. Select any cell in your datasheet. If one cell changes, all cells change.

2. Choose Font from the Datasheet menu.

   You see the dialog box shown in figure 8.11.

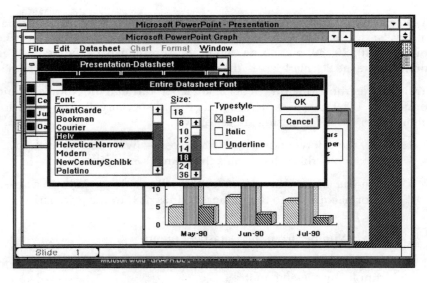

Fig. 8.11. The Entire Datasheet Font dialog box.

You can change the font, the size, and the typestyle.

3. Click on the scroll bar arrows to see the list of fonts and sizes.

   Choosing large numbers from the Size option increases the size of the letters and numerals in your database. The default font is Helv, which stands for Helvetica; the default size is 18. The numbers under the Size option refer to point size. The three type styles are Bold, Italic, and Underline. Bold is the default, as the X in the box next to the word Bold indicates.

4. Choose any option by clicking on it. For the example, change from Bold to plain.

   To get a plain typestyle, remove the X next to each of the three options (Bold, Italic, and Underline). All three options also can be on at the same time, if you want.

5. Click on OK to accept your changes, or click Cancel to revert to the original.

When you exit the dialog box, the cell entries display the new attributes.

Changing Column Width

Sometimes the standard column width is not wide enough to accommodate your numbers and text. (If you enter text that is too wide, PowerPoint Graph widens the cell. If you enter numbers that are too wide, PowerPoint represents them with a formula.) To change the width of one or more columns, do the following:

1. Select the columns or cells you want to change. Here, select the third column.

   If you select a cell rather than a column, Graph changes the width of all cells in that column.

2. Choose Column Width from the Datasheet menu.

   You see the dialog box shown in figure 8.12.

   The standard width is 9. If you forget the standard, PowerPoint provides a box in the lower left labeled Standard Width. Click on this box when you want to revert to the standard.

3. Type a number from 1 to 255, representing characters per column. For this example, try 15.

4. Click OK or press Enter to accept your choice and return to the datasheet.

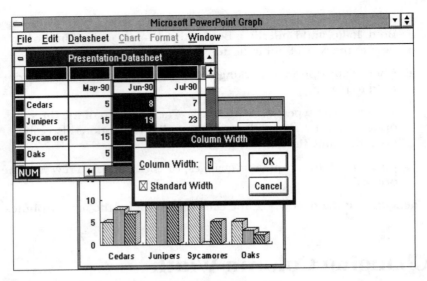

Fig. 8.12. The dialog box for changing column width.

The chosen columns change to the new size. A more straightforward way to change column widths is shown in these steps:

1. Place the mouse pointer between the black rectangles above the columns. Here, point to the line after the third column.

    The shape of the pointer changes to a black cross with arrows on the horizontal line.

2. Hold down the mouse button and drag the line to change its location. Drag the line to the right to widen the column; drag to the left to narrow the column. Here, drag the line to the left to revert to the standard column width.

3. Release the button when the column width looks right.

Try dragging the line instead of specifying a number when you want to see the exact width of a column.

Chapter 13, "Using Advanced Features of Graph," discusses many additional features of datasheets. The rest of this chapter covers the Chart window, the companion window to the Datasheet window.

Creating the Graph

The reason you use PowerPoint Graph is to produce graphs. Adding entries to the datasheet provides the raw data to display in the graph (or "chart," in PowerPoint's terminology). What you see in the Chart window, except perhaps for size, is what you finally see when you exit Graph and return to the current slide. You can change almost everything in PowerPoint as many times as you like, but you will save time if you get the graph attributes right when you start.

In the following sections, you see how to display the same datasheet information in different kinds of graphs, how to select objects on a graph, and how to modify graphs with different colors and patterns, line styles, and fonts. Finally, you learn to insert the graph into your PowerPoint slide.

To open the Chart window if you are now in the Datasheet window, change to the Chart window by clicking on the visible portion of the Chart window. Alternatively, press Ctrl-T or Ctrl-F6.

In the example, you now see something similar to figure 8.13.

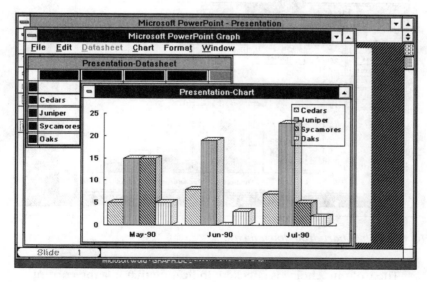

Fig. 8.13. *The Chart window.*

When you change to the Chart window, the Datasheet menu in the menu bar turns gray. The Chart and Format options turn black, indicating that they are now available.

Choosing a Graph Type

Graphs enable you to see overall relationships among complex data. Six different kinds of graphs are available in PowerPoint Graph: Column, Area, Bar, Line, Pie, and Scatter. Suppose that you do not know which kind of graph to use and you want to look at them all. Follow these steps to see how they look:

1. Choose Chart from the menu bar.

    You see the drop-down menu shown in figure 8.14.

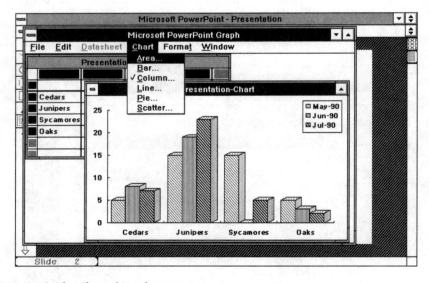

Fig. 8.14. *The Chart drop-down menu.*

The Column choice is checked, indicating that it is the current choice. (Column is also the default choice.) Each kind of graph is available in different styles.

2. Click on any of the six types of graphs to see the graph styles. Click on Column, for instance, and the dialog box shown in figure 8.15 appears.

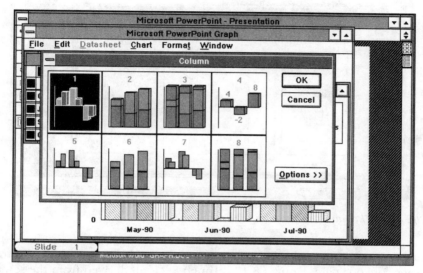

Fig. 8.15. *The Column option dialog box.*

In this dialog box, you can choose from eight graph styles. All graph types have eight styles, except Scatter, which has five. One style always has a black background, meaning that it is the current choice (the default choice if you are using it for the first time in a session). (The Options button in the lower right part of the window enables you to choose more options, such as Stacked or 3D Axis. See Chapter 13, "Using Advanced Features of Graph," for discussion of these additional options.)

3. Click on the style of your choice and then click on OK. Choose the rectangle numbered 2 and you see a graph similar to the graph shown in figure 8.16.

In the example, the application of style number 2 creates a graph that still arranges the numbers of trees planted per month in columns, but now the different kinds of trees are grouped in a single column per month. Before, each kind of tree appeared in a separate column.

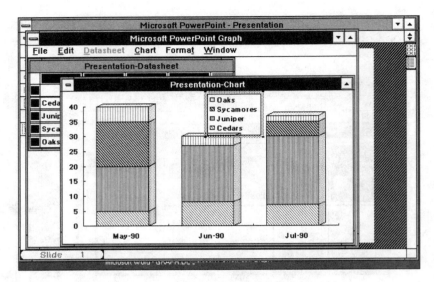

Fig. 8.16. *The number 2 style in the Column dialog box.*

Each graph type and display style can focus attention on some significant aspect of your data. Figures 8.17 through 8.21, all derived from the same datasheet that produced figure 8.16, illustrate the different kinds of graphs available in PowerPoint—area, bar, line, pie, and scatter. (See figure 8.16 for an example of a column graph.)

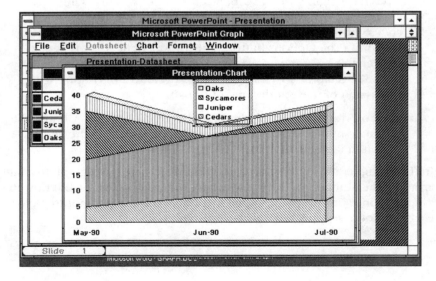

Fig. 8.17. *An Area graph.*

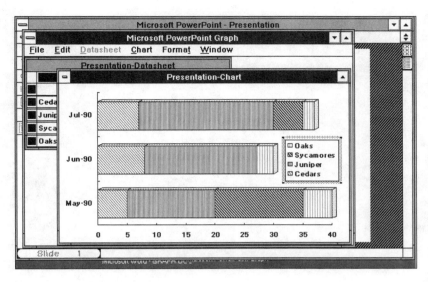

Fig. 8.18. *A Bar graph.*

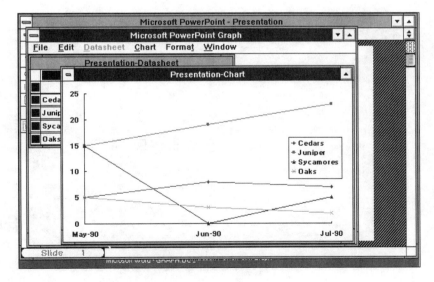

Fig. 8.19. *A Line graph.*

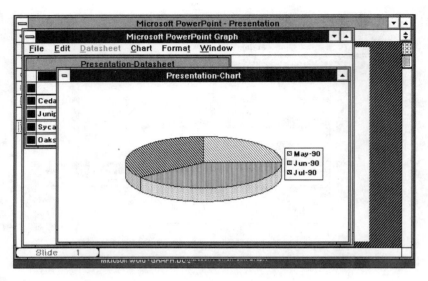

Fig. 8.20. A Pie graph.

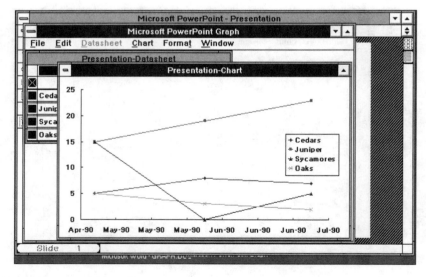

Fig. 8.21. A Scatter graph.

Seeing the different kinds of graphs in association with different kinds of data is the best way to discover which graph type best suits your needs. Table 8.2 gives a summary of the advantages of each kind of graph. You also can customize each graph form by applying options like 3D Axis for a column graph or drop lines for a line graph. Chapter 13, "Using Advanced Features of Graph," explains the options.

Table 8.2
Choosing a Graph Type

Graph	Advantages
Area	An area graph is useful for showing the parts in proportion to the whole, often plotted against time on the horizontal axis.
Bar	Use a bar graph to compare the parts to each other. A bar graph does not emphasize the flow of time as strongly as a column or area graph.
Column	A column graph emphasizes change in the parts over time.
Line	A line graph emphasizes change over time, but highlights trends rather than the actual numbers.
Pie	The pie graph always shows only one series of data. In PowerPoint Graph, if you choose Series in Rows from the Datasheet window, the pie graph for that datasheet uses the data in the columns. If you choose Series in Columns, then the pie graph uses the data in the rows. The pie graph is the best graph to show the proportion of parts to the whole. No time measure is given.
Scatter	Scatter graphs have numbers rather than labels along the axes. Use scatter graphs to show the relationship between two or more series.

Elements of a Graph

Most graphs have certain elements in common: a vertical and horizontal axis, a legend box, tick marks, tick mark labels, data points, and data labels. Figure 8.22 shows you the positions of these elements in a column graph.

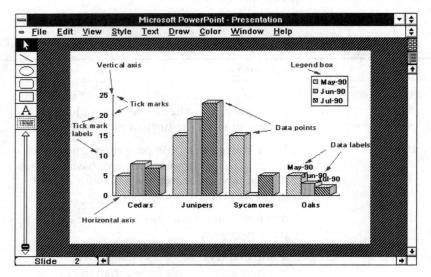

Fig. 8.22. *The elements of a graph.*

In this example, the datasheet is set as a series in columns, so that the column headings, May-90, Jun-90, and Jul-90, appear in the legend box, and the row headings appear along the horizontal axis. If the series were in rows, this situation would be reversed. The vertical axis is the measuring stick. In the example, 23 is the highest number in the datasheet and 0 the lowest, so the vertical axis includes both these numbers and has a scale of 0-25. The tick marks increase by increments of 5 in this example; the tick mark labels identify the tick marks. The data points (the tops of the columns in this type of graph) correspond to the numbers that appear in the datasheet. In the example, the group of columns representing cedars have data points of 5, 8, and 7 for May, June, and July. The numbers are not marked on this graph, but trace the top of the columns to the vertical axis, and you see that the correspondence is good. Data labels show the legend box labeling in "close-up," i.e., against the actual columns in this case.

See the following sections and Chapter 13 for discussions of all the formatting options available in the Chart window.

Selecting Objects on a Graph

You can change almost everything you see on a graph—color, pattern, line style, and so on. To change an object, you first must select the object. You can select any of these items on a graph: either axis; any lines, points, or columns that represent your data on the graphs; the labeling; the gridlines; the legend; and column frames. All graphs except the pie graph have these features, although some features, like gridlines, you must activate yourself. The pie graph is different from other graphs because it can represent only one series of numbers at a time. This fact means that features other than labeling and the legend box are redundant. To select an object, click on the required object. For this example, select the top line from the line graph shown in figure 8.19.

Figure 8.23 shows a selected line, the top line from figure 8.19. The three open square boxes along the length of the line indicate that the line is selected.

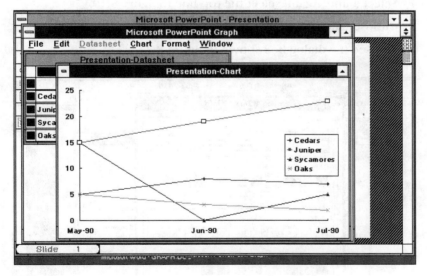

Fig. 8.23. *A selected line starting at the tick mark labeled 15 on the vertical axis.*

Selection in a graph in PowerPoint Graph is similar to selection in PowerPoint itself. For a discussion of selecting objects in PowerPoint, see Chapter 4,

"Adding Text to a Presentation." The important thing to remember is that you must select something in order to use Line Style, Fill, and Font.

After you have selected an object, you can change it. In the next section, you learn how to color and style an object in a graph.

Choosing Line Styles

Use the Line Style option to change the color or thickness of a line or the color or appearance of a marker. Markers mark the exact data points on a line to distinguish them from the rest of the line, which connects the data points. When you select a line, the square boxes show the position of the markers, as you see in figure 8.23. (An axis line does not have markers, so you cannot change its markers, but you can change its thickness and color.)

Change the line styling as shown in these steps:

1. Select a line. Again, select the top line in figure 8.19.

2. Choose Line Style from the Format menu.

   You see the dialog box shown in figure 8.24.

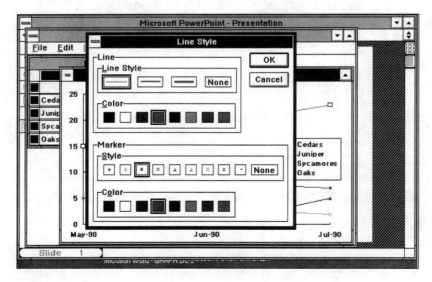

Fig. 8.24. *The Line Style dialog box.*

Only the top half of the box would appear if your selected line were an axis line. The marker options would be left out because the axis line has no markers. The default color for lines and markers is black. The default line thickness is the thinnest line, and the default marker varies. Style 2 of the Line options has no markers. Other styles have markers automatically selected.

3. Choose the colors, thickness, and marker appearance that you want, and click on OK to accept them. Try thicker lines for the example.

The colors available in the Line Style dialog box are quite dark. You can use the Recolor Picture option discussed in Chapter 14 to change them to brighter colors after you return to the slide.

Choosing Fill Colors and Patterns

Fill colors can provide strong contrast between series and parts in a graph. Selecting the object and changing the colors and patterns is easy. The way patterns and colors combine is less straightforward. To change Fill Colors and Patterns, do the following:

1. Click on an object in a graph; for instance, click on any enclosed area from figure 8.17, 8.18, or 8.20.

2. Choose Fill from the Format menu.

   Graph displays the dialog box shown in figure 8.25.

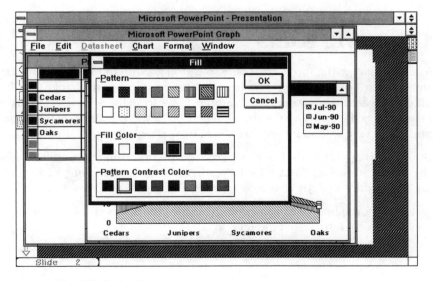

Fig. 8.25. *The Fill dialog box.*

The three choices are Pattern, Fill Color, and Pattern Contrast Color. Fill Color and Pattern Contrast Color are the primary and secondary colors of your graph, respectively. The pattern you choose combines them in a unique way. Use Fill Color to choose the main color of a pattern and use Pattern Contrast Color to choose the secondary color. Pattern shows how the two look when combined. ("Primary" and "secondary" are not used in the artist's sense of the term, i.e., the primary colors are red, yellow, and blue.)

3. To gauge the results, first choose the Fill Color and the Pattern Contrast Color. Try green and white, respectively.

   When you choose the colors, the Pattern choices change to reflect the new colors. These Pattern choices therefore show the actual final look of the selected graph objects.

4. Click on a Pattern. Try number 2, the white dots on a darker background.

5. Click OK if the pattern looks good to you.

Adding fill to your graph objects can make certain elements in the slide stand out. If you want to emphasize one slice in a pie, for instance, you can fill it with a bright, solid color.

You also can create different effects by changing the fonts for text and numbers, as explained in the next section.

Choosing Fonts

You can change the font, size, color, and background of numbers and text on graphs. Select a line or a legend box and you can change all the characters at the same time. For example, you can change the characters on labels along the axes and within the legend box and the characters on data and value labels. Remember that all characters are changed.

Suppose that your legend box overlays a graph line, and you want to make the words in the legend easier to read. The steps for changing fonts are similar to the steps for changing fills and line styles, as follows:

1. Select the line or object containing the characters you want to change. Here, select the legend box.

2. Choose Font from the Format menu.

   You see the dialog box shown in figure 8.26.

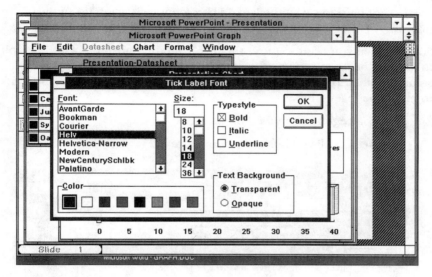

Fig. 8.26. The Font dialog box titled Tick Label Font.

3. Choose the different fonts, sizes, and colors by clicking them. Scroll down to see more choices.

   In the lower right corner of the dialog box, you see two choices for text background, Transparent and Opaque. Transparent is the default. When you choose Opaque, a solid rectangle encloses text selected on the graph so that background lines do not obscure the characters.

4. Choose Opaque when you want characters to stand out against a background. Choose Opaque for this example.

On the graph, an opaque background now surrounds the words in the legend box. Use the preceding steps to change font and size and to choose between opaque and transparent text backgrounds.

Moving the Legend

The legend is the box in your graph that identifies the different parts of a series. If you choose Series in Columns in the Datasheet window, the column headings appear in the legend box. The default position for the legend is in the upper right portion of the graph. You can choose to display this box in different positions, move it yourself, or not to display it at all. You do not have to select the legend box to move it when using the menu option.

Suppose that you want to move the box from the right side of a pie graph to the top, because you know that when you place the graph on the slide, some explanatory text will fall to the right of the graph. Follow these steps to move the legend box:

1. Choose Legend from the Format menu.

    You see the dialog box shown in figure 8.27.

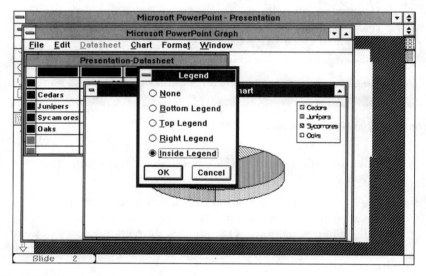

Fig. 8.27. *The Legend dialog box.*

The choices are None, Bottom Legend, Top Legend, Right Legend, and Inside Legend. Using Bottom Legend, Top Legend, and Right Legend places the legend outside the graph. The Inside Legend option enables you to move the legend around yourself (the other options do not).

2. Select any option. Here, select Top Legend.

You return to the graph, with the legend box in its new position along the top in this example. When the legend is inside the graph, you can move the legend box around in the usual way (described in Chapter 5, "Drawing Objects"). Click over the box, hold the mouse button down and drag the box to its new position. The capability to move the legend box is useful when legends get in the way of graph features.

You can use those two simple steps to change the positioning of legend boxes. See Chapter 13 for advanced features such as defining the scale for the vertical axis, changing the positions of an axis, displaying data labels, adding gridlines, and so on.

Inserting the Graph into Your Slide

When you have the graph you want, you insert it into your slide. To insert your graph, do the following:

1. Choose File from the menu bar.

2. Choose Exit and then Return.

The Graph windows close and you return to the presentation slide you were using in PowerPoint when you entered PowerPoint Graph. Figure 8.28 shows an example of a slide with a graph inserted into it.

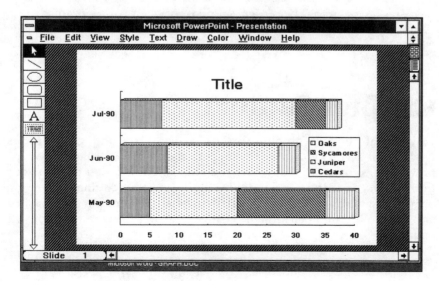

Fig. 8.28. *A slide with an inserted graph.*

The graph is now an object on a slide. You can move the graph, resize it, fill it, and so on, like other objects. You also can recolor the graph like a picture to make it blend in with the rest of your color scheme. You cannot, however, save a graph from the PowerPoint Graph window. You can save from the main PowerPoint window only (the main PowerPoint window contains the slide). If you haven't completed your graph in one session, exit Graph as shown in the preceding two steps, save your presentation (thereby saving your graph), and go back in again later, as shown in the section "Editing Your Graph," to complete your graph.

Editing Your Graph

You often need to return to Graph to edit your graph. You can return to Graph by placing the mouse pointer over the graph on the slide and clicking twice, or by clicking the graph to select it and then choosing Edit Graph from the Edit menu.

Either way, you return to Graph with the selected graph displayed. Follow the same steps described in this chapter to add data, change a legend, and so on.

> *Tip:* Do *not* use Insert Graph from the File menu to go into a graph that you already have pasted onto the slide. Insert Graph always creates a new graph. Use Insert Graph only when you want to add another graph to your slide.

Chapter Summary

PowerPoint reduces graphing to its basics—data and graph forms. PowerPoint enables you to work with both at once. In this chapter, you saw how to move between datasheets and graphs. You learned to insert data into the datasheet and to manipulate cells by selecting, cutting, and pasting data. You saw how to insert and delete rows and columns in the datasheet and how to use number formats, change text, and vary the width of your columns.

You also read how to choose the right graph for your purposes, how to select objects, and how to change line styles, fills, and fonts. You learned to move the legend box around in your Chart window. Finally, you saw how to return to a PowerPoint slide with your new graph inserted. Even more power is available in PowerPoint Graph, as you see in Chapter 13.

9

Creating Output

W hen most people hear the word *slide*, they think of the transparent, colored slide that you view with a slide projector. Everything you do in PowerPoint you do, ultimately, so that you can create a slide (or another form of output, such as an overhead transparency).

In this chapter, you find out about this last and most important step in creating your presentations: outputting your slides. You first find out how to set up your printer (a step you should perform before you create any slides with PowerPoint). You next find out how to set up the slides themselves. This chapter also shows you how to use the computer as a slide projector.

You find out how to print the slide to different kinds of output devices. You also learn to print the notes pages and handouts available with your slides. Finally, you find out how you can arrange to send your PowerPoint slides to Genigraphics by modem to have the Genigraphics slide service bureau create your slides for you.

Setting Up Your Printer

The first step in creating a PowerPoint presentation is to set up your target printer, because your choice of target printer determines which fonts are available when you create your slides and also the slide dimensions that appear in the Slide Setup dialog box. Although you usually do not print a slide until after you create your presentation, you need to plan for printing from the outset.

Before you can set up your printer, you must install it. To install the printer, copy into PowerPoint the software—called *printer drivers*—that PowerPoint needs to work with that printer. Use Windows operating system commands to install the printer. Start with the Control Panel and choose Printers. Refer to the Windows documentation if you need help installing your printer.

In PowerPoint, you work with a target printer and also, if you want, a draft printer. You print your final presentation on the target printer. Your choice of target printer determines the available fonts, the slide dimensions and orientation, and other settings in the Slide Setup dialog box. The draft printer is a printer you can use instead of the target printer during a given session. PowerPoint does not keep track of your choice of draft printer after you finish the session. See the section "Printing Your Slides" in this chapter to find out how to print to a draft printer rather than to the target printer.

Your target printer need not be a conventional printer. If you plan to send your files to Genigraphics to be made into slides, you can specify the Genigraphics driver as the target printer. (See the section "Linking with Genigraphics" in this chapter.) You also can specify Display as the primary target if you plan to deliver your presentation as an on-screen slide show. (See the section "Running a Slide Show on Your Screen" in this chapter.)

If you plan to print color transparencies or black-and-white overheads, install the appropriate printer and designate it as the target printer. Do the same if you plan to print on a film recorder. PowerPoint makes available different slide dimensions, different slide orientations, and different fonts, depending on your target printer. After you set up the output device, you use PowerPoint's menus and capabilities in the same way for any output device.

Suppose that you want to install a Hewlett-Packard LaserJet printer as the target printer for a presentation. Follow these steps to install the LaserJet:

1. Choose Printer Setup from the File menu.

    You see the dialog box shown in figure 9.1. Specify the target printer for your presentation. You also can specify a different target printer for notes and handouts.

    When you first open a new presentation, PowerPoint already has the Default Target as the target printer. With this setting, you can print to the following paper sizes: letter, legal, A4, 135, or slide. You also can print in portrait or landscape orientation. Use the default target printer to save time and trouble if you just want to print in draft mode.

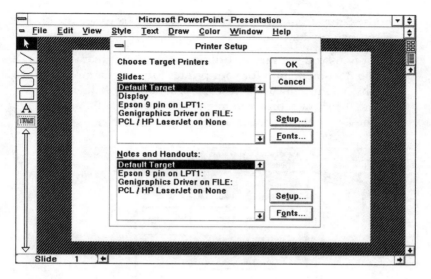

Fig. 9.1. *Printer Setup dialog box.*

Tip: If you have a color output device and a black-and-white printer, you can use the color output device as the target printer for the presentation and the black-and-white device as the target for notes and handouts.

2. Highlight the printer you want to use as your target printer for the presentation. Do the same to set up the target printer for notes and handouts.

   You can choose OK now and begin to create your presentation. The Printer Setup dialog box, however, offers two submenus—Setup and Fonts.

Setting Printer Options

By choosing your target printer, you provide PowerPoint with the information necessary to set up the right fonts and dimensions for your presentation. You also can set up additional options on your own. To set up other options, follow these steps:

1. Choose Setup from the Printer Setup dialog box to see the options for setting up your printer.

   The options you see vary according to the printer that you choose. See the documentation for your printer for explanations of most options. You usually use landscape orientation for slides. Figures 9.2 and 9.3 show setups you might have for a default target printer and the Epson 9-pin printer driver.

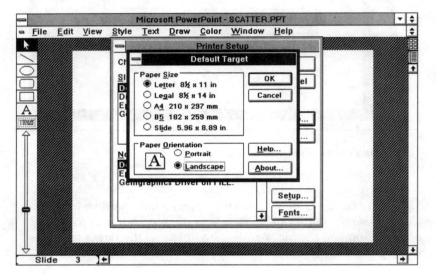

Fig. 9.2. A printer setup.

2. Choose OK after you set up your options.

3. Move the cursor to the second Setup box, at the bottom of the Printer Setup screen. Repeat the preceding steps to set up the options for the notes and handouts.

   You usually use portrait orientation for notes and handouts.

Choosing Replacement Fonts

After you set up your target printer, PowerPoint makes available the appropriate fonts for the printer. You do not have to set up the fonts yourself. If you do not print the presentation on your target printer, however, PowerPoint cannot use the fonts designed for the original target printer. You do not need to designate fonts for the replacement printer; PowerPoint automatically substitutes fonts that are compatible with your replacement printer for the incompatible fonts. (You can designate fonts from the Style menu within the presentation if you do not want to use the defaults throughout. See Chapter 4, "Adding Text to a Presentation.")

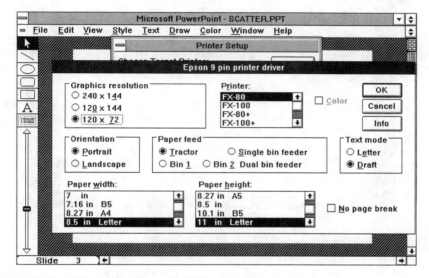

Fig. 9.3. *Printer setup for the Epson 9-pin printer.*

If you want, you can specify which fonts from the replacement printer to substitute for the incompatible fonts from the original target printer. The replacement is temporary. When you return to the original target printer, PowerPoint uses the original fonts.

Follow these steps to designate replacement fonts:

1. Choose a target printer from the Printer Setup dialog box.

2. Choose Fonts.

   You see the Fonts dialog box, shown in figure 9.4. On the left, under Replace, are the fonts you want to replace (those from the original target printer that the replacement printer cannot print). The fonts displayed in this dialog box (see step 4 for instructions on how to access the fonts) are the fonts available with the target printer. You must decide which font can be used with your replacement printer and whether the font is compatible with the replacement printer.

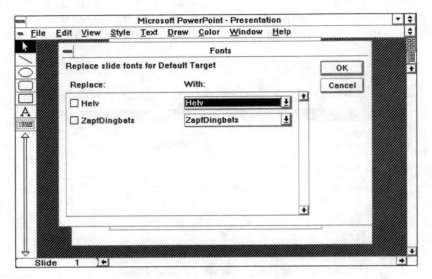

Fig. 9.4. The Fonts dialog box for specifying replacement fonts.

3. Select the fonts you want to replace in the Replace column. An X in the box indicates that you have selected the font. PowerPoint will replace all occurrences of those fonts when you use the replacement printer.

4. On the right side of the box, under the word With, click the arrow directly to the right side of the drop-down menu for the font listed.

   You see a list of replacement fonts (fonts that work on the replacement printer).

5. Highlight a replacement font to select it.

6. Choose OK. If you do not want to specify replacements, choose Cancel.

If you print the presentation and your printer does not have the fonts you choose for your target printer, PowerPoint will use the fonts you have specified as replacements rather than its automatic replacements. When you go back into this Fonts dialog box in the future, the replacement font always remains highlighted—it appears in the Replace column and is the highlighted option in the list of fonts available. You can, of course, change the replacement font at any time.

> *Tip:* Not all replacement fonts exactly duplicate the original fonts, even if they are the same point size. If you are using replacement fonts, look over the presentation carefully. You may need to make corrections where text spills over the end of the line or no longer follows the original alignment.

After you have set up your printer, PowerPoint sets up your slides to work with the printer. If you prefer, you can set up the slides yourself, as explained in the next section.

Setting Up Your Slides

Setting up your slides is similar to setting up your printer. When you specify a printer during printer setup, PowerPoint assigns dimensions and an orientation for the slides. If you want to change the default dimensions through Slide Setup, change them before you start to create your slides so that everything fits properly. You might want to change the setup to create special visual effects, such as space above and below the slide. To specify the slide setup yourself, follow these steps:

1. Choose Slide Setup from the File menu.

   You see the Slide Setup dialog box, shown in figure 9.5. Move through the box with the keyboard or mouse in the usual way. Table 9.1 summarizes the choices available in the box.

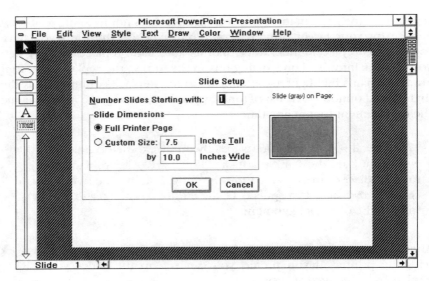

Fig. 9.5. *The Slide Setup dialog box.*

Table 9.1
Slide Setup Dialog Box

Option	*Action*
Number Slides Starting With	Type the number of the first slide, or accept the default (1). PowerPoint numbers additional slides in sequence.
Slide Dimensions	Specify the dimensions or accept the default. You can choose a smaller size, for example, to add more white space around the slide.
Full Printer Page	If you select this option, PowerPoint prints the slide so that it fills the entire page on your target printer.
Custom Size	In these boxes, you can specify a size for the slides other than the default. Type a number that represents units of measurement—inches or centimeters, according to your default Windows measurement units.

The rectangle at the right, labeled `Slide (Gray) on Page`, shows the effect that the dimensions you choose for your slides have on the output. The rectangle first shows the orientation (landscape or portrait). The outside edge of the rectangle corresponds to the edge of the paper. The inside edge represents the maximum area available for the slide image. A small margin always exists between the inner and outer rectangles. The gray area represents the actual dimensions you have set up for your slides. If you change the dimensions, click the rectangle to see how the new dimensions affect the slide. If you make the dimensions smaller, for instance, the gray area appears smaller inside the rectangle.

2. After you have the dimensions you want, choose OK.

You need correct slide dimensions before you start to work in PowerPoint. Changing the dimensions is basically an advanced technique, however, you seldom need to change them. You may need to change slide dimensions only to satisfy a special problem, such as outputting to paper of an unusual size.

Running a Slide Show on Your Screen

Not too long ago, you did not consider yourself finished with a presentation when you had created slides on your computer. You had to pay for 35mm slides and wait for a slide service to prepare them and return them to you.

You still may elect to use 35mm slides in making your presentation. Now, however, you also can run a slide show on your computer screen. If the presentation room at your company has the right kind of projection device, you can project the screen show from your computer to an entire room. If you do not have such a device, you can project the screen show on one computer to a small audience gathered around the PC. (If your computers are networked in the right way, you can display the screen show on several individual PCs at the same time.)

To run a screen show from your computer, open the presentation with the File and Open commands and follow these steps:

1. Choose Slide Show from the File menu.

   You see the Slide Show dialog box, shown in figure 9.6.

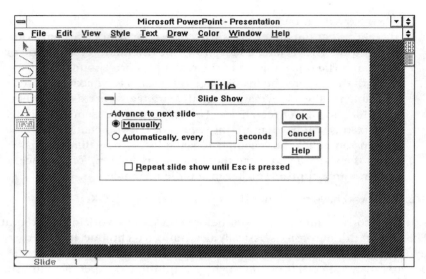

Fig. 9.6. The Slide Show dialog box.

2. **Choose** Manually **or** Automatically, Every [ ] Seconds. **For this example, choose** Automatically Every 5 Seconds.

   If you choose Manually, you can use the mouse or the keyboard to advance the slides one at a time or move backward through your presentation. If you choose Automatically, you can specify the interval between slides. (Five seconds is a good interval because it gives the audience time to read the slides.) Table 9.2 summarizes the keystrokes and mouse movements you use to move through the screen show.

3. If you want the show to repeat continuously (for example, for public announcements or an introductory screen at a trade show), select the box labeled Repeat Slide Show Until Esc Is Pressed. Do not click this box for the example.

4. Click OK.

The slide show runs on your computer.

Table 9.2
Navigating in the Slide Show

Activity	Using Mouse	Using Keyboard
To show next slide	Click left button	Space bar, N, right arrow or up arrow
To show preceding slide	Click right button	Backspace, P, left arrow or down arrow
To show a particular slide	None	Type the number and press Enter
To Show or Hide the pointer (toggle)	None	A or equal sign (=)
To invert the image	None	I or slash (/)
To toggle between a blank screen and a screen that is not blank	None	B or period (.)
To toggle between a white screen and a screen that is not white	None	W or comma (,)
To return to the Slide Show dialog box	None	Esc or hyphen (-) or Ctrl-Break dialog box
To start or stop the automatic show	None	S or + (plus sign)

Printing Your Slides

You make most of your choices about your target printer, fonts, and page orientation when you set up for printing. After you have completed the setup, you are ready to create your presentation. PowerPoint has recorded which fonts and dimensions to use.

When you are ready to print the presentation, you can make additional choices, such as whether to print to a draft printer or to a final printer. If you are printing expensive color transparencies or printing to a file recorder, for instance, you may want to print a draft first to make certain that your slide looks the way you want it to look.

Follow these steps to print a presentation:

1. Open the presentation that you want to print and choose Print from the File menu.

    You see the Print dialog box, shown in figure 9.7. The cursor appears first in the Copies box.

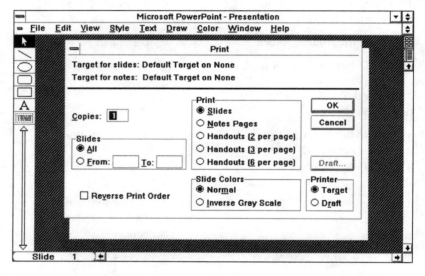

Fig. 9.7. The Print dialog box.

2. If you want, designate the number of copies you want to print. If you do not specify a number, PowerPoint prints one copy.

3. Choose whether you want to print all your slides or only specific slide numbers. Click All to print the entire presentation.

    You can print selected slides rather than the entire presentation. If you are trying to perfect one slide, slide number 5, for example, you can choose From 5 To 5 to print that slide.

4. If your printer stacks the pages with page one on the bottom, choose Reverse Print Order so that you don't have to rearrange the pages after you print them.

Tip: As you see later in the chapter, handout pages contain more than one slide per page. If you do not want to print all the handout pages, specify the slides (not the pages) that you want to print. To figure out which pages contain certain slides, you need to make some calculations based on the number of slides you are printing per page.

5. Under Print, choose whether you want to print Slides, Notes Pages (explained later in this chapter in the section "Printing Notes Pages"), or one of the choices for Handouts (explained later in this chapter in the section "Printing Handouts").

6. Under Slide Colors, choose Normal or Inverse Gray Scale.

   If you choose Normal, PowerPoint prints in color or in gray scale, if applicable to your presentation. If you are printing a black-and-white presentation, the printer prints black and white only.

   If you print your presentation and find that your printer has printed all colors and gray scale as black, use the Inverse Gray Scale option in the Slide Colors box. When you choose Inverse Gray Scale, PowerPoint reverses the usual match of colors and gray scale. Colors that are dark on the slide print as light on the gray scale and light colors print as dark. This option is useful if you want to create black-and-white overheads of color 35mm slides. Slides traditionally have light text on a dark background, whereas overheads usually have dark text on a light background. With Inverse Gray Scale, you can print as overheads slides you have designed as 35mm slides.

7. For Printer, choose either Target or Draft.

   You cannot specify a draft printer during setup; you can specify it during the current session only. To print to a draft printer, select Draft. The Draft Printers box appears, as shown in figure 9.8.

   The choices of printer depend on what you installed during PowerPoint installation. See the section "Setting Up Your Printer" for an explanation of the Setup option. Choose your draft printers, and choose Setup if you want to change options. You do not have a choice of replacement fonts for the draft printer as you do for the target printer.

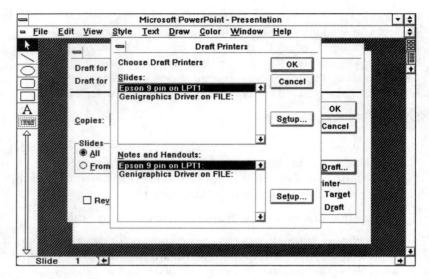

Fig. 9.8. *The Draft Printers dialog box.*

See the section "Setting Up Your Printer" for a discussion of the target printer.

8. After you have the settings you want, choose OK.

PowerPoint prints your document. You also can print notes pages or handouts rather than slides, as you see in the next sections.

If you want to produce overhead transparencies, you have a couple of alternatives. Some printers accept transparency film, which you can use to print your overhead transparencies directly. Another option is to print your slide on plain paper and then make it into a transparency by photocopying it onto transparency film.

Printing Notes Pages

In addition to the slides themselves, PowerPoint provides two other valuable ingredients for a presentation—notes pages and handouts, explained in this section and the next. For each slide you create, PowerPoint also creates a notes page, where you can add your own notes. The notes page contains a miniature of the slide and plenty of room for your notes.

Suppose that you want to work with the notes page for slide 7 in the sample presentation PRSPP16.PPT, which you worked with in Chapter 3. After opening an untitled copy of presentation PRSPP16.PPT in the SAMPLES subdirectory, follow these steps (always use an untitled copy to preserve your original sample presentations):

1. Select the slide you want to work with—slide number 7 in this case, shown in figure 9.9.

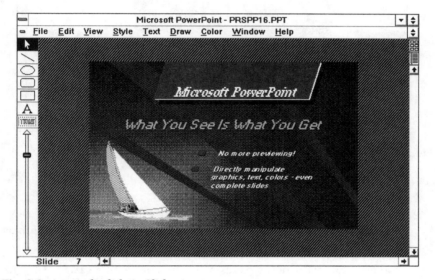

Fig. 9.9. *A sample slide in Slide view.*

2. Open the View menu and choose Notes. You see the notes page— a page with a miniature of the slide and blank space for you to add notes (see fig. 9.10).

Each slide in your presentation has an equivalent notes page, one page for every slide. Use text tools and other graphics tools to enter information when you are in the Notes view. The notes can be reminders to yourself, such as "Be sure to emphasize this point" or "Point to this as you speak."

PowerPoint creates a master for the notes pages just as it creates a master for the slides. You work with a notes master in the same way that you work with a slide master (explained in Chapter 3, "Creating a Presentation"). Put anything on the notes master that you want to appear on every notes page. You can set up a frame, for example, and enter the slide number, date, and time. The following steps show you how to use the notes master to put a slide number on each slide.

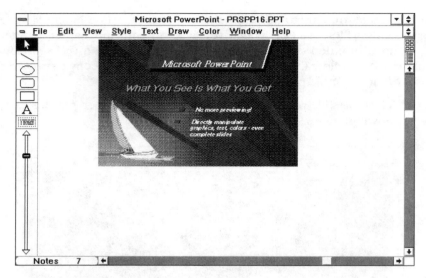

Fig. 9.10. *Notes view of a slide.*

1. Choose Notes Master from the View menu.

2. Type your notes. For the example, type ## in the upper right corner of the notes master. PowerPoint will place the slide number for each slide at that position on the notes page.

After you annotate your notes pages, you can print a notes page. To print the notes pages, choose Print from the File menu. Click Notes Pages in the Print dialog box, shown in figure 9.7. Although you usually print slides in landscape (horizontal) format, you typically print notes pages in portrait (vertical) format.

You may want a copy of each slide in your hands as you deliver the slide show to an audience so that you can refer to your remarks as you go along. You may want to give an annotated copy of the slides to someone who did not attend the slide show. You also may want to keep the annotated copy in your paper files as a backup and for future reference.

You need not use the notes pages as handouts, however. As explained in the next section, PowerPoint provides a more efficient format for handouts than notes pages—a sheet that can hold more than one slide per page.

Printing Handouts

Each handout page can hold two, three, or six slides. You can add notes—typically the date of the presentation, page numbers, or a business logo.

Just as you should set up the printer before you design your slides, you should decide how you plan to print your handouts before you create them. As you saw in figure 9.7, you use the Print dialog box to specify the number of slides per page on the handout page.

When you know the number of slides you want to use per page, you can see which areas of the handout page will be blank. You then can add text and other objects.

To create a handout page, do the following: With the presentation open, open the View menu and choose Handout Page. You see the screen shown in figure 9.11.

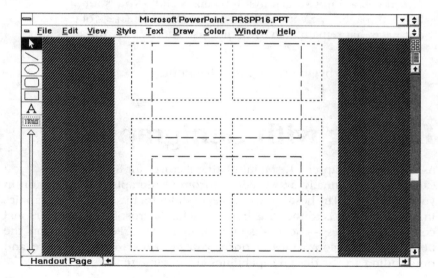

Fig. 9.11. *Format page for handouts.*

The dotted lines show how the handouts will look with two, three, or six slides per page. You do not specify which format to use until you print. You should decide on a format in advance, however, especially if you plan to use text or special characters on your handouts.

Although PowerPoint does not refer to the handout page as a master, the handout page works like the notes master or the slide master—whatever you type on the handout page appears on every handout page. For instance, you can use the symbols ## for page number, :: for time, and // for date just as you can on the notes master or the slide master. You may want to type the title of the presentation on the top of the handouts page.

Follow these steps to print the actual handouts:

1. Choose Print from the File menu.

   You see the Print dialog box, shown in figure 9.7. In the Print box, on the right side of the dialog box, you indicate how many slides you want per page.

2. Click the circle for the number of slides you want per page. Choose the default of 6 for the example.

> *Tip:* If you are not sure at first how many slides you want per handout page, type your notes in the sides and top areas of the handout page that remain blank whether you choose two, three, or six.

3. Click OK to begin printing your handouts.

Linking with Genigraphics

As you see in Chapter 11, "Manipulating Pictures for Special Effects," you can use professionally drawn clip art from Genigraphics Corporation in your own slides. The best-known maker of slides for business, Genigraphics in many respects is to the slide business what Microsoft is to the personal computer business—the undisputed leader. PowerPoint gives you the benefit of both companies at once; you get outstanding software and outstanding artistic design capabilities at the same time.

In addition to drawing on the expertise of Genigraphics and Microsoft to *create* your slides, you also can benefit from the expertise of both companies when you *output* your slides. PowerPoint and the Genigraphics software combine to produce your file. You can use Genigraphics as your "output device" and have slides sent back to you by overnight express.

You must have a Hayes-compatible modem to use the direct connection to Genigraphics. (If you prefer, you can take a disk to a Genigraphics office.

See your PowerPoint documentation for a list of Genigraphics offices around the country.) When you install printer drivers during setup, also install Genigraphics Driver on FILE. See the Windows documentation for information on installing printer drivers. To link with Genigraphics, when you begin to design your presentation, choose Printer Setup and select Genigraphics Driver on FILE as your target printer. When you create your slides, the fonts, slide dimensions, and orientation will be appropriate for processing by Genigraphics. Figure 9.12 shows the Genigraphics Setup dialog box, which you use to set up to print with Genigraphics.

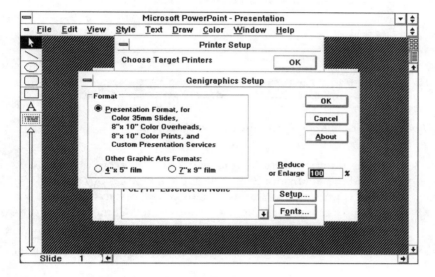

Fig. 9.12. *The Genigraphics Setup dialog box.*

Follow these steps to "print" your presentation with Genigraphics:

1. With Genigraphics as your target printer, choose Print from the File menu.

2. From the Print dialog box, choose OK.

    You see the Genigraphics Job Instructions dialog box, as shown in figure 9.13.

    You choose to have one or more copies made of one or more of the following types of output: 35mm slides on plastic mounts, 35mm slides on glass mounts, 8-by-10-inch overheads, and 8-by-10-inch prints.

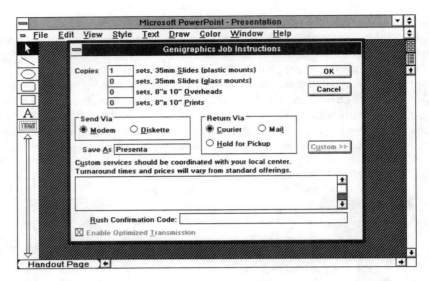

Fig. 9.13. *The Genigraphics Job Instructions dialog box.*

3. Type the number of copies you want of each type of output. You can send the file by modem or disk. Click Modem or Diskette. Modem is the default. You use the three options in the Return Via box (Courier, Mail, or Hold for Pickup) to tell Genigraphics how to return the slides to you.

4. Choose Courier, Mail, or Hold for Pickup. Now specify the name of the file.

5. Type the file name for your Genigraphics file in the Save As box (the default extension is .GNA). If you click the button on the bottom right, labeled Custom, you can type specific instructions regarding your print job.

6. Select the Custom option, and the screen opens out as shown in figure 9.13.

   A wide range of services and formats is available. Call your Genigraphics Service Center before you specify any custom service or format. After you speak with Genigraphics, you can type the necessary information about customization in the box that has the blinking cursor. If you need a rush order, get a number from the service center when you call, and type that number in the Rush Confirmation Code box. A box in the lower left labeled Enable

`Optimized Transmission` is set to on automatically. Do not turn off this option unless the Genigraphics Service Center tells you to do so.

7. Choose OK after you fill in the options in the Genigraphics Job Instructions box.

If you choose the Modem option, the Genigraphics driver saves the file to the Genigraphics directory. If you choose the Diskette option, you see the standard PowerPoint Save As dialog box. You can indicate there the directory to which you want to save your file.

The Genigraphics driver begins to save your slides. Next, you see the Genigraphics Billing Information dialog box, shown in figure 9.14.

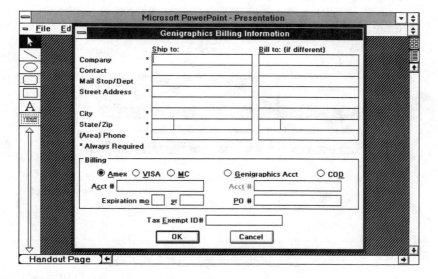

Fig. 9.14. *The Genigraphics Billing Information box.*

8. Fill in the fields in the dialog box as necessary.

The information includes the shipping (and billing, if different) address and name; and the form of payment—by credit card, Genigraphics account, or cash on delivery (COD). You also can type your tax-exempt ID number, if relevant.

9. Select OK after you finish.

If you choose the Modem option for transmission in the Genigraphics Job Instructions box, you receive a message to run GraphicsLink in order to transmit the file. The next section discusses how to use GraphicsLink.

Using GraphicsLink To Transmit Files

The preceding section tells you how to create a file in the proper Genigraphics format. You can create the file to send by modem or by disk. If you opt to send your file by disk, then this section is irrelevant to you. But if you want to send your files by modem, follow these steps:

1. Invoke the GraphicsLink program in the Applications window in Program Manager. You do this by double-clicking the GraphicsLink icon or by clicking once and then choosing Open from the File menu.

   You see the GraphicsLink dialog box, shown in figure 9.15.

Fig. 9.15. *The GraphicsLink dialog box.*

In this example, only one file, PRESENTA.GNA, appears on the list. The Status column displays the message Unsent, which changes to

Sent after you transmit the file; the date the file was last modified; and the estimated transmission time. At the bottom, you see three buttons: Job Instructions, Billing Information, and Transmitted Info. The latter is unavailable in this example because no file has been transmitted. When available, the Transmitted Info button gives information about transmitted files. If you choose the Job Instructions and Billing Information buttons, you see boxes identical to those shown in figures 9.13 and 9.14. You can change information in these two boxes as necessary. Before sending your file, you must choose Communications Setup from the File menu. The Communications Setup option enables you to change the default numbers for setup as necessary. The options include Modem Speed; Dialog Type; Port; Parameters; and special choices such as Initialization Command, Dialog Prefix, Disconnect Sequence, and Hardware Flow Control. Consult your modem manual for details on the options you need to use. In addition, you must specify the destination, which you choose from the list of Genigraphics Service Centers displayed on-screen. When you are satisfied with all the options, click OK to return to the main GraphicsLink menu.

To select a file or files to send, click the file name or click and drag the files.

2. Select the files that you want to send.

   You also can use the Edit menu options—Select All, Select Unsent, and Select Sent—to select files. Select All selects all files; Select Unsent selects only those file that you haven't sent.

3. After you have selected your file or files, click Send in the bottom right corner of the dialog box.

Transmission begins, and a special box provides you with a report of the progress made. At the end of the transmission, another message tells you whether the transmission was successful. You can try again if necessary. If unsuccessful, the message tells you when the transmission failed. If successful, a report replaces the file on disk. This report appears on the GraphicsLink screen under the same name as the file, and the message sent appears in the Status column.

Pricing for individual slides begins at $9.95 (as of April, 1991). Call Genigraphics before you send a file the first time to make certain that you have made all the proper arrangements. The phone number at Genigraphics Corporate Headquarters in Shelton, CT, is 1-901-795-9088.

Chapter Summary

In this chapter, you took the final step in creating presentations—you found out how to output your presentation to whatever device you choose. You first found out how to set up your slides for printing. You next saw how to run a slide show on your screen and how to print a slide show on the target printer or on a draft printer. You also saw how to print notes pages and handouts, and how to use the Genigraphics slide service.

You now have seen all the steps you need to know to create a presentation. PowerPoint, however, has advanced capabilities for text, graphs, and color, that were not discussed in Part I. In Part II of this book, you learn about PowerPoint's advanced features.

Part II

PowerPoint Advanced Features

Includes

Quick Start: Working with Pictures

Manipulating Pictures for Special Effects

Using Advanced Features of Text

Using Advanced Features of Graph

Using Advanced Features of Color

Creating Standard Business Charts

10

Quick Start: Working with Pictures

I n previous quick starts, you learned to create a presentation, add text and objects, and choose a color scheme. In this quick start, you use advanced PowerPoint capabilities to work with pictures and text. You turn PowerPoint objects into a picture and then crop the picture. You work with text boxes in new ways, import text from outside PowerPoint, and create a new text style.

In this chapter, you also work with PowerPoint's clip art, a feature that would be invaluable even as a stand-alone product. As you see in this chapter, you do not need much skill or experience to select and copy clip art onto your slides, but when you do so, you create the kind of slide that only a professional artist can create without predrawn art. The PowerPoint clip art library has a collection of well-drawn, well-colored objects. Using predrawn graphic objects can give you a "quick start" in many of the slides you create with PowerPoint.

Turning Objects into a Picture

Converting objects and text boxes into pictures makes them easier to manipulate. For example, you can turn many objects into one picture that you can move, recolor, resize, and crop. This section shows you how to create and set up a logo for a firm. You then see how to recolor the logo, cut or copy it, and paste it onto a slide as a picture. You can crop this new picture and resize it as necessary.

Suppose that you want to produce a logo like the one shown in figure 10.1.

Fig. 10.1. *An example of a logo.*

The elements of this logo—the text and drawn object—are parts of one picture, although each element was typed and drawn separately. Follow these steps to create this picture:

1. Draw an oval on a new slide. Make the frame width (line thickness) the second thickest width available (fifth from the top in the Line Style submenu) and choose the color YO5.

   You change the frame width through Line Style in the Draw menu and the color through Line in the Color menu. You can resize the oval later, if necessary.

2. Select the labeler tool and type *Golden Dome* inside the oval, then click on a position underneath the words `Golden Dome` and type *Landscaping*.

   By clicking again before you type *Landscaping*, you create two text boxes, one for *Golden Dome* and one for *Landscaping*, which you can move separately. You must reselect the labeler tool before you type the second piece of text because after you click, PowerPoint defaults back to the arrow tool. Next, change the size and color of the text.

3. Select the bottom text box and change the text size to 40 and the color to the BU3 blue of the default PowerPoint color scheme. Next, select the top text box and change the text size to 40 and make the color RD8.

   You change the text size by choosing Size from the Style menu and you change the color through Text in the Color menu. You now want to make individual letters larger.

4. Select the G in Golden and enlarge it to 72 points. Do the same with the D in Dome.

   You click to one side of a letter and then drag the mouse over the letter to select it. If necessary, rearrange the boxes on your slide to match the alignment shown in figure 10.1. The box with Landscaping lies on top of the oval frame. Follow step 5 to block out the frame.

5. Select the Landscaping box and make it opaque.

   To make the box opaque, choose Opaque from the Draw menu. The opaque box blocks out the frames of the other objects in the slide. You now have three boxes, two text and one drawn object, which you want to turn into one picture. Turning your logo into a picture is discussed in the next section.

Pasting as a Picture

You learned in Chapter 5 that after you copy or cut a graphic object such as an oval or a text box, you can use the Paste command in the Edit menu to paste the object onto other slides. The Paste as Picture command, also in the Edit menu, works similarly; you copy or cut and then paste. Afterward, however, PowerPoint treats as a picture the objects you selected and then pasted. This fact means that if you select and copy or cut more than one object, the objects are then combined into one picture that you can recolor with the Recolor Picture option, move around the slide as one picture, and "crop" (cover the edges).

In the example, you created an oval frame and two labeler text boxes. Follow these steps to change them into a picture:

1. Select all three boxes. Click over one box to select it, then hold down the Shift key and click over the other two boxes separately.

Your screen now looks something like figure 10.2.

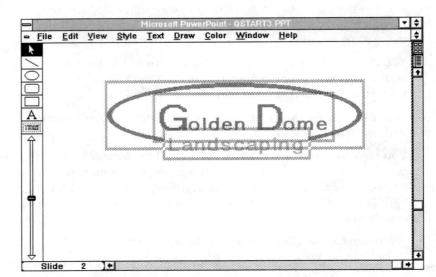

Fig. 10.2. Three selected boxes.

2. Put the objects into memory.

3. Choose Cut or Copy from the Edit menu. The next step creates the picture.

4. Choose Paste as Picture from the Edit menu.

PowerPoint pastes the objects back onto the slide as one picture. When you select the picture, you see one selection box, not three. In contrast, the Edit Paste function re-creates the three boxes. The picture is now exactly in the center of the screen. The Paste function puts the selected objects in the same position as on the slide from which you copied them. A centered picture is easy to crop, as you see in the next section.

Cropping a Picture

When you crop a picture, you block some of the picture, usually the edges, from view. You don't cut out anything. You can uncrop later and the picture returns to its original shape and size. Here, you want to trim the left and right edges of the oval. Follow these steps:

1. Select the new picture by clicking over it.

2. Choose Crop Picture from the Edit menu.

   The mouse pointer changes to the cropping tool, which is shaped like one V upside down on top of another with a rectangular space in the center.

3. Place the rectangular space over the top or bottom dots on the left side of the selected picture.

4. Press the mouse button and drag the left side over to the right. Block off about half the frame length between the left side and the word Golden. Use figure 10.1 as a guide, if necessary.

   You now need to block off the same amount of the frame on the other side of the picture. Here, use the guide lines to make the measurement exact.

5. Choose Show Guides from the Draw menu and measure the distance from the cropped left side of the picture to the left side of the slide.

   Figure 10.3 shows the guide line aligned with the left side of the picture.

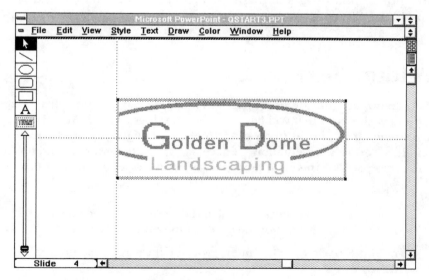

Fig. 10.3. *A half-cropped picture with guide lines.*

6. Note the left measurement and then drag the guide line to the same distance on the right side of the picture box. Crop the picture on the right side.

You end up with the logo shown in figure 10.1. To resize the picture, drag the corner dots with the arrow tool. You can make the picture smaller and place it on the slide master so that the logo appears on all slides in your presentation. The logo remains a picture and you can use the regular Paste function to paste it to your slides.

Creating Notes Pages

As you saw in Chapter 9, every slide has a notes page with the slide printed on it and room for text boxes and other objects. In the example in this chapter, you created a logo for your company. Suppose that you now want to include most of the information in the notes pages and use the slides as broad headlines for your slide-show topics. You insert text and drawn objects on notes pages in the same way you insert them on slides.

In this section, you draw a text box on a notes page and copy the text box to all other notes pages in the presentation. You next import text from another application and define a new text style to use in the notes pages.

Adding Text Boxes

You draw text boxes on notes pages in the same way you draw text boxes on slides. Suppose that you have created your logo. Type *A New World of Landscaping Opportunity* on slide 1 below the logo (refer to Chapter 4, "Adding Text to a Presentation," if necessary). You now want to add text to the notes page for this slide. Follow these steps to set up the text box:

1. Choose Notes (#1) from the View menu.

2. Select the word processor tool and draw a text box below the slide image covering most of the space in the notes pages.

   At 50% Size on the View menu, you see the screen pictured in figure 10.4.

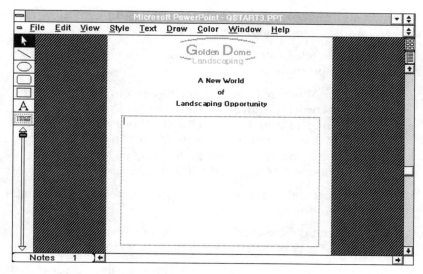

Fig. 10.4. *A 50% view of a notes page.*

You want to put a great deal of text on each notes page. Copy the text box from slide 1 to each notes page so that all the notes pages look similar.

3. Click outside the text box to get rid of the line cursor; then reselect the box and choose Copy from the Edit menu.

    Although the Sized to Text option is on by default, the box does not shrink in size because you have not entered any text yet.

4. Go to the next notes page (the PgDn key puts you there quickly) and choose Paste from the Edit menu.

The text box appears on the notes page. You next import text from another file.

Importing Text from Another Application

Use the import function to avoid retyping text that already exists elsewhere. In the preceding section, you set up your text blocks in the notes pages and you now want to import text from a Microsoft Word for Windows document. Follow these steps to import the text:

1. Switch to the Microsoft Word for Windows document from your PowerPoint presentation.

   First, use the Minimize button on the PowerPoint window (in the upper right corner, the arrow pointing down) to shrink your presentation to an icon. You can click the Word window to switch to the Word document if you have Word for Windows up and running. If not, you must return to the Program Manager, start Word for Windows, and open the relevant document.

2. Select the text and copy it into memory by choosing Copy from the Word for Windows Edit menu.

3. Exit Word and double-click the PowerPoint icon to get your presentation back on-screen.

4. Click in the notes pages text box to activate the line cursor.

5. Choose Paste from the Edit menu.

   The text flows into your notes pages text box, as shown in figure 10.5.

Fig. 10.5. *Imported text in a notes page box.*

Copying between Windows applications can be as easy as copying within applications. You next create a new text style and apply it to the text box.

Creating a New Text Style

To save time, create and use a new text style rather than change the font, size, color, and typestyle of your text individually as you go along. Follow these steps to create a new style for the notes pages text:

1. Choose Define Styles from the Style menu.

   You see the dialog box shown in figure 10.6.

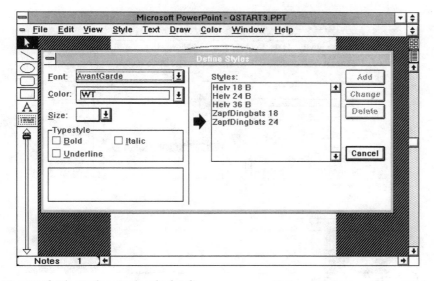

Fig. 10.6. The Define Styles dialog box.

   You choose the four elements that make up a style—font, color, size, and typestyle—from the left side of the dialog box. First, choose a font.

2. Click the arrow to the right of the font box.

   A drop-down menu of choices (the same choices available through Font in the Style menu) appears.

3. Select Bookman to choose it as your font.

4. Follow similar steps to choose BU3 and 14 as your color and size, respectively.

    In this example, you do not want to use bold, italic, or underline. You do not see plain listed as a choice because your text automatically appears in plain unless you choose another typestyle. A box underneath the typestyles displays the word `Sample` in the style you have chosen.

5. Select Add in the upper right corner of the dialog box to add the new style to your list of styles.

    The title, Bookman 14, then appears on the list. Your dialog box now looks like figure 10.7.

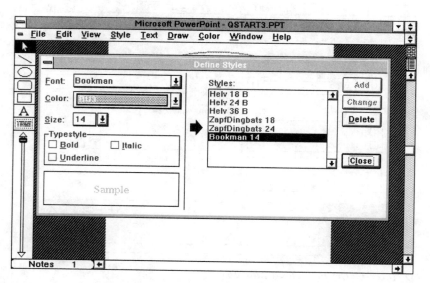

Fig. 10.7. A new style added in the dialog box.

6. Select Close to exit the dialog box.

7. Select your notes pages text box and choose the new style from Styles in the Style menu.

When you use a custom-designed style, you can save time and maintain a standard look. Another good way to save time is to use predrawn pictures. In the next section, you find out how to transfer clip art to your slides.

Using Clip Art

PowerPoint comes with a collection of clip art (predrawn pictures) to use with your slides. Transferring clip art to your own slide is easy. In this section, you transfer a picture of a bench to your presentation to illustrate your slide show about landscaping. You continue from the preceding section with your presentation open. Follow these steps to transfer a clip art picture:

1. Choose Open from the File menu; then go to the CLIPART directory through the Open dialog box. Choose the presentation HOUSEHLD.PPT.

2. Drag the marker down on the Slide Changer to go to slide number 9 in the presentation.

3. Select the bench by clicking over it. The bench is the only part of the picture you want to transfer.

    Your screen now looks like figure 10.8.

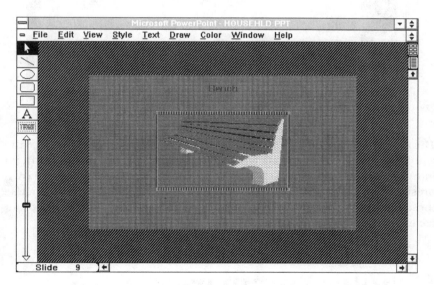

Fig. 10.8. A selected clip art object.

4. Choose Copy from the Edit menu.

5. Return to your own presentation.

You can return to your presentation through the Window menu or by closing the HOUSEHLD.PPT presentation.

6. Go to the slide where you want to copy the picture and choose Paste from the Edit menu.

The picture appears on the slide, as shown in figure 10.9.

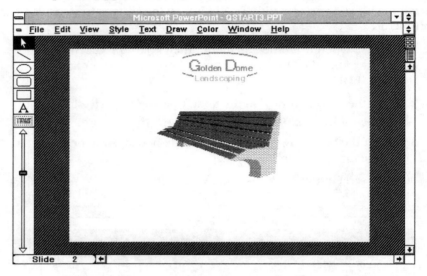

Fig. 10.9. The transferred clip art.

The clip art background did not transfer because you did not select the whole picture. To transfer the whole slide (including the background), go into the Slide Sorter view, select a slide, copy it, then return to your own presentation and paste it onto a slide (again from the Slide Sorter view). Use these simple steps to bring well-drawn pictures into your slides without having to create them yourself.

Chapter Summary

In this chapter, you drew an oval and two text boxes, then cut and pasted them onto the slide to make them into one object—a picture. You cropped, or trimmed, the new picture. You next drew a text box on a notes page and imported text from another application. You created a new text style and applied it to the imported text. Finally, you transferred a clip art object from a PowerPoint presentation to your slide.

11

Manipulating Pictures for Special Effects

I n Chapter 3, "Creating a Presentation," you learned to work with an entire multiple-slide presentation at one time. Often, however, you want to include something in your presentation from outside the presentation altogether.

In this chapter, you see how to cut clip art, text, and graphics from one presentation and paste them into another. You also see how to transfer between applications in Windows. You next go step-by-step through one of the most useful applications of the Paste From command—pasting from an outline to create a series of slides.

Whether you import multiple images or create them yourself, you sometimes end up with several objects on the screen at the same time. You may want to manipulate them as a single object to change their size, for example, or to copy them into another presentation as one object. You find out in this chapter how to combine several objects into one picture.

When you import or create pictures, you often need to adapt them to a fresh slide. One way to adapt a picture is to "crop" it—to block parts of the original picture from view. In this chapter, you find out how to crop a picture in PowerPoint. The last section of this chapter, on creating special effects, is for the more creative and adventurous among you, but it shows techniques you may well decide to use.

Pasting Pictures and Text

With PowerPoint, you can import data from other PowerPoint presentations and also from other Windows applications, such as word processors and paint programs. You can exchange data in two ways: through the Cut (or Copy) and Paste commands and through the Paste From command on the File menu. Paste From, when it applies, saves you time by eliminating the copy step. The Paste From command works with a whole file at a time. This command applies only with certain kinds of files, as discussed in the section "Using Paste From," later in this chapter.

You first see how to use the cut-and-paste technique.

Pasting Clip Art, Text, and Graphics

Just about anything—graphics, charts, text—that you can copy from a Windows application into the clipboard (or buffer or memory, to use other terminology), you can paste into a PowerPoint slide. You open your presentation, go to the file or application that contains the items you want to copy, copy them into the clipboard, return to your presentation, and paste them onto your slide. You can copy items from Windows applications only. You then can paste anything in your clipboard onto a PowerPoint slide.

In Chapter 10, "Quick Start: Working with Pictures," you copied text from a file produced with a word processor. The following steps use an example of copying a picture from the clip art subdirectory that comes with your PowerPoint software. Use steps similar to the following for all cutting and pasting:

1. Open your PowerPoint presentation and go to the file from which you want to copy. Here, open ANIMALS.PPT in the CLIPART subdirectory of POWERPNT.

    To go to a file in another Windows application such as Microsoft Word for Windows, simply open the application and then the file. If the application is already open, click on the window to make the application active. To go to another PowerPoint file, open the file through the File menu.

2. Select the items you want to copy. In the example, go to the Title Sorter view and select slide 8, Eagle.

   Your screen now looks like figure 11.1.

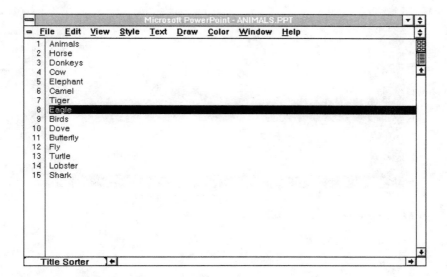

Fig. 11.1. The Title Sorter view of ANIMALS.PPT.

3. Copy or cut the items. Here, choose Copy from the Edit menu. Note that you do not have to display the slide first.

> **Tip:** Never cut from an original presentation in the CLIPART directory. Use an untitled copy of a CLIPART file or use the Copy command.

4. Return to the PowerPoint presentation. To return to the presentation in the example, choose Close from the File menu or choose the presentation from the Window menu.

5. Go to the correct slide and choose Paste from the Edit menu to paste your items.

   PowerPoint pastes your copied items onto the slide. In the example, the slide now looks like figure 11.2.

For a complete list of PowerPoint clip art, see Appendix C.

Fig. 11.2. *A pasted picture of an eagle.*

Copying between Applications

Copying between applications is as easy as copying within PowerPoint. Suppose that you want to copy text from Ami Pro, a Windows word processor. You need to have a text block in PowerPoint into which you can paste the text. Follow these steps to paste between applications:

1. Create a text box in PowerPoint to receive the imported text. If a box already exists, you can use that box.

2. Go to the application from which you want to copy.

   If the application from which you want to copy is open, you can make the PowerPoint window smaller and click the application window. If the application is not open, click the application icon. The program opens.

3. Select the items or text that you want to copy.

   Your screen should now look something like figure 11.3.

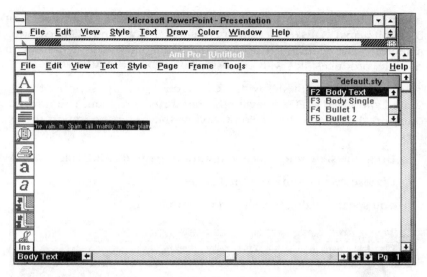

Fig. 11.3. *Selected text in Ami Pro with the PowerPoint window in the background.*

4. Copy the text items into the clipboard.

5. Return to the PowerPoint window.

6. Click in a text box to get the line cursor.

7. Choose Paste from the Edit menu.

If you have not selected a text box, PowerPoint places the text in the center right of the slide. You can move the text elsewhere, but placing it in the right position at first saves time.

Using Paste From

When you use the Paste From command, you paste an entire file onto a slide. You don't have to open the file or application that you want to paste, and you don't have to cut or copy. You just choose the Paste From command from the File menu.

Paste From works with the following file extensions: .PIC (Lotus 1-2-3), .CGM (computer graphics metafile—created by graphics programs and some others), .TIF (Tagged Image File Format—created by scanners), .EPS (encapsulated PostScript), .PCX (PC Paintbrush), .MSP (Microsoft Paint), .BMP (bit maps), .DIB (device independent bit maps), and .WMF (windows metafiles). The Paintbrush application that comes with Windows, for example, produces files with extensions of .PCX and .BMP.

Paste From works with files with these extensions only. Suppose that you created and saved a .PCX file with the Paintbrush program. You now want to import the file into PowerPoint. Follow these steps to import the PCX file:

1. Go to the slide into which you want to paste the .PCX file.

2. Choose Paste From from the File menu.

   You see the dialog box shown in figure 11.4.

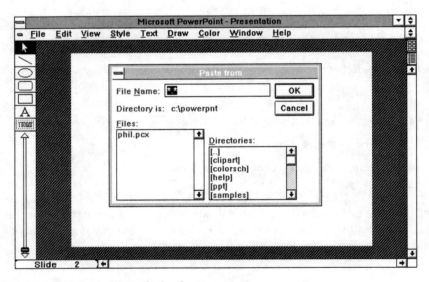

Fig. 11.4. The Paste From dialog box.

   The dialog box lists only those files in the directory on display that you can import with the Paste From command. PHIL.PCX is the only file listed in this case.

3. Open the directory that contains the file you want to import; then select and open the file.

   PowerPoint pastes the file onto your slide. In the example, your screen now looks like figure 11.5.

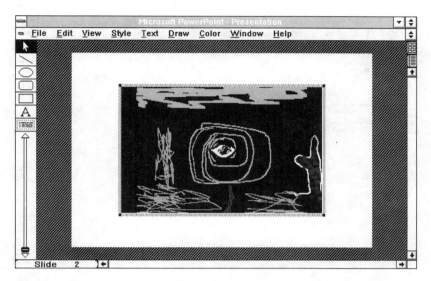

Fig. 11.5. *A picture pasted with the Paste From command.*

Use Paste From whenever possible when you want to paste complete files or files from outside Windows. The next section discusses a particular application of the Paste From command—copying text outlines.

Copying Text Outlines

Paste From has a feature that can save you a great deal of time. If you have text typed in a word processor, you can use PowerPoint to create new slides in a presentation using this text. The text must be in outline form. Some word processors, such as Lotus Manuscript and Microsoft Word, come with an outliner you can use to create an outline. You then can transfer the text of the outline to PowerPoint. If your word processor does not have an outliner tool, you can create an outline yourself with tabs (tab once for lower levels) and still use the PowerPoint Paste From command.

Suppose that you have text outlined as shown in figure 11.6. This particular example shows an outline created in Microsoft Word with the Microsoft Word outliner, but you also can use any outline or series of headlines created by tabbing.

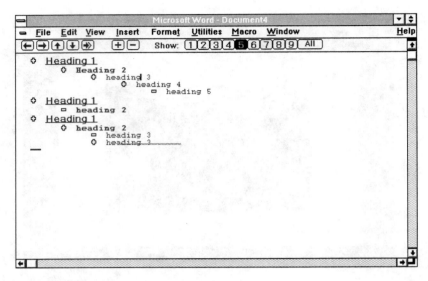

Fig. 11.6. Text outlined in a word processor.

Follow these steps to create slides in PowerPoint for every headline/outline level in a word processing document:

1. Save the outlined text to a text file (or an ASCII file). Make sure that the extension is .TXT.

   PowerPoint creates slides for every outline level.

2. Open your PowerPoint presentation and go to the Slide Sorter view.

3. Click (to get the line cursor) where you want to insert the new slides.

   If you have the default PowerPoint presentation open with one slide and you want to insert the new slides after this slide, your screen now looks like figure 11.7.

4. Choose Paste From from the File menu, and open the text file you just created.

In this example, PowerPoint creates 12 new slides, a slide for every outline level and a slide at the start that contains a list of the outline levels. Figure 11.8 shows the Title Sorter view after you paste in the outline. The first slide called Title already existed. The second slide called Title contains the names of the outline levels—in this case, Heading 1, Heading 2, and so on. Each subsequent slide contains the text of an outline.

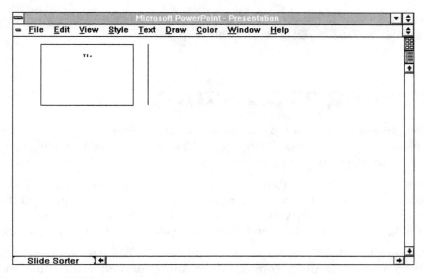

Fig. 11.7. *A Slide Sorter view.*

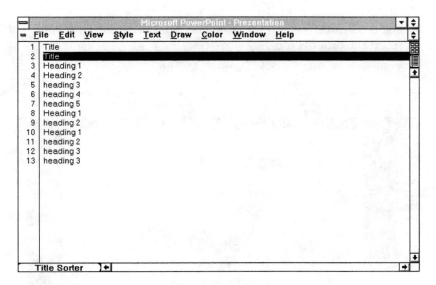

Fig. 11.8. *The Title Sorter view after you paste in the outline.*

The Paste From feature described in this section enables you to use the outliner in your word processor and then transfer the text to PowerPoint after you are satisfied with your sequence of slides. In the next section, you learn how to use Paste as Picture and crop pictures.

Pasting as a Picture

You can recolor and crop pictures (unlike drawn objects). When you crop a picture, you block parts of it from view. You can recolor and crop to create variations of an existing picture.

In the section "Pasting Clip Art, Text, and Graphics," you transferred a picture of an eagle to your presentation. Suppose that you encircled the picture and the text box that contains the word Eagle with an oval. You now have three different object boxes that you can turn into one picture.

Pasting different objects onto a slide as one picture is as easy as pasting any object onto a slide. Cut or copy the objects into your clipboard as usual, and choose a special paste option from the Edit menu. Follow these steps to change the three object boxes, text, oval, and picture of an eagle into one picture:

1. Select all three boxes. (Select one box and press the Shift key; then select the other boxes.)

   Your screen now looks something like figure 11.9.

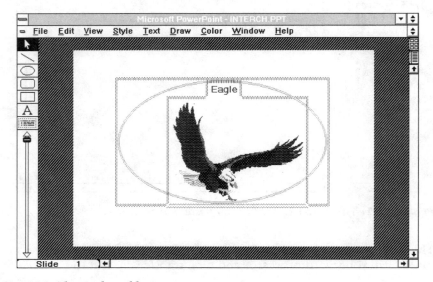

Fig. 11.9. *Three selected boxes.*

Now put the objects into your clipboard.

2. Choose Copy from the Edit menu. You also can use Cut.

3. Go to the slide where you want to paste your new picture.

   If you use the Edit Paste function here, you re-create three boxes in the same position as on the original slide. To create a single picture, use a different option.

4. Choose Paste as Picture from the Edit menu.

The Paste as Picture command always pastes the new picture into the center of a slide. The Edit Paste command pastes the object in the same position on the new slide as the object had on the original slide. In this example, the eagle, the text, and the oval are now one picture, as shown in figure 11.10.

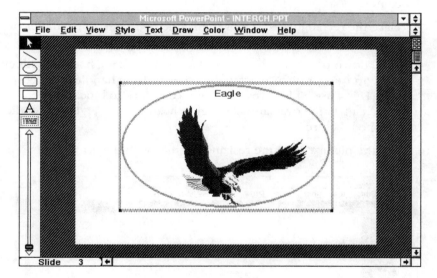

Fig. 11.10. *A picture created from three boxes.*

Select the picture. You see one selection box, not three. Because the picture is now exactly in the center of the screen, you can use the guides to crop your picture easily, as illustrated in the quick start in Chapter 10. The next section also discusses cropping the picture.

Cropping a Picture

When you crop a picture, you don't cut anything out; you block parts of the picture from view, and you can uncrop to return the picture to its original condition. For the example, suppose that you want to block out everything in the picture except the eagle's wings.

Follow these steps to crop the picture.

1. Select the picture.

2. Choose Crop Picture from the Edit menu.

   The mouse pointer changes to the cropping tool, shaped like one V upside down on top of another, with a rectangular space in the center.

3. Place the rectangular space over any one of the resizing handles on the four corners of the selected picture.

4. Hold down the mouse button and drag the resizing handle to block out part of your picture. Drag the other resizing handles, if necessary. Here, use all four resizing handles in turn to block off the word Eagle, the oval, and the eagle's head. Figure 11.11 shows the cropped picture.

To resize the picture, drag the resizing handles with the arrow tool.

Fig. 11.11. *A cropped picture.*

Creating Special Effects

If you want to be creative, you can create a variety of special effects with PowerPoint, including shading objects and shadowing text. Although PowerPoint provides templates with all these effects and more in the TEMPLATES directory, sometimes you want to custom-design your own effects. The process of creating special effects usually involves copying, pasting, and recoloring, and then repeating these steps as many times as necessary.

This section shows you how to create three kinds of special effects—shading an object, shadowing text, and creating repeating patterns for a background.

Shading an Object

As you know from Chapter 5, "Drawing Objects," you can fill an object like a circle or square with any color that you want. Suppose that you now want to have different shadings of the color in the object, as shown in figure 11.12.

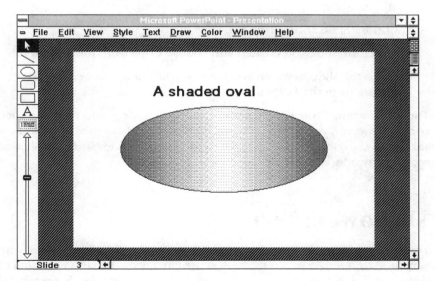

Fig. 11.12. A shaded oval.

Follow these steps to create the effect shown in figure 11.12:

1. Create a slide with a shaded background. In this example, the background color is white, and the shade background (set in Color Scheme) is horizontal.

2. Draw the shape you want. Here, draw an oval.

3. With the object selected, choose Opaque from the Draw menu.

4. With the object selected, choose Copy from the Edit menu.

5. Go to wherever you want to place the object and choose Paste as Picture from the Edit menu. In the example, go to a plain white slide with no shading.

   PowerPoint transfers the selected object with its shading. (Paste, as distinct from Paste as Picture, transfers just the object, not the shading.)

You can copy a whole slide (through the Slide Sorter view), paste it as a picture, and then resize it to achieve a similar effect. This method produces a rectangle because a slide is rectangular. After you have created the slide to copy (as shown in the preceding step 1), follow these steps:

1. Delete any text in the slide, including the word Title, present in all new slides.

2. Choose Slide Sorter from the View menu.

3. Select the slide you created and choose Copy from the Edit menu.

4. Go to the slide to which you want to paste and choose Paste as Picture from the Edit menu.

The shading that you copied covers the new slide completely. At each corner, however, you see the resizing handles. Use them to make your new shaded rectangle as small as you want. Figure 11.13 shows a shaded rectangle produced by the preceding steps.

Shadowing Text

You can use shadowed text to produce professional-looking slides with very little trouble. After you create your original text—usually a heading or slide title, you just copy, paste, move, and recolor. Suppose that you want to create a shadow effect like that shown in figure 11.14.

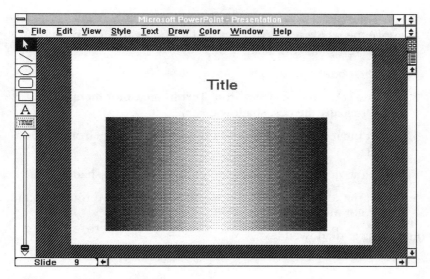

Fig. 11.13. *A shaded rectangle.*

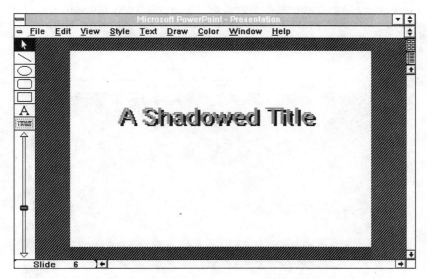

Fig. 11.14. *A shadowed title.*

The black-and-white representation in figure 11.14 does not do justice to the spectacular effect that you see in color (red and black, in this case). Follow these steps to create shadowed text:

1. Type the text that you want to shadow, here *A Shadowed Title*, and move the whole text box down and to the right of the position where you want your text.

   This first box is the actual shadow.

2. Choose your shadow color from Text in the Color menu. Here, use black (usually the best shadow color).

3. Select the text box and choose Copy and then Paste from the Edit menu.

4. Move the new text box above and to the left of the shadow text.

5. Select the text in the pasted box and apply a color through Text in the Color menu. Here, use RD8.

You now have shadowed text.

Creating Repeating Patterns

Simple repeating patterns on your slide can create a nice background effect. Use the copy and paste functions to create these patterns. Figure 11.15 shows an example of a background of repeating patterns.

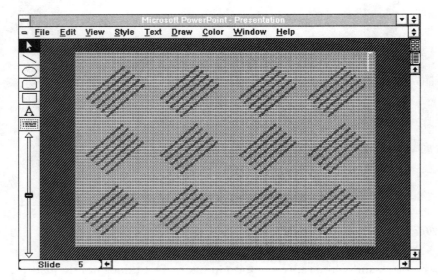

Fig. 11.15. A repeating pattern.

Usually, you want the colors in the pattern and the background to be similar. Otherwise, any text or objects that you draw on the slide become less visible. Follow these steps to create the pattern shown in figure 11.15:

1. Draw a diagonal line (use the Shift key) in the upper left part of your slide. Use Line Style in the Draw menu to make the line as thick as you want.

2. Color the line with the Line option on the Color menu. Here, use the color YW8.

3. Copy and paste the line three times. The Paste command in PowerPoint automatically places the pasted lines down and to the right. You can move the pasted lines if you want.

4. Select all four lines; then copy and paste three times.

5. Move the three copies along the row to place the sets of four lines along the top of the slide.

   You can repeat this pasting process another eight times and place each set of four lines in the slide as shown in figure 11.15. Step 6, however, gives you an easier way to create the effect shown in figure 11.15.

6. Select the four sets of four lines in the top row, copy them, and then use Paste as Picture from the Edit menu. Do this twice and move one of the pictures to the bottom of the slide.

You end up with the desired pattern. For the example, you used YW8 as the line color. YG8 is a good background color for this pattern. Use this pattern on your slide master and it repeats on all your slides. Alternatively, use the steps outlined in the section "Shading an Object" to copy the entire slide pattern to additional slides.

The presentation in the TEMPLATES directory has many slides created with techniques similar to the kind shown in this section. Open an untitled copy of a template and select objects on a slide. You can see how the objects are overlaid to create effects such as embossing, shadowed titles and patterns, 3-D objects, and so on.

Chapter Summary

When you use PowerPoint, you still can work with other Windows applications. When you cut from another application, you put the cut object into a common Windows clipboard and simply paste it into your new application.

In this chapter, you saw how to apply two standard PowerPoint techniques—cut-and-paste and Paste From—with applications outside PowerPoint. You then saw how to use Paste From to create new slides from text outlines. You also learned to turn a set of objects into a picture and to crop a picture. Finally, you learned how to create special effects such as shading an object, shadowing text, and drawing repeating patterns on the background of your slide.

In the next chapter, you learn about advanced features of PowerPoint text.

12

Using Advanced Features of Text

PowerPoint offers flexibility in word processing beyond that of many word processors. So many combinations and possibilities are available in PowerPoint that ordinary capabilities such as indenting and line spacing can become quite complicated. You do not need to know everything about these capabilities, however, to use them quite well. After you do feel comfortable with the basics, you may want to move to advanced capabilities, such as using decimal tabs in sublevels of a text box.

In this chapter, you first find out how to set indents and tab stops and then how to apply them in creating a table. You next find out what options PowerPoint provides for line and paragraph spacing, and you see how to save your settings as defaults. You learn how to set up a custom dictionary in your spelling checker, and finally, you see how to create a text style of your own that you can choose from the PowerPoint menus.

Setting Indents and Tab Stops

The text ruler enables you to change indentation and tab stops for up to five indentation levels. The indentation point defines where the left margin of the text begins. Tab stops are additional indentation points where a line of text begins after you press the Tab key.

You can change indents and tab stops individually or in pairs. In addition, you can set up extra tab stops that align text from the right, from the center, and from a decimal point, as well as from the customary left.

295

See figure 12.1 for an example of multilevel indenting.

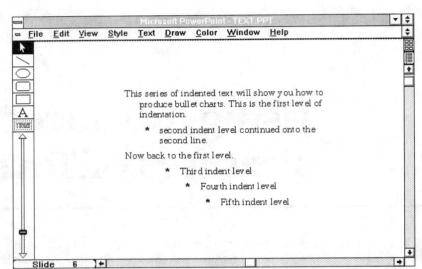

Fig. 12.1. Multilevel indenting.

Chapter 4, "Adding Text to a Presentation," explains indentation and tab stops and shows you how to create a bulleted chart with multilevel indenting. In this chapter, you learn to change indentations.

Changing Indentation

You can select and indent text that is already typed or you can set up the ruler in a text box so that the indents are already in effect as you type. You can insert a ruler after you have begun typing and it will apply to text that you type afterward.

Suppose that you want to change the indentation in the box shown in figure 12.1. To work on this example yourself, you can type the text shown in figure 12.1. Refer to Chapter 4 to learn how to produce a text block like this one, step-by-step. You first want to align the text on the second and third lines with the text on the first line. Follow these steps to align the text:

1. Select the text box you want to indent.

2. Choose Show Text Ruler from the Text menu.

   The ruler appears above the selected text box as shown in figure 12.2.

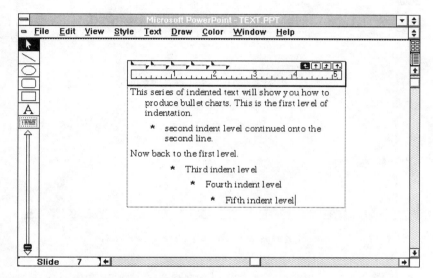

Fig. 12.2. The Text ruler.

On the ruler you see five sets of paired black triangles, one set pointing up, one set pointing down. These triangles enable you to set five different levels of indentation within your text.

The upward-pointing triangles set the indentation for the first line at each level. The inverted triangles set the indentation for additional lines at each indent level. A dotted line links each inverted triangle to an upward-pointing triangle so that they are connected in pairs, totalling five pairs for the five indentation levels in PowerPoint. For the example, align the first set of triangles so that they are exact mirror images of each other.

3. To move an indent, click it and drag it to the new position. Here, drag the first inverted marker to the far left, underneath the first upward-pointing marker.

The relevant text at this level, the first level in the example, follows the marker. Your text now looks like figure 12.3.

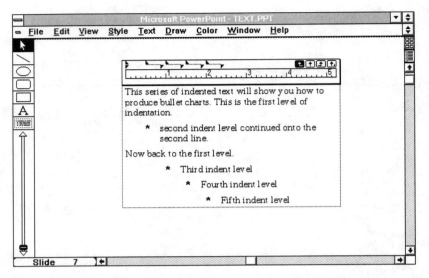

Fig. 12.3. First paragraph text realigned with the lower marker.

In addition to moving the paired markers independently, you can move them together, without altering their relative positions. Suppose that in the example you want to move the second indent level to the right.

4. Click the dotted line between the markers and drag it to the new position on the ruler. Here, drag the second pair of markers to the right.

You end up with something like figure 12.4.

Notice that you cannot move the set of markers for the second level past the markers for the third level. If you drag the second level markers farther to the right, you also push the third level markers farther to the right.

You can move your text from one indentation level to another, as discussed in Chapter 4. To move text from the first level to the second, choose Indent>> from the Text menu. (The shortcut is Ctrl-R.) To move text "up" one level at a time, choose Indent<< or press Ctrl-L.

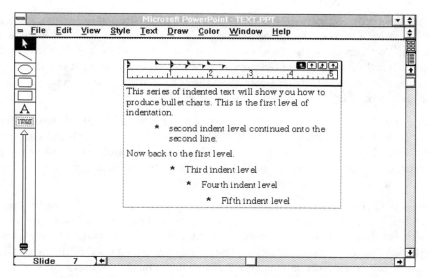

Fig. 12.4. Text with the second indentation level dragged to the right.

The markings on the ruler denote inches on a printed slide, not on the screen. If you have set your operating environment for the metric system, the marks on the ruler represent centimeters. Change between the measuring systems using the International option in the Control Panel in the Program Manager. See your Windows manual for full instructions. If you want to learn to set additional tabs for each indentation level, keep the ruler on-screen and go to the next section. If not, switch off the ruler.

5. To switch off the ruler, click outside the text box.

Using indents gives you a great deal of flexibility in setting up bulleted charts and tables. In addition to using indents, you can set up four kinds of tabs. You next learn to use the text ruler to manipulate tabs.

Using Tabs

Like text alignment when you begin typing, the default for tabs is to work from the left side. You can change them, however, to work from the right, the center, and a decimal point.

The tab tools, located on the far right of the text ruler, are the little boxes that contain arrows. In PowerPoint, you can set tabs in your ruler in two ways. You can click the type of tab you want to use (if it is not selected already); then click at the bottom of the ruler where you want the tab stop to appear. Alternatively, you can drag the tool to the place where you want it on the bottom of the ruler.

The first tab box contains an arrow pointing left and is the default. This arrow is the left-aligned tab marker. The second box, with a straight arrow, is the tool for center-aligned tabs. The third box, containing an arrow facing right, is for right-aligned tabs. The fourth box, the decimal tab marker, has a period next to the arrow.

Figure 12.5 shows four different text boxes with left-, center-, right-, and decimal-aligned text, all produced using tabs. The left tab left-aligns text typed at that tab (the most familiar use of tabs for most of us). The right tab right-aligns text typed at the tab. (The text appears to the left of the tab.) The center tab center-aligns text typed at the tab. The decimal tab right-aligns text (usually numerals) before a decimal point and aligns the remaining text at the tab stop.

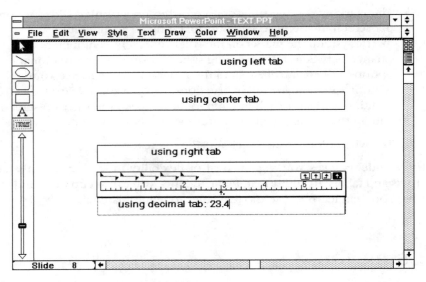

Fig. 12.5. *Four examples of tabbing.*

All four boxes in the figure have the tab set at the same point—at the 3-inch mark. The bottom box shows the text ruler with the decimal tab highlighted to the right and the tab marker under 3.

Follow these steps to set and use tabs:

1. Create a text block and display the text ruler.

2. Select one of the tab tools (left, center, right, or decimal) from the right side of the screen. Left is the default. For the example, stay with the left.

   Now position the actual tab.

3. Place the mouse pointer at the point underneath the rule line in the text ruler box where you want the tab stop to appear. Click once. For the example, click under 3, or if you use centimeters, click somewhere to the right of the indentation triangles.

   You produce an arrow, in this case an arrow pointing left, because you are using the left-align tab. Now, use this tab stop. As mentioned, this tab is an additional way to align text, besides the indentation levels set with the indentation markers.

4. Click in the text box at the start of a line.

5. Press the Tab key twice.

   You move first to the indent marker for the current level, then to the tab stop.

6. Type your text. In this example, type *using left tab*.

   The text starts at the 3-inch mark and continues to the right. When you use the center-align tab, the text (as shown in the second box in figure 12.5) spreads in both directions from the tab stop. When you use the right tab, the text goes to the left of the tab stop. When you use the decimal tab, the text falls to the left of the tab stop until you type the first period, and then whatever else you type falls to the right.

7. Set center, right, and decimal tab stops in the same way you set left tab stops. Here, reproduce the bottom three text boxes by choosing each tab in turn, placing the marker at 3 inches, and typing your text after tabbing to the marker.

Moving a Tab Stop

To move a tab stop created with one of the four tab tools (left, right, center, or decimal), just click it and drag it to where you want it to go. Experiment with this procedure in the four text boxes created in the preceding section and watch the text move to the new position.

Deleting a Tab Stop

Sometimes you need to delete tab stops. To delete a tab stop created with a tab tool, follow these steps:

1. Click the marker and drag it above or below the ruler line.

   The background turns dark.

2. Release the mouse button.

   The tab stop disappears.

Tip: You cannot place one kind of tab in exactly the same position as another (a left over a center, for instance). If you have a reason to put two tabs in the same place, such as creating a text chart with some text centered at the tab and some left-justified, create two separate text boxes. See the next section of this chapter for an example.

Tabs are useful in creating tables, as shown in the next section.

Creating a Table

If you often present numbers, you may want to display them in a table. Perhaps you want to use the table along with one of the chart forms described in Chapter 8. The table might show the "raw" figures, while a pie graph might show how the figures compare as parts of the whole.

PowerPoint's selection of predrawn charts in the Graph program does not include a table. If you want to use a table, you must create your own. Creating a table may take some time, but PowerPoint provides the tools for you to set up the table exactly the way you want.

Suppose that you want to produce a table of figures like that shown in figure 12.6.

The headlines are set in a box separate from the numerals. Each column head—North, South, East, and West—has a separate tab stop created with the center tab. Follow these steps to create the headlines:

1. Create a text box and display the text ruler.

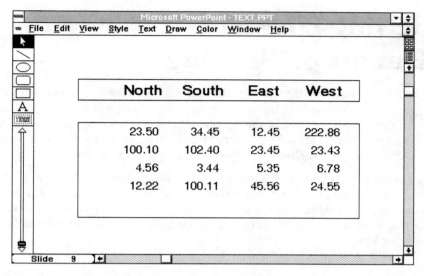

Fig. 12.6. *A table set up with center and decimal tabs.*

2. Set center tab stops for each column headline. Here, set tabs at 1, 2, 3, and 4 inches.

3. Tab to the tab stops and type your text, in this case, *North*, *South*, *East*, and *West*.

Follow these steps to set up the numbers:

1. Create a text box and use the guides to align the left side with the headline text box. See Chapter 5, "Drawing Objects," for information about using the guides, if necessary.

2. Display the text ruler and set four decimal tabs to align with the column heads in the headline text box. Here, place the markers at 1, 2, 3, and 4 inches.

3. Tab and type your numbers.

Add a frame if you want, as explained in Chapter 5. After you have completed the table, you can save it and reuse it as the data changes. Making the table may take some time, but you can create the exact table that you want.

Setting Line and Paragraph Spacing

Line spacing refers to the number of blank lines you leave between lines of type. In one sense, setting up line spacing and paragraph spacing is a simple matter of specifying the number of blank lines you want between lines or paragraphs. For slides such as bulleted lists or simple text slides, you want to leave enough space between lines to make the text easy to read.

PowerPoint gives you the flexibility to set up line spacing in almost any way you want. You do not have to use the full PowerPoint capability to be able to set up adequate line spacing. If you want to get fancy, however, you can (perhaps by setting up different line spacing for each of several levels in a word chart).

Setting Line Spacing

The Line Spacing dialog box sets the amount of space between lines and paragraphs. This dialog box works with the five outline levels (or levels of indentation) discussed in the preceding sections of this chapter. You can set different line and paragraph spacing for every level, if you want.

Figure 12.7 shows you an example of indented text in which levels 1, 2, and 3 each have two paragraphs:

Suppose that you want to increase the line spacing within level 1, decrease it within level 3, and increase the paragraph spacing between all levels. Follow these steps to use the Line Spacing dialog box:

1. Select the text box in which you want to change line spacing. Here, select the box in figure 12.7.

2. Choose Line Spacing from the Text menu.

   The Line Spacing dialog box appears, as shown in figure 12.8.

   In this case, the dialog box obscures the text box. If you want to see the text box at the same time, you can click the title bar of the text box and drag it to a more visible location on the left, as in figure 12.8.

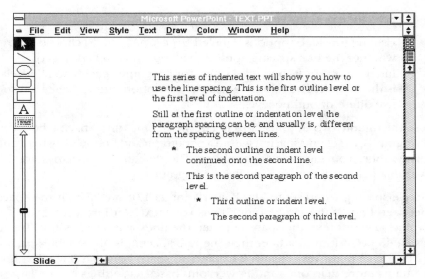

Fig. 12.7. A text box with different outline or indentation levels.

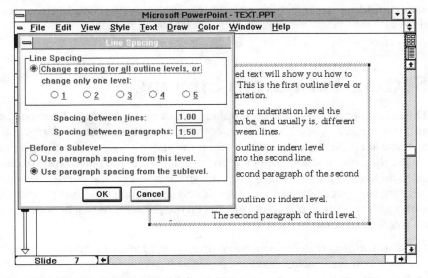

Fig. 12.8. The Line Spacing dialog box.

3. Select the options you want.

Use the top set of options, labeled `Line Spacing`, to choose whether the line spacing applies to all outline levels (levels of indentation) or to one level only. Applying line spacing to all levels is the default. The numbers next to the option buttons refer to the five different outline levels.

Use the middle two options, Spacing between Lines and Spacing between Paragraphs, to set line spacing within a paragraph and line spacing between paragraphs. You can type any number. The default line spacings are 1.0 within a paragraph and 1.5 between paragraphs.

Single-spacing (represented by PowerPoint as 1.0) means that the space between lines is the same point size as your text. For instance, if you are typing 12-point text, the space between the lines will be 12 points. If you use a 48-point font in a line, then the line spacing is 48. Double-spacing (2.0) for 12-point text creates 24 points of space between lines. If a line contains more than one font, PowerPoint bases its settings on the largest font in the line.

Line spacing also affects paragraph spacing. Before setting line spacing, you also should consider paragraph spacing, which is explained in the next section.

Setting Paragraph Spacing

The actual space put between paragraphs is a multiple of the line spacing and the paragraph spacing. If you set the spacing between the paragraphs at 1 and keep the line spacing at 1, then the space between the paragraphs will be the same as the space between lines. If you set the paragraph spacing at 2 and keep the line spacing at 1, the space between the paragraphs will be twice the space between the lines. If you set the line spacing at 2 and the paragraph spacing at 2, the space between the paragraphs will be four times the size of the text.

These settings can drive you crazy until you figure out how the system works. If you set spacing between paragraphs at 2, you do not necessarily end up with two spaces between paragraphs. The number 2 for Spacing between Paragraphs does not refer to number of lines, but is the factor by which you multiply the number in Spacing between Lines.

Use the bottom set of options, labeled Before a Sublevel, to set up the spacing between the higher level paragraph (the "parent") and a sublevel. The space between the levels could be either that of the higher level or that of the lower level. The default is the spacing of the sublevel. This option is meaningless when you are setting line and paragraph spacing for all outline levels (as distinct from level 2, for instance).

Use the following steps to set line spacing for the first level:

1. From the Line Spacing dialog box, select the level number. For this example, select 1.

2. Set the number for Spacing between Lines. To set the number, click the number box and type the new number. Here, type *1.2* to increase line spacing.

    Now set the paragraph spacing between levels 1 and 2.

3. Select the desired Before a Sublevel choice: either Use Paragraph Spacing from this Level or Use Paragraph Spacing from the Sublevel. Here, select Use Paragraph Spacing from this Level.

    In the example, this setting increases the paragraph spacing between the levels slightly because the line spacing has gone up in level 1. In the example, you don't want to change level 2 line spacing, but you do want to decrease 3.

4. Select the level number (3 in this instance), and set the line spacing, here 0.8.

    This step also decreases the paragraph spacing within level 3. You don't want this new paragraph spacing to apply between 2 and 3, so follow step 5.

5. Select the level number, here 2, and select Use Paragraph Spacing from this Level in the Before a Sublevel section of the dialog box.

    This choice maintains the paragraph spacing between levels 2 and 3 at 1.5. This number comes from the default settings of 1.0 for Spacing between Lines and 1.5 for Spacing between Paragraphs. Multiply these together and you get 1.5, the paragraph spacing at level 2.

6. Press Enter or click OK to exit.

    The result is shown in figure 12.9.

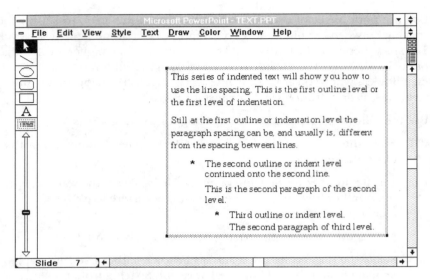

Fig. 12.9. The text box with new spacing.

Use the Line Spacing options to make your text easier to read. White space can make slides easy for the audience to see. Try various spacing intervals and see how they look. Be careful about varying the spacing too much, even though PowerPoint gives you the power to do so. You should always have a clear reason for changing the spacing, such as to distinguish between a section of main text and another section of less important text.

Creating New Default Settings

After you have set up indents, tab stops, line spacing, and paragraph spacing, you can reuse the settings in other presentations. The Set as Default option on the Text menu enables you to carry over text ruler (tabs, indents) and line spacing settings throughout your presentation. Use the Set as Default option, and the settings of your chosen text block override PowerPoint's defaults and are used in any text boxes you draw later.

If you decide to set your own new defaults, follow these steps to use Set as Default:

1. Select the text block that contains the settings you want to use as new defaults.

Tip: Be careful about setting your choices as defaults. The PowerPoint defaults are traditional and acceptable for many situations. Your own variations may be good for one presentation but not necessarily all. Before setting your formatting and indenting choices as defaults, ask yourself if you are sure that you want to lose the originals. You cannot recover the original defaults.

2. From the Text menu, choose the Set as Default option.

    A box appears with the following question:

    ```
    Set the default text ruler and line spacing to be
    those of the selection?
    ```

    The box gives you two options, Set It and Cancel.

3. Choose Set It to carry over your defaults.

Text blocks you have drawn previously remain unaffected by the new defaults. All new text blocks use these settings until you set new defaults.

Creating a Custom Dictionary

With PowerPoint's spelling checker, you can create your own dictionary of specialized words that are not included in the standard dictionary. You can add surnames, for example, or technical words that you do not want to verify every time you use the spelling checker. If you are not sure how to use the spelling checker itself, refer to Chapter 4.

When you run the PowerPoint spelling checker, it compares your spellings with a dictionary file, LEX-AM.DAT. The spelling checker also compares your words with those in a custom dictionary. You can use only one custom dictionary at a time, an important reason to limit the number of custom dictionaries you create. When you use a custom dictionary, PowerPoint does not identify words in your text (words such as NASA, IBM, or Thomas) as misspelled if they are listed in the dictionary.

PowerPoint saves your custom dictionary to a file called STDUSER.DIC. If you want, you can open additional dictionaries and keep them in separate files, but using STDUSER.DIC for your custom dictionary is best because the PowerPoint spelling checker automatically looks for this file.

> **Tip:** If you create extra dictionary files, store them in the same directory as PowerPoint. When you check spelling, PowerPoint can hunt for files in that directory.

You cannot add words to the standard dictionary file. Follow these steps to create a custom dictionary and add words to it:

1. Open the presentation you want to spell check. Here, open an untitled copy of PRSPP16.PPT from the SAMPLES subdirectory as an example of a presentation with a great deal of text.

2. Choose Spelling from the Text menu and then select the Check Spelling option.

   In the example, the first word found is *PowerPoint*. The word in this case is not misspelled; it simply is not included in the standard dictionary. Your screen should now look like the screen represented in figure 12.10.

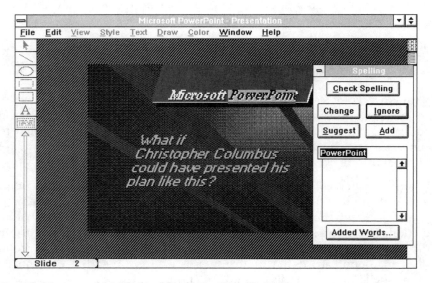

Fig. 12.10. *A word highlighted in the Spelling dialog box.*

If the word is spelled correctly, you can add it to your custom dictionary, and the PowerPoint spelling checker will not question its spelling again. You can add specialized words, foreign words, proper names, place names, and other categories of words. (You can add any word, but be careful not to add misspelled words to your dictionary, or PowerPoint will no longer identify them as misspelled.)

3. Select the Add button.

   The first time you select the Add button, no custom dictionary exists yet and the Added Words dialog box appears and informs you that no dictionary is open, as shown in figure 12.11.

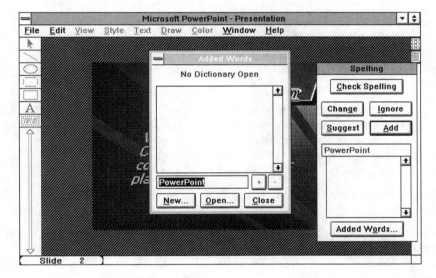

Fig. 12.11. *The Added Words dialog box.*

4. Choose the New option in the bottom left corner of the dialog box.

   If you want to open some other already-existing custom dictionary, use Open (in the same way that you open a PowerPoint file). When STDUSER.DIC exists, PowerPoint opens it automatically.

   Another dialog box opens, similar in appearance to the Save As box in the File menu.

5. Type the name of your new dictionary in this box or accept the default and select Save. The default name for the custom dictionary is STDUSER.DIC.

Now your custom dictionary is open. You return to the Added Words box, where the word `PowerPoint` is still highlighted. To the left of the highlighted word are two buttons with + and – signs on them. You use these to add and delete words to and from your custom dictionary from the Added Words box.

6. Choose the + option to enter the selected word into your custom dictionary.

   Use the + option to add words from the Added Words dialog box. You can add as many words as you want at one time; just keep typing them and pressing the + button. You also can delete words here. Highlight the word and click the minus sign button. At the end, select Close to exit the Added Words dialog box.

7. Select Close to exit this dialog box and return to the Spelling dialog box.

   After you create STDUSER.DIC (as shown in the preceding steps), PowerPoint adds the words to that file unless you specifically create or open another custom dictionary. To add words through the Spelling dialog box, select Add from that box. The spelling checker continues its search for misspelled words.

8. Choose Close from the Control menu to exit the Spelling dialog box.

Creating a custom dictionary can save you time. Do not create too many custom dictionaries, though. If you have several careers, you might be tempted to open a custom dictionary for each career. Even with such multiple demands, however, you might do well just to use one custom dictionary, because PowerPoint can use only one dictionary at a time.

Creating a New Text Style

Text style includes four characteristics: font, color, size, and typestyle (for example, plain, bold, underline, or italic). PowerPoint provides five ready-made styles for you, accessible through the Styles option in the Style menu. Three of these styles use the Helvetica font, the other two use Zapf Dingbats. You also can create your own style to add to the list.

Suppose that you want to create a text style using the Avant Garde font in dark green. Follow these steps to create this style:

1. Choose Define Styles from the Style menu.

   You see the dialog box shown in figure 12.12.

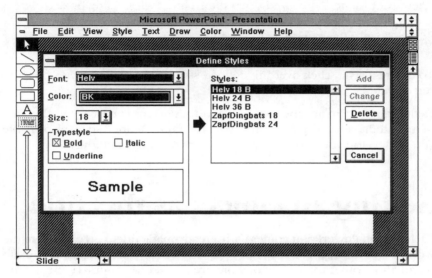

Fig. 12.12. *The Define Styles dialog box.*

On the left side of the dialog box, you see boxes from which to choose the font, color, size, and typestyle. In the middle of the dialog box, PowerPoint displays the existing styles—in this case, the five styles that come with PowerPoint. Any new styles appear in this dialog box after you create them.

2. Click each option on the left side of the dialog box—Font, Color, Size, and Typestyle—and make your choice. Here choose the Avant Garde font, GN3 color (through the Other option), a size of 24, and Bold.

   If necessary, refer to Chapter 14, "Using Advanced Features of Color," to find how to use the Other color option. A sample of your new style then appears in the lower left corner of the dialog box.

3. If you like the style, select the Add button.

Your style is added to the list, in this case as AvantGarde 24 B. You can use your style whenever you want. To apply a defined style to a text box, select the text box and choose the style through the Style menu.

> ***Tip:*** You also can set up a new style directly in the text box. Type your text in the new color, font, size, and typestyle; then select the text (not the text box) and open the Define Styles dialog box. Your new characteristics appear as the four choices on the left side of the box. To add this new style to your list, just select Add.

To delete a style, click over the defined style in the Define Styles box and select Delete.

Defining a style in advance as shown in these steps can save you the time of repeatedly setting up a style that you use often. Defined styles also enable you to develop your own unique look for your presentations.

Setting an Object as the Title

Each slide in PowerPoint comes with a ready-made title. You can delete the word Title inside a title box, but you cannot delete the box itself. You can set anything other than a line or a picture as the title to replace the default title. For example, you can set an oval or rectangle, a text block, or a label as your title. After you set an object as the title, as shown in the steps below, you cannot delete the selection box because the object becomes the new title. You can, however, make the selection box invisible by "unframing" an oval title, deleting words in a text box title, and so on.

To set an object as a new title, follow these steps:

1. Select the object you want to set as the new title. Try an oval (with or without words) as an example.

2. Choose Set as Title from the Edit menu.

The selected object is your new title. In the Shade Background option in the Color Scheme dialog box (see Chapter 7), one option is to shade the background color of your slide from the location of the title box. This capability can create a nice effect when you have a special text box or object that you want to highlight.

Chapter Summary

In this chapter, you learned to use features in the Text and Style menus that were not covered in Chapter 4, "Adding Text to a Presentation." You first learned to use the text ruler to change indents and tab stops. You then saw how to use the left, right, center, and decimal tab tools on the text ruler to create additional tabs in text boxes. You saw how to create a table of numbers. You next learned to change line and paragraph spacing in text boxes and to save spacing (and indent) settings as the new defaults. You then saw how to set up a custom dictionary and add words to it. Finally, you saw how to set up a text style to suit your own needs.

Just as you can go beyond the basics with text as you become familiar with PowerPoint, you can fine-tune your graphs as well. In the next chapter, you find out about advanced possibilities with graphs.

13

Using Advanced Features of Graph

PowerPoint Graph reduces graphing to its two basic elements—data and graph forms, which express the data. (Note that this book uses the term "graph" where PowerPoint documentation often uses the term "chart.") Chapter 8, "Creating Basic Graphs," shows you how to build almost any kind of graph you can imagine from the two basic elements. As you also see in Chapter 8, you have many options even when you work with just one of the basic elements. You can expand or contract the datasheet and display the data in different fonts and formats. You can choose six different graph types and (in most cases) eight different styles for each type (for a total of 48 initial graphs from which to choose). Chapter 8 introduces you to the power and flexibility of PowerPoint Graph. This chapter goes beyond Chapter 8 to cover the more advanced features that are available to you in the datasheet and graph forms.

In this chapter, you learn about Datasheet window features not covered in Chapter 8: creating new number and date formatting, excluding and including rows and columns, and changing the series in the horizontal axis for a scatter graph.

You also learn about Chart window features not covered in Chapter 8: how to move the axes and change their scale and how to change the markers and the tick marks to suit your own requirements. You learn about gridlines, putting labels directly on items in the graph, and copying the whole graph to other applications, such as Microsoft Word.

Finally, you find out about two procedures that apply to both the graph and the datasheet—replacing the default datasheet and graph that appear when you first enter Graph, and importing data from other applications, such as spreadsheets. The section "Importing Data" includes a special section on importing from Microsoft Excel directly onto your slide.

Customizing the Datasheet

You can use a number of advanced features when you work in the datasheet. You can design a custom format, include or exclude rows, or format the axes for a scatter graph. This section discusses these options.

Designing a Custom Format

As you saw in Chapter 8, PowerPoint Graph comes with an impressive array of number formats. You may find, however, that the available formats sometimes do not meet your needs. If you need another format, you can create your own. This section shows you how to create a number format for cells when the existing formats don't fit the bill.

Table 8.1 lists some of the symbols you use to modify Graph number formats. Table 13.1 adds to the list of symbols you can use to customize Graph's number formats.

Table 13.1
Symbols for Numeric Formats

Symbol	Use	Examples
– + ( ) space	Use these symbols when you want them to appear in the cell without typing them.	Format with –#0.00 and *17* appears as -17.00; Format with (#,###) and *8* appears as (8).
"" and \	These symbols display the characters	Use "No" ## and *8* appears as No 8;

Symbol	Use	Examples
	of your choice automatically. The double quotes display as many characters as you want; the backslash displays the next character (one only) in the format.	Use \>## and *8* appears as >8.
*	This symbol repeats the character that follows it to fill the column.	Use *>## and *8* appears as >>>>>>>>>>>>>>8.
[color]	The cell contents appear in the requested color in the brackets. The available colors are black, white, red, green, blue, cyan, yellow, and magenta. Some of the colors are quite dark and can look much like black itself.	Use [red]#,### and the number in the cell appears in red.

Creating a Custom Format

Suppose that you want to exclude a column of cell numbers temporarily from your graph (see the section "Including and Excluding Rows and Columns" later in this chapter). You can change the color of the column numbers and put them in parentheses to distinguish the column from other columns in the graph. Follow these steps to create a new cell format for your numbers:

1. Select the cells you want to format. For the example, select the column labeled 4th Qtr in the default Graph datasheet.

2. Choose Number from the Datasheet menu.

   You see the dialog box shown in figure 13.1.

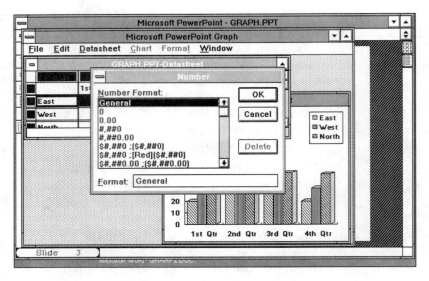

Fig. 13.1. The Number dialog box.

3. Choose the format that looks most like the one you want to create. This step is not essential, but can save you time. Here, choose #,##0.

   The chosen format appears in the Format box, located at the bottom of the dialog box. If you do not select a format, the default format, General, appears in this box.

4. Click over the format displayed in the Format box, and the mouse pointer changes to a line cursor. You now can change the format.

5. Use the arrow keys, Del key, and character keys to create the format you want. For the example, change #,##0 to [green](#,##0).

6. Choose OK when you are satisfied with the new format.

The new format now applies to the numbers in the selected cells. The next time you open the Number dialog box, you will see the newly created format at the bottom of the list of formats.

Deleting a Custom Format

You might find that a format you created earlier needs to be changed to a new format. You can delete any formats that you create by following these steps:

1. Choose Number from the Datasheet menu.

2. Select the format you want to delete by clicking on it.

   You sometimes need to scroll down to see your format.

3. Click the Delete button to delete the format.

You can delete only formats that you create yourself. You cannot delete formats that come with PowerPoint Graph.

Including and Excluding Rows and Columns

Including and excluding rows and columns is different from deleting rows and columns, which is covered in Chapter 8. You exclude rows and columns as a temporary measure so that you later can include the row or column without retyping the data. You might want to exclude a row or column if some data in your datasheet is irrelevant or superfluous to a particular graph you are creating. By excluding data that is irrelevant, you draw more attention to the displayed data that is relevant. Later, you may produce a graph that includes the previously unused (excluded) data. If you excluded rather than deleted the data, you need not retype the column or row in your new graph. Follow these steps to exclude a row or column:

1. Select either a row or column. For example, select the column labeled 4th Qtr in the default Graph datasheet.

2. Choose Exclude Row/Columns from the Datasheet menu.

   You see the dialog box shown in figure 13.2.

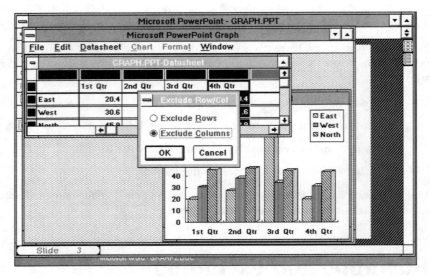

Fig. 13.2. The Exclude Row/Column dialog box.

When you select a column, the Exclude Columns button is active; when you select a row, the Exclude Rows button is active.

3. Click on OK.

The selected row or column on the datasheet turns gray. The data in the excluded row or column does not appear in the graph. For example, if you exclude the 4th Qtr column, your graph looks like the graph in figure 13.3.

Follow these steps to include the row or column that you excluded:

1. Select the row or column you want to include, here, the 4th Qtr column.

2. Choose Include Row/Column from the Datasheet menu.

3. Click on OK, and the row or column entries return to the graph.

Excluding and including columns and rows can save you the time and trouble of retyping them.

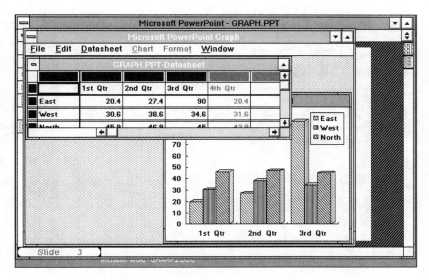

Fig. 13.3. The default graph with the fourth column excluded.

Formatting Scatter Graphs

Scatter graphs show the relationship (or lack of relationship) among sets of data. Scatter graphs, unlike other kinds of graphs, do not plot labels on one axis and numeric values on the other. Instead, two numeric values, an x and a y, determine the position of each point "scattered" on the graph. Because each point must have two values, you must have at least two series on your database for a scatter graph.

You can use the Plot on X Axis option, however, to determine which values plot on the x-axis and which plot on the y-axis. (The x-axis is the horizontal axis; the y-axis is the vertical axis.) See figure 13.4 for a sample scatter graph.

Use the Plot on X Axis option to change the series that Graph represents on the horizontal axis. In figure 13.4, the Holes/Time row is represented on the x-axis, as indicated by a white X against the black rectangle on the far left side of the row. Change the x-axis row as follows:

1. Select the row you want to represent on the x-axis. For the example, select the row labeled `Irishman`.

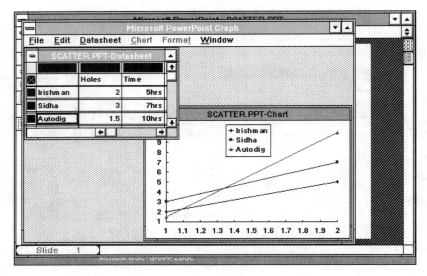

Fig. 13.4. *A scatter graph.*

2. Choose Plot on X Axis from the Datasheet menu. Note that your graph must be formatted as a scatter graph in order for the Plot on X Axis option to be available.

The white X moves to the selected row, and the graph changes as shown in figure 13.5.

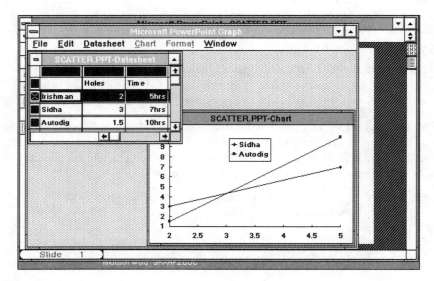

Fig. 13.5. *The new x-axis.*

In this example, the series is in rows. When the series is in rows, you can choose only rows to plot on the x-axis. Put the series in columns and you can choose only columns.

Customizing Graphs

PowerPoint graphs consist of the graph itself and the axes and legends that accompany the graph. As you have come to expect of PowerPoint, you can customize all the ingredients.

In the next section, you learn about additional options for the kind of graph you choose, such as using three-dimensional effects in columns or angling the slices of your pie graphs. You learn to move and scale the two axes found in most graphs, and how to change the appearance of their markings. You also see how to use gridlines in graphs to make the graphs easier to read. You learn to apply labels to the graph figures themselves (as distinct from the axes or in the legend boxes). Finally, you learn to copy graphs into memory to transfer them to other applications.

Adding Special Effects

In Graph, you can choose different categories of graphs, such as column and pie graphs. You also can customize your graphs by adding three-dimensional effects and putting additional space between columns. Choose these options through the Chart menu. Figure 13.6 shows the default graph in Graph in an enlarged window.

Suppose that you want to add three-dimensional effects to the default PowerPoint graph. The following steps show you how to change display options for the graph:

1. Click on the graph to switch from the Datasheet window.

2. Choose Chart from the menu bar.

3. Choose the Column option.

   You see the display of styles available for the Column graph, as discussed in Chapter 8.

4. Choose Options.

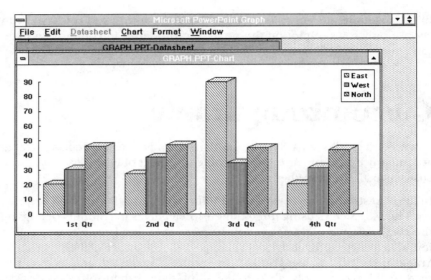

Fig. 13.6. *The Default PowerPoint Graph graph.*

The dialog box opens to display the available options, as shown in figure 13.7.

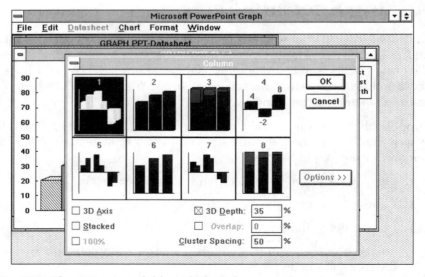

Fig. 13.7. *The options available with the Column graph.*

The six options available with a Column graph are 3D Axis, 3D Depth, Stacked, Overlap, 100%, and Cluster Spacing. In this particular example, you are using the Column graph style number 1, as indicated by the black background in the box that displays the style. The 100% and Overlap options appear in gray, which means that these options are not available for this graph style.

The X in the box to the left of 3D Depth and the number 50% in the box to the right of Cluster Spacing indicate that these options are selected. If you look at the graph in figure 13.8, you can see that each column has depth, giving the graph a three-dimensional effect. The number, 35% here, in the box to the right of 3D Depth specifies how much depth (up to 100%) you want. The 3D Axis option gives depth to the vertical and horizontal axes. Cluster Spacing adds space between groups of data.

The dialog box seems to indicate that Stacked, which appears in black, is available with this graph style. If you choose Stacked, however, the graph changes to a style 2 column graph after you click OK. Stacked, 100%, and Overlap are discussed later in this section.

5. Click on an option to select it. To change a number in a box, double-click on the number to highlight it, then type the new number. For the example, select the 3D Axis option, change 3D Depth to 70%, and change Cluster Spacing to 100%.

6. Click on OK.

You end up with the graph shown in figure 13.8.

Bar graphs have the same options as Column graphs. Other graph types have additional options. Scatter graphs have no options. Table 13.2. lists the options and summarizes their effects on the graphs. In the table, the phrase "groups of data" refers to natural groupings or clusters of values. For example, in figure 13.8, 1st Qtr, 2nd Qtr, 3rd Qtr, and 4th Qtr are groups of data that contain the individual values for East, West, and North.

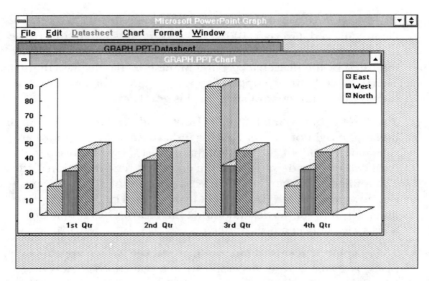

Fig. 13.8. *A column graph with 3D Axis, 70% 3D Depth, and 100% Cluster Spacing.*

Table 13.2
Definitions of Graph Options.

Option	Effect on graph	How to activate
3D Axis	Available with Area, Bar, and Column. Gives three-dimensional depth to to both axes.	Click on an option with the mouse or press A from the keyboard.
3D Depth	Available with Area, Bar, Column, and Pie. Gives three-dimensional depth to the object that represents the actual graph data.	Click with mouse or press D to activate or deactivate this option; then type a percent.
Stacked	Available with Bar, Column, and Line. Stacks groups of data on top of each other rather than beside one another.	Click with the mouse or press S to activate or deactivate this option.

Option	Effect on graph	How to activate
Overlap	Available with Bar and Column. Values within groups of data overlap by a given percent. If 100%, you have perfect stacking, because the values are on top of one another. A minus percent puts space between the values.	Click with the mouse or press O to activate or deactivate; then enter the percentage.
100%	Available with Area, Bar, and Column. One of the axes is numbered to 100, representing percent, and each individual value within a group of data is displayed visually as a percent of the total group value.	Click with the mouse or press 0 (zero) to activate or deactivate.
Cluster Spacing	Available with Bar and Column. Adds or takes away space between groups of data.	Click with the mouse or press C; then type the percentage in the box..
Drop Lines	Available with Area and Line. Draws vertical lines to the highest value in each group of data.	Click with the mouse, or press L to activate or deactivate.
Hi-Lo Lines	Available with Line. Draws a line from the highest to the lowest value in each group of data.	Click with the mouse or press H to activate or deactivate.

continues

Table 13.2 *(continued)*

Option	Effect on graph	How to activate
Angle of First Pie	Available with Pie. Your pie graph rotates clockwise according to the number (representing degrees) that you enter here. For example, 180 rotates the pie halfway around. The maximum number you can enter is 359 (360 is the same as 0.)	Click in the box to the left of degrees, type a number.

Choose the options that suit your purpose. If you want to emphasize a particular slice in a pie, for example, you can put that slice in the upper right. If you want a three-dimensional effect, you can choose the appropriate option. If you want the bars in a graph, for example, to represent the data precisely, however, you may elect not to have them appear in 3-D. In general, trust your own eye and your own sense of what you want to communicate.

In addition to manipulating the graphs themselves, you can change the axes of the graphs, as explained in the next section.

Changing the Axes

You can change the axes of a graph in a number of ways. For instance, you can change the positions of the x- and y-axes or make the axes disappear. You can draw the axes to different scales of measurement, and you can alter the position and appearance of tick marks (markers). In the following sections, you see how to vary the axes.

Repositioning the Axes

Figure 13.9 shows a graph with the horizontal axis along the bottom of the graph and the vertical axis along the left side.

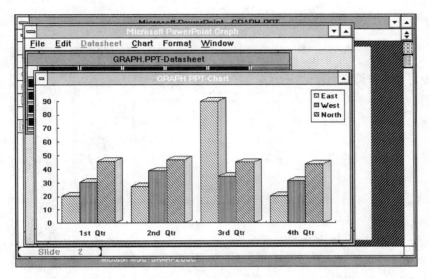

Fig. 13.9. *A graph showing the conventional positions of the horizontal and vertical axes.*

This format is the conventional way to show the axes. You can move either axis—horizontal to the top, for instance, or vertical to the right side—or you can remove the line that represents the axis. You sometimes have good reasons to move an axis. For example, if you have negative values on the graph and do not want to show them going below the bottom of the graph, you can move the point where the horizontal axis crosses the vertical to below the negative data. (Be sure that you have a good reason to change your axes and that you explain your changes clearly. Such variations can create misleading impressions.)

You must be in the Chart window of Graph to change the axes. Suppose that you want to move the vertical axis to the right side of your graph because you know that the graph will appear on the right side of a slide. Follow these steps to change the position of an axis:

1. Make the Chart window active.

2. Choose Format.

    Two options in the drop-down menu refer to the axes: Vertical Axis and Horizontal Axis. Both options work in the same way.

3. Choose Vertical Axis or Horizontal Axis. For this example, use the Vertical Axis.

You see the dialog box shown in figure 13.10.

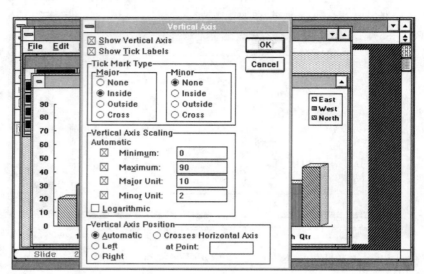

Fig. 13.10. *The Vertical Axis dialog box.*

In this example, the Horizontal Axis dialog box would give you fewer choices than the Vertical Axis dialog box. You would not have the scaling choices in the middle of the box, because the Column graph does not have scaling on the horizontal axis. The situation is reversed with a Bar graph, where the Vertical Axis option shows no scaling choices and the Horizontal Axis option does. The options on display vary according to the type of graph and the type of axis—horizontal or vertical. You use the options in the same way in all cases, however, as demonstrated in the following sections.

The X in the box to the left of the Show Vertical Axis option at the very top of the dialog box indicates that this choice is active. Click this box. The line representing the axis disappears from the graph, but the labels and tick marks remain.

At the bottom of the dialog box, you see the four options for moving the axis: Automatic, Left, Right, and Crosses Horizontal Axis at Point (with a box in which to type the exact crossing point). Automatic is the default. In this case, Left is identical to Automatic. In the fourth option, the exact point of intersection on the horizontal axis is difficult to gauge in this example because the horizontal axis has no scale marked on the graph! Try a few numbers to see where the axis appears. Type *2* here and the vertical axis crosses the horizontal axis somewhere near the center of the horizontal.

4. Choose one of the positioning options and then click on OK to see the result. In this case, choose Right.

   The axis moves to the right side of the graph, as shown in figure 13.11.

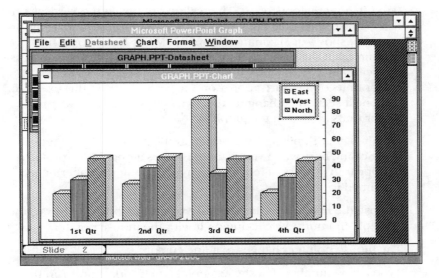

Fig. 13.11. The vertical axis on the right.

Scaling the Axes

In addition to changing the position of an axis, you can change its scaling (or ruling). You can focus on a small section of the graph, or you can adjust the units of measurement that the tick marks represent. You can change the scale to pinpoint exactly the data points displayed on the graph.

To continue with the example, suppose that you want to see only the data between 5 and 50 on the vertical axis. To show this data, follow these steps:

1. Choose Vertical Axis from the Format menu to access the Vertical Axis dialog box.

Figure 13.10 shows the dialog box. Toward the center of the box, you see the five Vertical Axis Scaling choices: Minimum, Maximum, Major Unit, Minor Unit, and Logarithmic. Graph sets the first four choices automatically, but you can change the numbers shown in the boxes to the right. The squares to the left of the first four choices indicate whether the automatic numbering choice is on. If Xs appear in the squares, as is the case when you first enter the dialog box, then the numbering is automatic.

In the example, the label numbering on the vertical axis runs from 0 to 90 in increments of 10. The scaling options in the Vertical Axis Scaling box reflect the label numbering: Minimum (the starting number) shows 0; Maximum shows 90; Major Unit shows 10, meaning that the principal (and in this case only) numbers increase by increments of 10; and Minor Unit shows 2—even though no minor units of measure appear on the vertical axis in this example. (The next section, "Changing the Tick Marks," explains why no minor units appear in the graph.)

Use the Logarithmic option, located at the bottom of the Vertical Axis Scaling box, when you want the values along the vertical axis to appear in powers of ten. You change the other numbering as explained in steps 2 through 4:

2. Choose the first box in the Vertical Axis Scaling box (the box to the right of Minimum) by clicking on it with the mouse pointer.

    The mouse pointer changes to a line cursor.

3. Type a new number. For the example, type 5, 50, 5, and 1 in the boxes (from Minimum to Minor Unit, respectively).

    Notice that the Xs in the squares to the left disappear when you type a new number.

4. Click on OK.

    Figure 13.12 shows the result.

The scaling now runs 5, 10, 15, and so on, up to 50. Any portion of the data above 50 and below 5 is cut off, although the relative heights of the columns remain the same. The minor units of scaling still do not appear. The next section explains how to bring the minor units on-screen and how to change the tick marks.

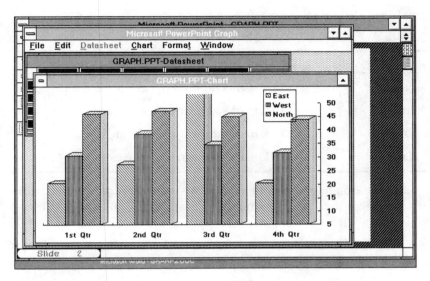

Fig. 13.12. The default graph with new scaling.

Changing the Tick Marks

The tick marks are the horizontal lines opposite the labels on the vertical axis. You can place the tick marks inside or outside the axis, and you can make either the major or minor (or both) units of measure disappear. Follow these steps to place the major units outside the axis and the minor units inside the axis:

1. Choose Vertical (or Horizontal) Axis from the Format menu to enter the dialog box shown in figure 13.10.

   Toward the top of the dialog box, you see the Tick Mark Type box and its options.

   Show Tick Labels, located above the Tick Mark Type box, is one option. The labels are the numbers, 5, 10, and so on, on the graph in the example, that identify the tick marks. The labels appear by default. To switch off the labels, click Show Tick Labels so that the X in the square to the left disappears.

   The two categories of Tick Mark Type options, Major and Minor, refer to the major and minor units of measure on the axis. Both Major and Minor have four options: None, Inside, Outside, and Cross. The default option for Major tick marks is Inside. Table 13.3 explains the effect of each of the tick mark options.

Table 13.3
Tick Mark Type Options

Option	Effect
None	Tick marks do not appear on the graph.
Inside	Tick marks appear inside the axes.
Outside	Tick marks appear outside the axes.
Cross	Tick marks fall across the axes.

In the example, the circle next to None under Minor is black. (This setting is the reason no minor units appear on the graph in the preceding section.)

2. Choose an option for Major and an option for Minor. For example, try Outside for Major and Inside for Minor.

3. Click on OK to see the graph.

Figure 13.13 shows the result.

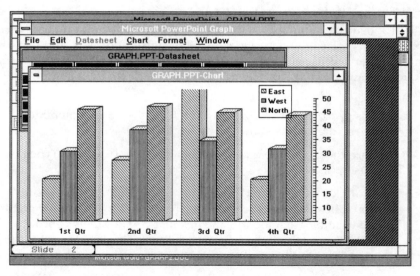

Fig. 13.13. *A graph with major unit tick marks outside and minor unit tick marks inside the axes.*

Notice that the minor units of measure now appear on the graph. You can use grids to draw more attention to the units of measure, as explained in the next section.

Using Gridlines

Gridlines work with major and minor units of measure on both the horizontal and vertical axes of your graph. Gridlines are lines that cross the graph at the tick mark units. Use gridlines to help you see how the units of measure apply to the graph. You also can use the Gridlines option to draw a rectangular frame around the graph, as if you had four and not two axes, as shown in the following steps.

Suppose that you want to draw as many lines as possible across your graph to make the exact data amounts easy to read. Follow these steps to draw the lines:

1. Choose Gridlines from the Format menu.

   You see the dialog box shown in figure 13.14.

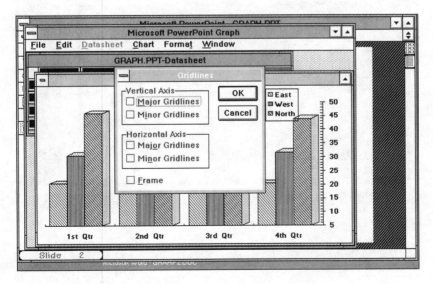

Fig. 13.14. *The Gridlines dialog box.*

You see five options—Major Gridlines and Minor Gridlines for the Vertical Axis, Major Gridlines and Minor Gridlines for the Horizontal Axis and—on the bottom—a Frame for the graph. If you choose Major Gridlines in the Vertical Axis part of the dialog box, for example, PowerPoint draws straight lines across the graph from the major tick marks. Minor Gridlines, when activated, draws lines across the graph from the minor tick marks. Similarly, in the Horizontal Axis options, choosing Major Gridlines draws lines vertically from the horizontal axis major tick marks; activating Minor Gridlines draws lines from the minor tick marks.

2. Click any option, then click on OK to see the result.

If you choose the top four options, the result will be similar to the graph in figure 13.15. If you choose Major Gridlines in both the Vertical Axis and Horizontal Axis options, the lines automatically create a frame, so you don't need to select the frame option in that case.

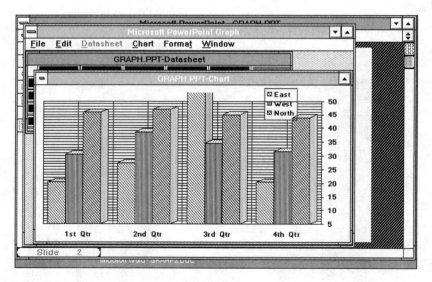

Fig. 13.15. *A graph showing all gridlines.*

Gridlines help your audience see the scale at any point on your graph. The next section discusses an even more direct way to emphasize data values—attaching labels directly to graphs.

Showing Labels

Sometimes entries in a legend are difficult to match with the corresponding items on a graph, especially if the legend box contains many entries. To avoid this problem, you can use the Data Labels option to label the data points and pie slices directly. You can show values, names (such as labels like 1st Qtr), or percentages (particularly useful with pie graphs). Suppose that you have a pie graph and want to label the percentages of the individual slices. To label the slices' percentages, follow these steps:

1. Choose Data Labels from the Format menu.

    You see the dialog box shown in figure 13.16.

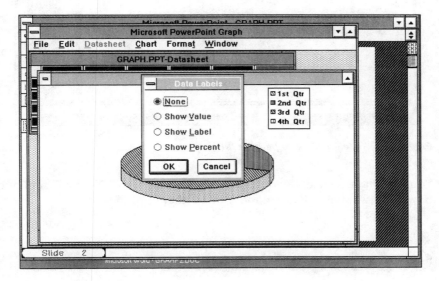

Fig. 13.16. *The Data Labels dialog box.*

The four choices available for a pie graph are None, Show Value, Show Label, and Show Percent. Show Percent is not available for any other graph type, though the other three choices are available for all other types. Show Value refers to the values shown in the cells in the datasheet. Show Label refers to titles such as East, West, and 1st Qtr. Show Percent refers to the overall percentage going to each slice in a pie graph. The None option is the default.

2. Choose an option. You can choose only one option at a time. Here, choose Show Percent, and click on OK to see the result. You see the graph in figure 13.17.

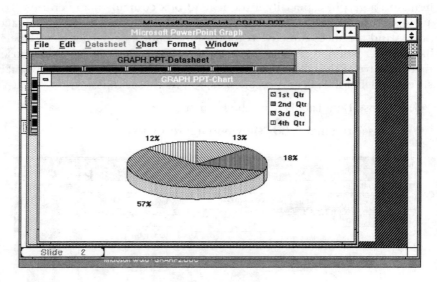

Fig. 13.17. *A pie graph with percent labels.*

You now have seen all the options in the Format menu. Next you find out how to copy a PowerPoint graph into another application.

Copying a Graph to Other Applications

In addition to drawing a graph on your slide (as you saw in Chapter 8, "Creating Basic Graphs"), PowerPoint Graph also can copy a graph into the clipboard. You can transfer the graph from the clipboard to other applications, such as word processors. You can transfer a graph, but you cannot transfer a datasheet.

Suppose that you want to transfer one particular graph to Microsoft Word for Windows to illustrate an article. Follow these steps to make the transfer:

1. From the Chart window, choose Edit from the menu bar.

   Copy Chart is the only choice available in the drop-down menu.

2. Choose Copy Chart.

   PowerPoint copies into the clipboard whatever is currently in the Chart window.

3. Go to the application into which you want to copy the graph, and use that application's paste function in the usual way.

When you copy between applications in this way, you can incorporate a graph into your word processor (or other application) with a single keystroke. You need not worry about file compatibility between your graphics program and your word processor. Thanks to Windows, which loads multiple applications into memory at once, you can incorporate the graph into another application as easily as into a PowerPoint presentation. Note, however, that you can copy between Windows applications only.

So far in this chapter, you have seen how to enhance the datasheet and, separately, the graph. You also can use advanced capabilities that apply to the graph and datasheet together. In the next sections, you find out how to replace the default graph with a default of your own and how to import data into Graph from other files.

Creating Your Own Default Graph

The default datasheet and graph give you an immediate idea when you first enter Graph of how a datasheet and graph look and how they interact. Every time you choose the Insert Graph option on a PowerPoint slide, you automatically see the default datasheet and the corresponding graph. If you prefer, you can have a graph and datasheet of your own design appear when you first start Graph. Perhaps you often use a standard pie graph with basic sales figures. You can set that graph as your default.

Changing the default can be useful, too, if you have formatted your cells to certain specifications. You also can delete all rows and columns in the datasheet (the Chart window goes blank) and save the blank datasheet and graph as the new default. If you delete all rows and columns, your screen looks like figure 13.18 when you first enter Graph.

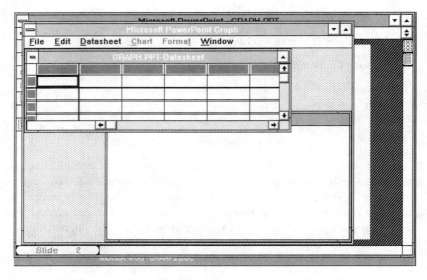

Fig. 13.18. *A blank datasheet and graph.*

Suppose that the blank datasheet and graph shown in figure 13.18 is your preference as a starting point when you enter PowerPoint Graph. Follow these steps to save the blank datasheet and graph as the default. Follow the same steps if you want to save a formatted datasheet and graph. You save everything, including numbers, when you create and save a new default datasheet and graph.

1. Choose File from the menu bar.

2. Choose Set as Default Chart.

You then have a new default datasheet and graph. PowerPoint creates a file called DEFAULT.PPG, to which Graph refers from then on when creating a new graph setup.

To revert to the standard PowerPoint default, delete DEFAULT.PPG in the main PowerPoint directory through DOS or Windows.

The final section in this chapter explains how to bring data from other files into Graph.

Importing Data

You often may want to produce a PowerPoint graph from data in a spreadsheet such as 1-2-3, Symphony, or Excel. When you use Power-Point's Import Data function, you do not have to retype data from another application. Table 13.4 lists the types of data and files you can import into PowerPoint.

Table 13.4
Data Files You Can Import

File	Extension
ASCII text-only files that use commas or tabs to separate fields	.TXT
Lotus 1-2-3 (version 1A) and Microsoft Works files	.WKS
Lotus 1-2-3 files, Version 2.0	.WK1
Symphony files	.WR1
Excel spreadsheets	.XLS
Excel graphs	.XLC
Multiplan, Excel, and other symbolic link (SYLK) files for exchanging data between spreadsheets and applications	.SLK

All formatting is imported automatically also. Formulas are not imported—just the current number in the formula cell.

PowerPoint was designed to work with Excel Version 2.1. If you use Excel Version 3.0, you cannot import directly into PowerPoint Graph. You must first go into the Excel spreadsheet that you want to import; save the spreadsheet as Excel 2.1—this option is in the Save and Save As boxes in Excel; then return to PowerPoint Graph and follow the steps in the paragraph below to import the new spreadsheet file.

Tip: You can import files up to 128 rows by 128 columns in size.

Suppose that you want to use data from a Symphony file, MOVILLE.WR1, in PowerPoint. Follow these steps to import data into Graph:

1. Activate the Datasheet window and select the beginning cell for the data. Here, select the blank first cell, top left, under the row of black cells.

2. Choose Import Data from the PowerPoint Graph File menu.

   You see the dialog box shown in figure 13.19.

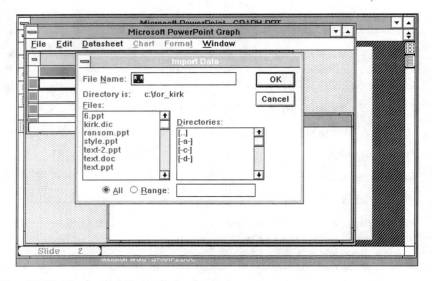

Fig. 13.19. The Import Data dialog box.

3. Follow the standard Windows procedure to select the file you want to import: Go to the correct directory and then choose the file.

   You need not import all the data in the file. At the bottom of the dialog box you see two buttons: All and Range. The All option is the default. Follow steps 4 through 6 to select a range of data.

4. Click the circle next to Range, then click in the box next to Range.

   The mouse pointer changes to a line cursor.

5. Type the cell range, separated by two periods. For example, type *C1..G200*. You also can use a range name, if appropriate. (For Excel, type *C1:G200*.)

6. Choose OK, and the imported data pours into the cells.

Sometimes labels are not imported with the data. When this happens, you can copy the labels from the file of origin, enter Graph, and paste the labels into the datasheet.

Importing Graphs and Worksheets from Excel

If you have Microsoft Excel for Windows on your hard disk, then the options in the File menu on the main PowerPoint screen change slightly. If Excel is not installed, the seventh option down is Insert Graph. As you saw in Chapter 8, this option takes you to the PowerPoint graph window. If Excel is installed, the option is Insert. Choose Insert and a submenu opens, as shown in figure 13.20, with three options: Excel Chart, Excel Worksheet, and Graph. Choose Graph when you want to go to PowerPoint Graph. You can use the other two options, Excel Chart and Excel Worksheet, to import graphs and worksheets directly onto your slide, where PowerPoint pastes them in as pictures.

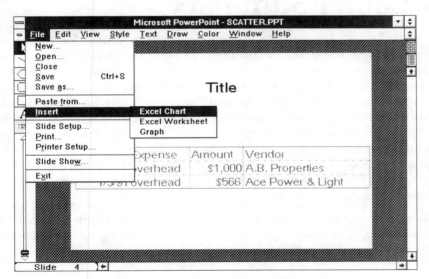

Fig. 13.20. *Additional options under the File menu when Excel is installed.*

Follow these steps to use the Excel Chart and Excel Worksheet options:

1. Choose Insert from the File menu and then choose either Excel Chart or Excel Worksheet.

   If PowerPoint can find the file EXCEL.EXE (or if Excel is already open), the Excel screen (Chart or Worksheet screen, depending on your choice) appears. If PowerPoint cannot find EXCEL.EXE, PowerPoint prompts you for its location. The file could be on drive D, for example. Type the location.

2. From the Excel window, open the Excel file from which you want to copy.

3. Select and copy the cells or graph you want to transfer to PowerPoint.

4. Return to PowerPoint (by exiting Excel or clicking on a portion of the PowerPoint window) and paste the contents of the clipboard onto the slide.

Chapter Summary

In this chapter, you saw how to use advanced Graph features for datasheets only, for graphs only, and for datasheets and graphs together. In the section on datasheets, you saw how to create new number and date formatting for your cells. You learned how to exclude rows and columns temporarily from graphs. In addition, you read how to change the series on display in the horizontal axis. In the section on graphs, you learned to move your axes, to change their scale, and to change the type of tick marks. You then learned to use gridlines, to put values directly onto graphs, and to copy a whole graph to another application. Finally, you saw how to create a new default graph and how to import data from other applications, including how to import directly onto your slide from Excel.

As with graphing, PowerPoint offers even more power in its use of color than you have seen so far in this book. In the next chapter, you find out about advanced uses of color.

14

Using Advanced Features of Color

As visual artists know, using color can offer endless possibilities for enhancing your presentation. In certain ways, PowerPoint offers endless possibilities, as well—you can, for instance, create and use any color you want. In Chapter 7, "Using Basic Color," you learned some of the basic techniques for using color in PowerPoint, such as copying the color scheme from a template, creating a unique color scheme to suit your own needs, and coloring individual objects. PowerPoint does not stop there, though. As you learned in Chapter 7, the eight colors you use most often make up the color scheme. These eight colors are directly available through the color menu options.

In this chapter, you find out how to go beyond the eight colors in the color scheme. You can go beyond the basics whether you choose the eight colors of your color scheme yourself or you accept the default PowerPoint color scheme. You learn how to use the many additional colors already available in PowerPoint and, beyond that, how to create new colors of your own. You find out how to use colors on a one-time basis and how to add colors to the menu so that you can use them in the same way that you can use any other colors.

Like much else in PowerPoint, using color can be simple or complex. As you become confident with the basics, PowerPoint provides you with the tools to use color in more sophisticated ways. For instance, after you create special colors to use in your own color scheme, you can use your color scheme in other presentations, as you find out in this chapter. You also learn how to create two or more color schemes within one presentation

347

and apply them to groups of slides or to individual slides. Finally, you learn to recolor pictures imported from other applications. PowerPoint always leaves the colors in these imported pictures as it finds them (even if the colors don't exist in PowerPoint), although you can recolor them.

Using Other Colors

As you saw in Chapter 7, the color scheme gives you eight basic colors with which to work. Suppose, however, that you want to use other colors. PowerPoint, through features available on the Color menu, gives you ample opportunity to make use of and even to create the exact colors you need.

Specifically, you can use the many colors already available in PowerPoint through the Other option (usually for one-time use) and through the Add Extra to Menu option (for permanent use). See the sections "Using the Other Option" and "Adding an Extra Color" in this chapter. You can create your own new colors with the More Colors option, which is available in certain dialog boxes, as explained in the section "Creating a Color."

Viewing Existing Colors

You can see the colors in the current color scheme through most options in the Color drop-down menu. Follow these steps to view the existing colors in the color scheme:

1. Choose Color from the menu bar to see the drop-down menu options.

   You can choose any of the first six options—Fill, Line, Shadow, Pattern Contrast, Text, and Color Scheme—to see the color scheme.

2. Choose Fill, for example, and you see the color choices as displayed in figure 14.1.

   PowerPoint always displays the color scheme in the same order, with the background color on top and the foreground color second. As you saw in Chapter 7, each color has its own use on the slide.

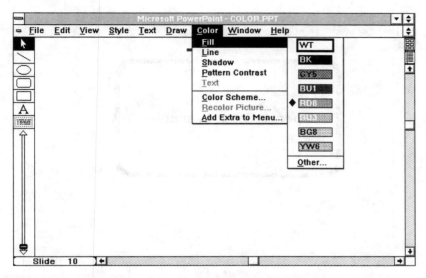

Fig. 14.1. *The eight colors of a color scheme and the Other option (shown in varying shades of gray in the black-and-white figure).*

3. Click anywhere on the slide or press Esc twice to exit the drop-down menus and return to the slide.

You need not use the existing colors in the color scheme. In the next section, you see how to use the Other option to make use of the many additional colors available in PowerPoint.

Using the Other Option

You generally use the Other option when you want to use the color only once, to color a specific drawn line or object or a piece of text, for example. You can use the Other option in other ways (to set a default color, for instance), but the Add Extra to Menu option from the Color menu is better to use in those cases. If you add the extra color to the menu, you can use it again easily by selecting it from the menu.

The Other option is available when you choose Fill, Line, Shadow, Pattern Contrast, or Text from the Color menu. You use the Other option in exactly the same way for all these commands. In the example here, you see how to use Other to change the color of the frame of the rectangle shown in figure 14.2.

Fig. 14.2. A rectangle with a black frame.

Suppose that you want to use a brighter color to draw attention to a special offer. To change the color of the rectangle, follow these steps:

1. Select the drawn object. Here, select the rectangle containing the words `Special Offer Available!`

   In the default color scheme, PowerPoint draws the frame in black.

2. Choose Line from the Color menu.

   Below the list of colors representing the color scheme, you see the word `Other`.

3. Choose Other.

   You see the screen shown in figure 14.3.

   This screen may look familiar to you. It is identical to the Change a Color screen discussed in Chapter 7, "Using Basic Color." Chapter 7 explains the options available on this screen. Along the top of the dialog box in this example, you see a black frame around the Line rectangle, which shows the current frame color. This black frame color also appears in the large rectangle to the right, labeled `BK` (for "black") in this example.

4. Choose any color on display to be the new color for the selected frame. Here, use GN8.

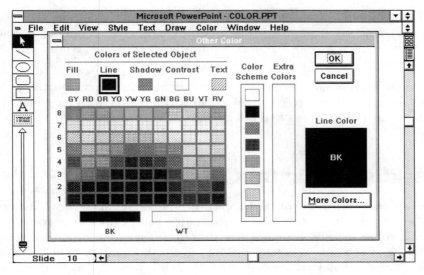

Fig. 14.3. The Other Color dialog box.

5. Click on OK (or press Enter).

On the slide, the frame now appears in the new color, as shown in figure 14.4. Although figure 14.4 is not a color figure, you can see the lighter shade of gray in the frame.

Fig. 14.4. The rectangle with a new frame color.

If you choose Color now, and then Line (without deselecting the rectangle), a diamond or a check will appear beside the Other option, indicating that the frame color is now contained under Other and is not included in the color scheme colors.

Sometimes you want to color more than just a single object. You may want to have an additional color available for use throughout your presentation. In the next section, you find out how to add such a color.

Adding an Extra Color

Any extra colors that you add appear on the Fill, Line, Shadow, Pattern Contrast, and Text menus beneath the color scheme colors. You can use the extra colors from these menus. The procedure for adding an extra color is similar to changing a color or using a color through the Other option. Suppose that you want the text Special Offer Available! to appear in a special new color, and that you intend to use this color for other text in this slide. Unlike the Other option, which applies only to what you have selected on your screen, the Add Extra to Menu option is available whenever you want to use it in the presentation.

Follow these steps to add a color to the menu:

1. Choose Add Extra to Menu from the Color menu.

   You see the screen shown in figure 14.5.

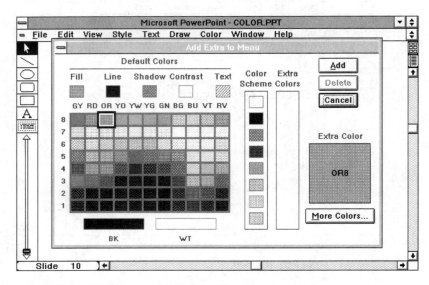

Fig. 14.5. *The Add Extra to Menu dialog box.*

The Add Extra to Menu dialog box is identical to the Other Color dialog box you saw in the preceding section and the Change a Color dialog box you saw in Chapter 7, with one difference. Here, in place of OK in the top right, you see two other buttons: Add and Delete.

2. Select any color. Use OR8 for the example.

   As soon as you select a color, the word Add in the Add button changes from gray to black. The Add button is active. Now that you have selected a color, you have the option of adding it. (If you don't select a color to add, the Add button changes and becomes a Cancel button.)

3. Select Add.

   A rectangle containing the color that you added appears in the Extra Colors column. You can add up to eight colors.

   To delete a color, click any color in the Extra Colors column, and then click the Delete button. The color disappears from the column.

4. After you add your colors, choose Close to return to the current slide.

All the colors you added (one in the example) now appear in the Fill, Line, Shadow, Pattern Contrast, and Text submenus underneath the Other option. Choose Color and any one of those five submenus to see something similar to figure 14.6.

To change the text to the new color, select the text, choose Text from the Color menu, and choose the new color at the bottom of the available options. (Note that the Text option on the Color menu appears in black only when text is selected—you can change the color of text only after you have selected it.)

You now have seen how to add an extra color to your menu of permanent color choices. You also can create a new color to add to your choices in Extra Colors, as you see in the next section.

Creating a Color

You can create additional colors with the More Colors option. You access More Colors through a box that could be called the color palette dialog box. This box has three different names in PowerPoint: Other Color, Change a Color, and Add Extra to Menu. The box has a different name depending on how you access it, but the palette from which you choose is the same.

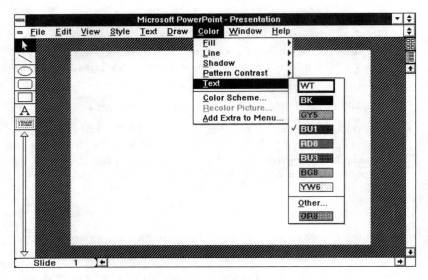

Fig. 14.6. *An extra color (OR8) in the Text submenu.*

Table 14.1 summarizes how you use the Other Color, Change a Color, and Add Extra to Menu dialog boxes.

You find the More Colors option in all three boxes mentioned in table 14.1—Other Color, Change a Color, and Add Extra to Menu. Because you already have looked at the Other Color and Add Extra boxes in this chapter, this section illustrates the use of the More Colors option with the third box, Change a Color. You use More Colors the same way in all three dialog boxes.

In Chapter 7, you saw how to use the Change a Color option to change a color in your color scheme. Here, you see how to change a color by creating another color to replace it. To continue the example from the preceding section, suppose that you want to fill the rectangle with color and decide that the current fill color, RD8, is not suitable. You can create a new color by following these steps:

1. Choose Color Scheme from the Color menu.

2. Select the color you want to replace—for the example, the fifth color down (RD8 in the default color scheme).

3. Select the Change a Color button.

    You reach the Change a Color box, which is identical, except for the name on top, to the Other Color box shown in figure 14.3. Now you are ready to create a color by accessing More Colors.

Table 14.1
Using Other and Extra Colors

Use option	And then option	To access the color palette box called	Effect
Fill	Other	Other Color	Changes an object's color
Line	Other	Other Color	Changes an object's color
Shadow	Other	Other Color	Changes an object's color
Pattern Contrast	Other	Other Color	Changes an object's color
Text	Other	Other Color	Changes an object's color
Color Scheme	Change a Color	Change a Color	Changes a color in the color scheme
Add Extra to Menu	—	Add Extra to Menu	Adds/deletes colors that you can choose from the menu

Tip: When you use Change a Color and Other Color to access the More Colors box, a color is always selected when you get there. This selection is not true of Add Extra to Menu. To help you create your new color, select a color close to the one you want to create before you access the More Colors button. Choosing a color initially can help you create your color the way you want it, because you create the new color by shading the previous color.

4. Choose the More Colors button.

   You see the dialog box shown in figure 14.7.

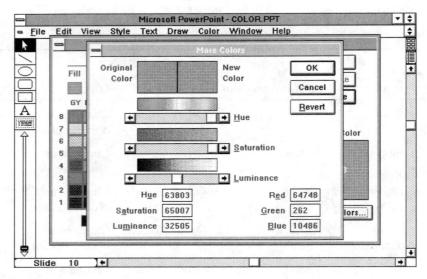

Fig. 14.7. The More Colors dialog box.

On top, you see two boxes, labeled `Original Color` and `New Color`. At first, both colors are the same. As you change the color, the New Color box changes, but the Original Color box does not. You therefore have a good comparison of old and new at all times. In this example, the original color is the red labeled RD8.

Below the two top boxes, you see three scroll bars: Hue, Saturation, and Luminance. The bar of colors above the Hue scroll bar shows the spectrum of colors available in PowerPoint. The position of the Hue scroll bar square reflects the color in New Color. In this example, the scroll bar square is to the far right of the scroll bar. Slide the square on the Hue scroll bar, and you change the color.

5. Click on the left or right arrow in the Hue scroll bar to see the color change.

   Saturation refers to how intensely the color is depicted. Far left is least intense; far right is most intense.

   Luminance shows how much black and white has been added. Far left of the scroll box makes the color all black. Far right makes the color all white.

6. Click the arrows in the Saturation and Luminance scroll bars to change your color.

As you change the color, notice that the numbers change in the boxes on the bottom of the screen. One set of boxes is labeled Hue, Saturation, and Luminance. The numbers in these boxes change one at a time as you alter the respective scroll bars. The other set of boxes, Red, Green, and Blue, represent the amount of red, green, and blue on an RGB monitor. The numbers in these boxes also change as you move the scroll bar boxes.

7. To change a number in any of the number boxes, choose the box with the keyboard or the mouse.

8. Type your new number and then choose the New Color box to put the number into effect. For the example, type *65000* in Red, *35000* in Green, and *45000* in Blue.

    You need to change only one set of numbers—Hue/Saturation/ Luminance or Red/Green/Blue—and the other changes automatically. Experiment with the features in this dialog box.

    If you want to retrieve your original color, choose Revert or choose Original Color. Either way, the original color goes back into the New Color rectangle and the scroll bar positions and numbers revert to what they were when you first entered this dialog box.

9. After you are satisfied with your new color, choose OK. Choose Cancel to discard what you have done.

    You return to the dialog box from which you entered, in this example, the Change a Color dialog box. The new color appears in the Color Scheme column and in the large rectangle on the right labeled Scheme Color.

10. Choose OK or Cancel or accept or reject the new scheme color.

    If you accept the new color, the new color replaces the old in the Color Scheme dialog box. Exit this screen by choosing This Slide, Matching Slides, or All Slides; apply the new scheme; and then exit the box. The fill color in the rectangle changes to the new color you created.

In this section, you have seen how to create a color in PowerPoint. This chapter and Chapter 7 use the term *matching slides*. The next section explains how to create matching slides.

Creating Matching Slides

Creating a color scheme that fulfills all your needs can take time and trouble. You may want to use your new color scheme with other presentations, either existing or new. Alternatively, as explained in Chapter 7, you simply can take advantage of color schemes that PowerPoint provides in the COLORSCH subdirectory. The color schemes in this subdirectory were created by professionals and blend colors according to established artistic principles.

If your presentation has slides that naturally divide into groups, you can apply a different color scheme to each group. You thereby create matching slides—groups of slides within the same presentation that have the same color scheme.

When you create a default template, you also can create a default color scheme, which becomes the color scheme for any new slides. In Chapter 1, you saw how to open a new presentation from within an open presentation and use the open presentation's defaults, including the color scheme defaults.

In Chapter 7, you saw that you can copy a color scheme by starting with the slide that has the unique color scheme you want to copy. You follow an almost identical procedure to create matching slides within a presentation. For the example, suppose that you want to create two matching slides with a new color scheme and leave the rest of the slides with the default. Follow these steps to create matching slides:

1. Go to the slide whose color scheme you want to copy, and choose Color Scheme from the Color menu.

    The Color Scheme dialog box appears.

2. Click on the slide. The dialog box disappears but is still open. (Do not close the dialog box.)

3. Use the Slide Changer, the Slide Sorter, or the Title Sorter to move to the slide to which you want to copy.

4. Choose Window and then choose Color Scheme.

    The Color Scheme dialog box comes back into view.

5. Choose This Slide and then choose Apply.

    The color scheme now applies to the current slide. When you create the matching slides, you apply the color scheme to one slide at a time. Now you have created a set of two matching slides with identical color schemes. Do this for as many slides as you need.

6. After you create matching slides, close the Color Scheme dialog box.

> *Tip:* If you want to create a custom color scheme for a presentation, do so on your first slide; you then can create subsequent slides based on the first one. Be sure to apply the color scheme using the All Slides option after you have changed it on the first slide. To make the change, choose New Slide from the Edit menu (or press Ctrl-N).

> *Tip:* When you copy color schemes to other presentations and to slides within a presentation, remember to keep the Color Scheme dialog box open. Even when the Color Scheme dialog box is not visible, always access it through the Window menu in the menu bar, never through the Color menu. If you use the Color menu, the Color Scheme dialog box contains the current slide's color scheme.

You now have seen how to transfer color schemes between slides within a presentation to create matching slides. The next section explains how to recolor pictures that you import into PowerPoint.

Recoloring Pictures

Pictures, as PowerPoint defines them, include logos, maps, photographs, and colored artwork. As you saw in Chapter 11, you can copy and move pictures between presentations. A special menu option on the Color menu enables you to recolor pictures, one color at a time. Black and white are colors, so you can change them to another color, as well. You cannot add to the number of colors already in the picture—you are limited to two colors in a black-and-white picture, for example. In addition, you can add color to pictures that use patterns rather than colors.

Suppose that you want to include an illustration in your presentation to inform your audience that your firm sponsors a local soccer team. The SPORTS.PPT file in the CLIPART subdirectory has a picture of a soccer player (shown in fig. 14.8) that you have pasted into your presentation slide. (See Chapter 10 for a discussion of how to paste in clip art.)

Fig. 14.8. The soccer player picture.

Suppose that you now want to change the colors to green and orange. Follow these steps to recolor an image:

1. Select a picture that you already have pasted onto a slide. Here, select the picture of the soccer player.

2. Choose Recolor Picture from the Color menu.

   You see the dialog box shown in figure 14.9.

   Your selected picture appears on the left of the box. As you change colors, you can use the Preview button at the bottom of the box to see how the picture looks with the new colors. Nothing changes on the actual slide until you use the OK button to exit the dialog box.

   To the right, you see three columns titled, from left to right, Change, From, and To. If the color is actually changed, an X appears in the boxes beside the colors in the Change column. The From column shows the colors as they are. The To column shows the new colors after you have changed them. Initially, the colors in the From and To columns are the same. PowerPoint displays only seven colors at a time, so, when necessary, use the long scroll bar on the right to bring extra colors onto the screen.

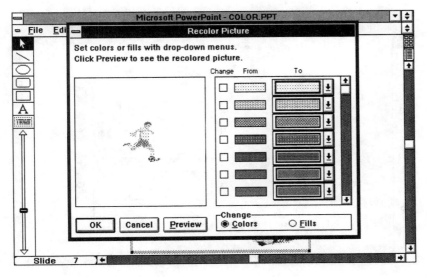

Fig. 14.9. The Recolor Picture dialog box.

One more set of buttons appears on the screen. Along the bottom right, you see a box titled Change, which contains two buttons: Colors and Fills. Before you change the picture, choose one of the two buttons. Colors refers to the solid colors in a picture. Fills refers to the pattern colors (the nonsolid colors). With some pictures, the Fills button (and less frequently the Colors button) is gray, indicating that it is not available. This condition means that the picture itself was created without any fills (or straight colors if the Colors button is gray). When you choose Fills, the colors in Colors remain unchanged and vice versa.

3. Choose Fills or Colors. Colors is the default. Here, stay with Colors.

4. To change a color, click the down arrow to the right of the To column. Here, click the top color, the color of the player's jersey.

   A scroll bar containing colors to choose from drops down, as shown in figure 14.10.

   The list is the color scheme in the current slide plus any extra colors you have created (OR8 here is an extra color). The Other option is also available.

5. Select as the new color any color on view, or choose Other to see the Other Colors dialog box and then select one of those colors. For the example, select the color GN8 through Other.

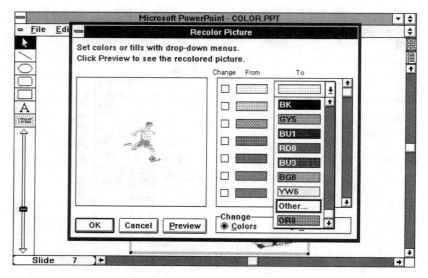

Fig. 14.10. *The drop-down menu list of colors to choose from in the To column.*

You also can create a new color through the More Colors option in the Other Colors dialog box in the usual way.

After you select a new color, the drop-down menu of colors disappears.

Your new color appears in the To column, and PowerPoint places an X in the Change column box.

6. Click Preview to see the effect of your new color.

Change as many colors as you want in the same way. Here, you can change the third color down in the From column to OR8, the color that you want for the shorts.

After experimenting, you may decide to use some colors and not others. To revert to the original color in any color choice, click the Change box beside any color. The X disappears. The To color stays as it was, showing the new color. But without the X, PowerPoint no longer actually applies the new color to the slide picture.

7. After you change colors, choose OK to apply the colors to your picture, or choose Cancel to leave the picture as it was.

On the slide, your picture has changed as required. The soccer player now has the colors displayed in figure 14.11.

***Fig. 14.11.** A recolored picture.*

You can recolor as many times as you need to get the best result. The Recolor option is not available, however, with objects you draw yourself in PowerPoint, such as ovals and squares.

Chapter Summary

In Chapter 7, you learned to use enough of PowerPoint's powerful coloring capabilities to enable you to select from a multitude of existing color schemes and to change the colors in those color schemes. With PowerPoint, however, you can use even more colors. In this chapter, you saw how to create colors not listed in the color scheme—literally any color you want. You learned how to add a color to your permanent list of available colors. You also saw additional uses for color schemes beyond those given in Chapter 7. You found out how to use a color scheme with other presentations and with matching slides in the same presentation. Finally, you saw in this chapter how to use the Recolor Picture option to change the color of pictures you import into PowerPoint.

Creating Standard Business Charts

In this book, you have seen all the graphics tools available in PowerPoint—those for text, drawing, color, and graphing. You can use those tools, of course, in any way you want. Chances are, though, that you will want to create certain standard business charts. Although you can see how to use the tools in previous chapters in the book, you still may want to find out how to apply PowerPoint's graphics tools toward certain specific objectives—such as creating an organization chart or creating a frame for a chart.

In this chapter, you find out how to use PowerPoint to create certain standard charts. Unlike previous chapters, this chapter does not list all the detailed steps for creating the charts, but rather gives you an indication of which tools to apply and how to apply them. (For details on using any of the tools, see the chapters in the book dedicated to that tool.)

In the first section of the chapter, you see how to create one of the most widely used business charts—the organization chart. You then see how to create some of the most popular standard graphs—bar, line, and pie graphs. (Again, this book often uses the word "graph" where the PowerPoint documentation uses the word "chart.") Most graphics presentations use text charts, and often rely on them quite heavily. In this chapter, you review four forms of text charts—title charts, bulleted lists, column text charts, and table charts.

Useful as words may be, a pictorial representation of a concept is often invaluable. This chapter reviews the concept of a chart as a way to make the abstract concrete. Because presentations often concern geographical locations, in the final section in this chapter you see how to use PowerPoint to add maps to your slides.

Creating an Organization Chart

An organization chart shows the structure of a company or business group. The chart shows the relative relationships of the members of the group— president, vice president, managers, sales people, and so on—and shows the lines of authority. Organization charts are particularly valuable to human resource departments when they plan the staffing of the organization and the career paths of its employees.

Slide 7 in the PowerPoint Guided Tour, COLUMBUS.PPT, is an organization chart (see fig. 15.1).

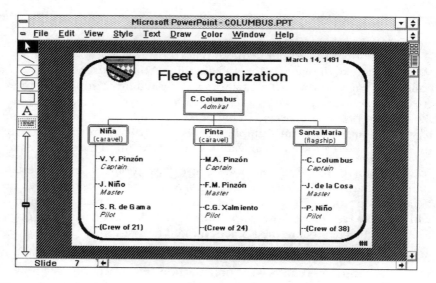

Fig. 15.1. *Sample Organization Chart.*

Like any graphic, an organization chart can become quite complex. The boxes can be shadowed or unshadowed and can have lines of various widths. You can do all the things with text fonts that you can do when using the word processing and labeler tools. Text within boxes can appear in multiple columns. Creating an organization chart can test your ingenuity in many ways. Nevertheless, the basic procedure for creating an organization chart is simple:

1. Create the boxes you need. Use the drawing tools, usually the rectangle or rounded-corner rectangle tools, to create the boxes. If you want all your rectangles to be the same size, you can create one box and use the Copy command from the Edit menu to create others identical to the first.

2. Draw lines to connect the boxes. Draw lines between the boxes with the line tool.

3. Fill the boxes with text. Add text with the labeler or the word processing tool. (Remember that if you use the labeler, the text remains attached to the box if you move the box; this characteristic is an advantage if you plan to change your organization chart.)

Tip: The Show Guides command from the Draw menu can help you place your boxes exactly where you want them on-screen. You also can use the grid to make the boxes snap into place precisely.

Creating Standard Graphs

The most widely-used graphs are probably the line graph, bar graph, and pie graph. You saw how to create all these graphs in Chapter 8, "Creating Basic Graphs." If you want, however, you can use the drawing tools to draw your own graphs. For a line graph, for instance, you can draw the axes, draw the lines that represent data, put in data points, add labels, and so on. Chances are, however, that you will never choose to create the graphs yourself in PowerPoint. The software does all the design work for you, so that you need only enter the data and choose a chart form to represent it.

Tip: You may want to use a bar, pie, or line graph that does not represent data exactly but is a "generic" graph. You can find such charts in the GRAPHS subdirectory under the TEMPLATE subdirectory in PowerPoint. To use a generic graph, paste it into your presentation and add labels.

Slide 4 from the presentation COLUMBUS.PPT, for example, shows how you might include a pie graph in a slide in your presentation (see fig. 15.2).

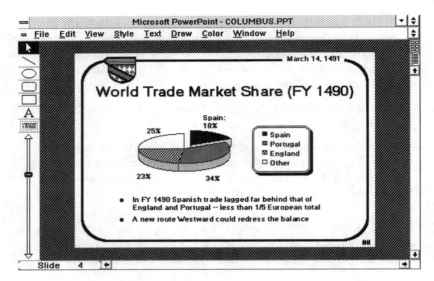

Fig. 15.2. *A pie graph in a presentation.*

To create the graph itself, follow these steps:

1. Choose Insert from the File menu.

2. Choose Graph.

3. Enter your data into the datasheet and choose your graph type from the Chart window.

Creating a line, bar, or pie graph is as simple as choosing Line, Bar, or Pie from the Chart menu. As you become confident in using PowerPoint options, you can apply such enhancements as 3-D effects (shown in the sample in figure 15.2) and stacking.

Remember that the finished graph becomes one pictorial element in your completed slide, as you can see in figure 15.2. Feel free to add text, symbols, arrows, borders, and so on, as you create a complete slide around the chart.

Creating Text Charts

Although the term "graphics" suggests pictures, most PC graphics are in fact text slides. Business people use graphics to communicate. A picture may be worth a thousand words, but you often cannot prove it from business graphics. In business graphics, words continue to hold a valued place—often the dominant place—because pictures merely support the words. In the following sections, you see how to create some of the most widely used types of text charts.

Creating a Title Chart

Like the cover of a book, the title page of a slide show sets the tone for the entire show and gives a direction to all that follows. A title chart is usually simple but powerful, with one word or, at most, just a few words, set in large type. Other graphic elements, such as the background, call attention to the title. Often you may want to add a clip art picture to a title page to create a professional look and to suggest the theme of the presentation. For example, the Genigraphics artists have created the title slide shown in figure 15.3 for the presentation titled PRSPP16.PPT in the PowerPoint SAMPLES subdirectory.

Fig. 15.3. A sample title slide.

When you begin any slide in PowerPoint, the title is already selected. In this way, PowerPoint prompts you to add the title to the slide and to format the title. To create a good title slide, think about concise wording for what you want to say, then use this procedure:

1. Type the text.

2. Use the Style menu to experiment with boldface, large type sizes, attractive fonts, and other ingredients to make the title stand out.

Creating a Bulleted List

Bulleted lists are probably the mainstay of most slide and overhead presentations. The purpose of the presentation, after all, is to communicate information in a number of clear, specific points. The PowerPoint ruler, in fact (described in Chapter 12), is designed with the bulleted list in mind.

To create a bulleted list, follow this procedure:

1. Use the ruler to set your indentation levels.

2. Select the bullet you want to use from Zapf Dingbats.

3. Type your text with the word processor tool.

Slide 6 in PRSPP16.PPT, for instance, shows how you can create a bulleted list with the first point indented the farthest, then each successive point closer to the left margin (see fig. 15.4).

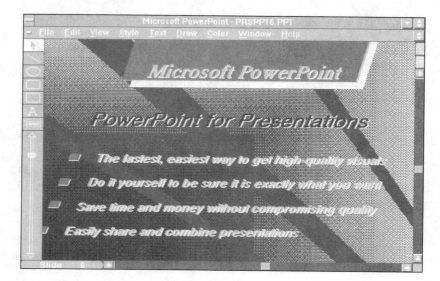

Fig. 15.4. *A sample bulleted list.*

Tip: You can use color to create a "build chart," with which you show a number of points but call attention to just one point at a time. Use a bright color for the point to which you want to call attention and a dim color for all the other points.

Creating a Column Text Chart

Column text charts are excellent for making comparisons. For example, in one column you can make all your points about "apples." In the second column you can make similar points about "oranges." A chart can be both a column chart and a bullet chart, as you see in figure 15.5, slide 6 from the COLUMBUS.PPT presentation. In the example in the figure, the presenter uses the column chart to present arguments in the first column and responses to them in the second.

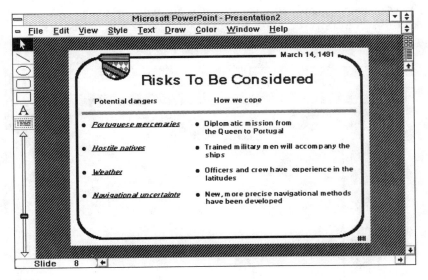

Fig. 15.5. *A column text chart.*

PowerPoint gives you more than one way to create the column chart. You can draw a single text box with the word processor tool and type one column at one indent level, the second at another indent level. You can use tabs, which can become harrowing if you have many columns, particularly when the text takes up more than one line in the column. An easier way to create the multiple columns, however, is to create a separate text box for each column.

> *Tip:* A quick way to create two or more matching columns is to create the first column with the word processor tool, select the column, choose Copy, then choose Paste to create a second column (or third or more columns). Use the Guides to line up the columns exactly. Keep the bullets, but delete the text from the second and additional boxes. Type new text for those additional columns.

Creating a Table

A table is similar to a column chart. A table, however, may have more rows and columns than a column chart and you may be more likely to draw lines between the rows and columns and around the table itself. Slide 9 in the COLUMBUS.PPT presentation, for instance, has three columns, as shown in figure 15.6.

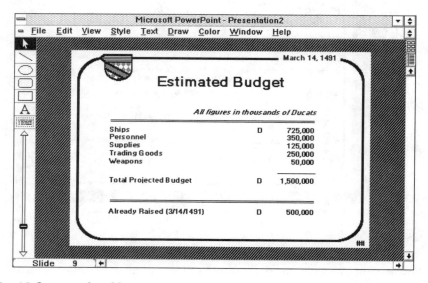

Fig. 15.6. A sample table.

One of the best ways to create a table, of course, is to use Excel or another spreadsheet. You may want to create the table in the spreadsheet, then import the table into PowerPoint.

Creating a Concept Chart

"Concept chart" is a broad term used to describe many kinds of charts that make abstract ideas concrete. The organization chart, discussed earlier in this chapter, is one form of concept chart. Concept charts often include symbols combined with arrows that show the flow of a process or the flow of information.

Any time you have to teach others, chances are that you can use a concept chart. You can use a concept chart to show how to sign on to a computer or to present the sales cycle at your company. After you begin to think in terms of concept charts, you are likely to find that you can translate abstractions into pictures easily. Audiences are often thankful for your efforts, because concept charts enable them to focus on something concrete while you present ideas that are abstract.

The communications network shown in figure 15.7 is a concept chart. The chart appears in the file named TOKEN.PPT in the PowerPoint SAMPLES subdirectory.

To create your own concept charts, follow this procedure:

1. Choose pictures from the clip art library (or simply create objects such as ovals and rectangles).

2. Add lines or arrows to show the flow of the concept.

3. Add text with the labeler.

Creating Maps

Maps are useful if your presentation has something to do with geography. Geography is relevant, for instance, if you are discussing sales territories, planned military invasion routes, air travel routes, or the history of a particular region. You may want to add a map to a slide first, then put data on top of the map. You can show a map of the United States, for example, then show sales for each sales region of a national company.

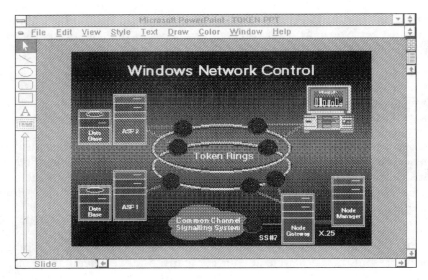

***Fig. 15.7.** A sample concept chart.*

The clip art file MAPS.PPT contains fifteen maps, such as the map of the Middle East shown in figure 15.8.

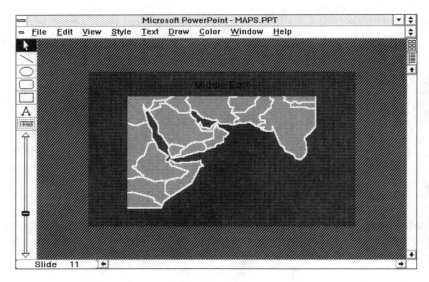

***Fig. 15.8.** A sample map from the clip art library.*

Tip: If you want to use only part of one of the maps—perhaps just Israel from the map of the Middle East—cover the remainder of the map with an opaque object that matches the background color.

In the sample presentation COLUMBUS.PPT, slide 2 uses a map, as shown here in figure 15.9.

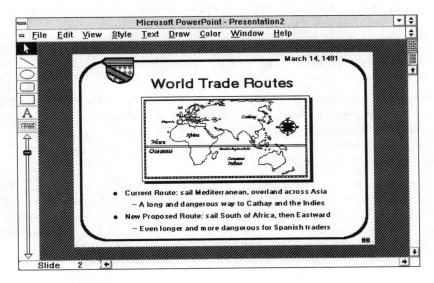

Fig. 15.9. A sample slide with a map.

To create your own map, follow this procedure:

1. Choose the maps you need from the clip art maps file, MAPS.PPT.

2. Paste the maps into your PowerPoint slide.

3. Add labels with the labeler tool.

Chapter Summary

Not all charts fit into neat categories, of course. A chart often contains elements of more than one chart form—such as a table and a pie graph, for instance, or a table, a pie graph, and a map and text. Broad categories such as "concept chart" and "text chart" contain many kinds of charts within themselves.

The value of learning the categories of charts is that you then can refer to those categories when you try to think of graphic ways to illustrate your ideas. Rather than ask yourself, "Can I create a graphic here?" you can ask, "Could I use a concept chart here? A map? A bar chart?"

As with much else in PowerPoint, using the capability is easy after you know that the capability is available and that it applies to your purposes. After you start looking for opportunities to use maps in your slides, for instance, you are almost certain to find many such opportunities. Copying the map from the clip art library is then a minor matter.

In this chapter, you went over some of the kinds of charts you may want to use in your own presentations—organization charts, standard graphs, text charts, concept charts, and maps.

You now have completed *Using PowerPoint*. You have seen all the PowerPoint capabilities and, in this chapter, you saw some of the many possibilities for creating your own graphics using those capabilities. As you continue to use PowerPoint, such possibilities increasingly become second nature for you.

PowerPoint lives up to its name, and indeed does offer a great deal of "power." The more PowerPoint capabilities that you learn to use, the more likely that additional capabilities will unfold for you. You can continue to learn more and more about PowerPoint for many months as you continue to use it and make discoveries about what you can do with it.

Installing PowerPoint

As you probably know, PowerPoint runs under Windows only, so you must have Windows installed on your hard drive before you can attempt to install PowerPoint. If you haven't installed Windows, you should do so now before you continue with this section. Refer to your Windows documentation for Windows installation instructions.

Copying Your Source Disks

To keep your original disks safe, copy the PowerPoint disks to another set of disks before you install the program. Keep the original disks in a safe place and use the copies. If you damage any disks during installation, you still have the originals. Follow these steps to copy your disks:

1. Label the target disks (the disks onto which you copy the files) with something like "PowerPoint Working Copies." Number them 1, 2, 3, 4, and 5 (or 1–4 if you're using 3 1/2-inch disks).

2. At the DOS prompt, type *diskcopy* followed by the floppy disk drive letter typed twice; for example, type *diskcopy a: a:*.

    DOS displays this message:

    ```
    Insert source diskette in drive A:
    Press any key when ready...
    ```

3. Put the original PowerPoint Disk 1 into the floppy disk drive and press any key.

After a short time you see another message:

```
Insert target diskette in drive A:
Press any key when ready...
```

4. Insert the target disk (use disk number 1 the first time) into the floppy disk drive and press any key.

DOS then copies files onto this disk. PowerPoint may prompt you to change source and target disks several times because of the large number of files involved. When you have copied all the files to the target disk, you see the following message:

```
Copy another diskette (Y/N)?
```

5. Press Y to indicate yes and repeat these steps to copy the remaining PowerPoint disks. Don't forget to use disks with matching numbers (disk 2 with disk 2, and so on).

6. When you see `Copy another diskette (Y/N)?` after all files on all disks have been copied, press N.

Now use the working copies to install PowerPoint, as explained in the next section.

Installing PowerPoint on Your Hard Drive

To install PowerPoint, you first run Windows. Follow these steps:

1. Insert the PowerPoint Working Copy Disk 1 into your floppy disk drive.

2. Start Windows (type *win* from the DOS prompt).

The first window you see in Windows is the Program Manager window, with menu items along the top row.

3. Select the File menu.

4. Choose Run.

A box appears with the words `Command Line` preceding the cursor.

5. Type *a:setup* and press Enter.

A message says `Please wait while Setup copies its working files to your hard disk`. This copying may take up to a minute. You then see the first screen in the Setup installation program.

> *Tip:* If you want to exit the Setup program (and thereby stop the installation) from any of the following screens, press F3.

You have two choices now, as shown on the screen: `Install PowerPoint Using Defaults` or `Install PowerPoint Using Options`. The first choice is the simplest. Use it to install the standard program, fonts, and so on, on your hard disk. The second choice enables you to choose what to install, as demonstrated in the following steps. If you choose which files to install, you can leave out what you don't need, which frees disk space. Follow these steps to install PowerPoint:

1. Click on the top box next to the words `Install PowerPoint Using Defaults` or on the box next to `Install PowerPoint Using Options`.

   The decision you make now is not irreversible. You can invoke Setup at any time to make changes such as adding screen or printer fonts. If in doubt about what to do, choose Install PowerPoint Using Defaults.

   Setup asks: `Where would you like to install PowerPoint Options?`, and gives a default of C:\POWERPNT. If you choose to install PowerPoint with its defaults, you see the message `Where would you like PowerPoint installed?`

2. Click the OK button or type a new subdirectory; then press OK.

   If you chose the Using Defaults option at step 1, skip to step 4.

   If you chose Using Options, you see the Setup install screen, which shows options to select or deselect.

   The Setup program offers seven options that represent various parts of PowerPoint. Setup automatically chooses six of the seven options, including Install PowerPoint. You know that an option has been selected by the `X` in the box to the left of the option. The final option, Install Bitstream Presentation Fonts, has not been selected. To deselect or select any option, click the box with your mouse pointer. Table A.1 lists the installation options.

Table A.1
PowerPoint Installation Options

Option	Installs
Install PowerPoint	This option installs PowerPoint applications, PowerPoint Graph, dictionary, help files, tutorials, default driver, and some screen fonts.
Install Graphics Import Filters	With these files, you can import other files (such as TIFF, CGM, HPGL) into PowerPoint.
Genigraphics Driver and GraphicsLink	These files enable you to use the Genigraphics slide production service. The driver creates a file in the proper format. GraphicsLink sends the file by modem if you prefer.
PowerPoint Templates	These files provide professionally designed formatting to use with your own presentations.
PowerPoint Sample Files	These presentations give you an idea of the possibilities available in PowerPoint.
Clip Art Files	These files contain clip art that you can transfer to your own presentations.
Presentation Fonts	This option loads different screen and printer fonts that are useful for different slides and purposes.

The Install PowerPoint option is mandatory if you want to run the PowerPoint program. Choose Install Graphics Import Filters if you think that you will need to import graphics from other applications. You might not need both the Bitstream Presentation font and the Genigraphics Driver and GraphicsLink, depending on how you intend to show your presentations. Use the fonts option when you want to print transparencies and overheads. Use the Genigraphics Driver and GraphicsLink if you want to produce slides.

Most people consider the templates, sample files, and clip art files essential to their needs. These files give you a head start to producing good presentations.

The Instructions box at the bottom of the screen gives information about the options. To scroll the box down to see descriptions of the options, click the down arrow in the scroll bar on the right. For instance, the Instructions box describes the Bitstream Presentation Fonts as: High quality screen and printer fonts in sizes suitable for presentation.

If you want to install Bitstream presentation fonts, follow step 3.

3. Click the Select Fonts box to the right of the Install Bitstream Presentation Fonts option.

Whether you came from step 3 or step 2 (by choosing the Using Defaults option at step 1), you see the Install Bitstream screen.

If you click the OK box at this stage, none of the Bitstream fonts will be installed (no option boxes have Xs). As before, to select any option, simply click the box to the left of the option.

The top option, Install Bitstream Fonts in Large Sizes, gives you the normal fonts (Helvetica, Times, and Zapf Dingbats) in the large sizes. The definition on-screen will be better if you use this option for these type sizes.

The lower options are for Printer Fonts. First, you should pick a printer. The default is HP LaserJet II or compatible. Click the arrow to the right to see the full list of printers. If the printer for which you want to create fonts is not included, you need to install it. To install the printer without leaving the Setup Program, press Alt-Esc to call up the Program Manager.

If you do not want to install a printer, go to step 10. To install a printer, follow steps 4 through 9.

4. From Setup, press Alt-Esc to call up the Program Manager.

5. Choose Control Panel.

6. Choose Printer.

7. Select the Add Printer button on the Printers dialog box.

You see a list of printers in a scroll box. The list is long, but if your printer is not there, choose Unlisted Printer; then specify the driver name and directory.

8. Choose your printer and then select the Install option.

   A dialog box tells you to insert Windows disk 5 into your floppy disk drive. Windows reads from the disk and installs the printer driver. The name of the printer appears in the list of Installed Printers in the upper right part of the dialog box.

9. Choose OK to exit the dialog box.

   Your printer is installed.

10. Click OK to exit the Bitstream screen.

    If you chose the Using Defaults option at step 1, the Setup program immediately continues with installation, as described in step 5.

    If you chose Using Options at step 1, you return to the screen with the seven options.

11. Click OK and the installation procedure continues.

    A message appears on-screen: `Setup is copying files.` As each file is copied, the name and the percentage of the total files to be transferred are displayed on-screen. Installing PowerPoint can take quite a while—up to an hour or more, in fact—depending on how many options you have chosen to install.

    After Setup copies the contents of the first disk to the hard drive, Setup prompts you for the second disk. Insert the second and other disks as prompted. If you haven't asked for the complete set of options, Setup may not prompt you for the fifth disk in your set.

    After the installation, Setup sends a message:

    `The PowerPoint Setup is complete.`

    Setup also gives you the choice to go straight into PowerPoint (`Start PowerPoint`) or to exit to **Windows** (`Return to the Program Manager`).

12. Click one of the boxes and you exit Setup.

The Setup program automatically installs PowerPoint within Windows. The PowerPoint icon now appears within the Windows Applications group window.

B

PowerPoint Defaults

Defaults can be helpful to keep you oriented as you go along. You can change the defaults easily, as you see in Chapter 3 and elsewhere. Defaults are a safety feature; they conform to rules of good usage. From time to time, you may want to refer to them or restore some or all of them.

The presentation that you see when you enter PowerPoint has default settings in most of the menus. This appendix lists these defaults under menu headings: Style, Text, Draw, and Color. For explanations of the meanings of any of the terms used, refer to the appropriate chapters in the book.

Printer Defaults

The printers for slides, notes pages, and handouts are the current printers for your operating system, and they use the orientation, paper size, and other options set in your operating system.

View Defaults

The slide scale is initially 50 percent. The slide master has a centered title at the top, set in boldface in Swiss SWA 18 point (if available). The notes master centers a reduced 50 percent scale slide at the top of the notes page (for portrait orientation) or at the left (for landscape orientation). The default handout page contains no text or objects.

383

Style Defaults

The default text style is Swiss SWA at 18, 24, and 36 points (if available).

Text Default

Only one default exists in the Text menu: Left positioning, as distinct from Center, Right, or Justify. Label and word processor objects are unframed, sized to text, left-aligned, and boldfaced, in Swiss SWA 18 point (if available).

Draw Defaults

In Draw, the default settings for a drawn object are transparent (not opaque), framed, unfilled, and unshadowed. The default pattern is all black, which means that only the primary color shows if you subsequently choose the fill option. The default line style is the thinnest line in the menu, without arrowheads.

Any text box drawn receives the Sized to Text feature.

In addition, the Grid option on the Draw menu is automatically turned on, the guides do not show, and the edges of drawn objects do not show unless you choose this option yourself.

Color Defaults

The eight colors available in the default color scheme are white (WT), black (BK), GY5, BU1, RD8, BU3, BG8, and YW6. The latter six are variations on gray, dark blue, red, blue, blue/gray, and yellow, respectively.

The default fill color is RD8; the default line and text color is black; the default shadow is GY5, and the default pattern contrast is white.

Fill, Line, Shadow, Pattern Contrast, Text, and Title are all set to the colors of the current Color Scheme. The slide background is the first color in the scheme, as is the Pattern Contrast. Slide foreground, line, and text are the second color in the scheme. Shadows are the third color, title text the fourth color, and fill the fifth color.

The Clip Art Slides
by Presentation

T he following is a complete list of the individual slides in the CLIPART
subdirectory in PowerPoint. You should find it quicker to glance
through this list first rather than go straight into the presentations in the
CLIPART subdirectory to find the kind of illustration you want. The CLIPART
subdirectory contains 16 presentations in all:

- ANIMALS
- ARCHITEC
- BACKGRND
- BUSINESS
- EDUCATIO
- ENTRTNMT
- HOUSEHLD
- INTERNAT
- MAPS
- PEOPLE_1
- PEOPLE_2
- PRESHELP
- SCIENTFC
- SPORTS

- TECHNAL
- TRANSPOR

This appendix lists each slide in these presentations.

Each clip art presentation starts with a title slide (the number 1 slide), which is the same in all the clip art presentations.

The slide numbers in the following lists therefore begin with slide 2 in each case.

ANIMALS.PPT (Animal Slides)

2   Horse

3   Donkeys

4   Cow

5   Elephant

6   Camel

7   Tiger

8   Eagle

9   Birds

10 Dove

11 Butterfly

12 Fly

13 Turtle

14 Lobster

15 Shark

ARCHITEC.PPT (Architecture Slides)

2   Bird's-Eye View

3   Cityscape

4   High Rise

5   Court House

6   Capitol

7   Government Building

8   Barn

9   Factory

10 Mansion

11 Victorian House

12 House

13 Outhouse

14 Brick Wall

15 Opening Door

16 Pine

17 Tree

18 Palms

19 Leaves

20 Rose

BACKGRND.PPT (Background Slides)

2   Ribbons

3   Clouds

4   Laurels

5   Weighted Lines

6   Neon

7   Marquee

8   Lines

9   Fleur De Lis

10 Computer Screen

11 Shadowed Neon

BUSINESS.PPT (Business Slides)

4   Credit Cards

5   Typewriter

6   Crystal Ball

7   Office

8   Improved Stamp

9   Mail

10   Briefcase

11   In/Out Basket

12   Hard Hat

13   I Beams

14   Forklift

15   Hoe

16   Pipeline Valve

17   Money

18   Coins

19   3-D Dollar Sign

20   Pot of Gold

21   Safe

22   Liberty Bell

23   Eagle

24   Torch

25   Scales of Justice

26   Uncle Sam

27   Lincoln Memorial

28   Mt. Rushmore

29   Statue of Liberty

EDUCATIO.PPT (Education Slides)

2   Open Binder

3   Open Book

4   Book

5   Book with Tabs

6   Bookshelf

7   Books

8   Bookshelves

9   Mortarboard

10   Fish

11   Lecture 1

12   Lecture 2

13   Classroom

14   Pencil

15   Ink Bottle

16   Design Tools

17   Drafting Table

ENTRTNMT.PPT (Entertainment Slides)

2   Spotlight

3   Top Hat and Cane

4   Magician

5   Clown

6   Cards

7   Grocery Cart

8   Salt and Pepper Shakers

9   Cheese

10   Hamburger

11   Desserts

12   Apple

13   Fruit

14   Beer

15   Drink

16   Champagne

17   Conductor

18   Keyboard

19   Banjo

20   Radio

HOUSEHLD.PPT (Household Slides)

2   Clock

3   Stopwatch

4   Shoes

5   Glasses

6   Toilet Paper and Tissues

7   Faucet

8   Bedroom

9   Bench

10   Saw

11   Screwdriver

12   Toolbox

13   Paintbox

14 Gears

15 Keys

INTERNAT.PPT (International Slides)

2   Australia

3   Austria

4   Belgium

5   Brazil

6   Canada

7   China

8   Denmark

9   Egypt

10 Federal Republic of Germany

11 Finland

12 France

13 German Democratic Republic

14 Greece

15 Hungary

16 Ireland

17 Israel

18 Italy

19 Japan

20 Korea

21 Luxembourg

22 Mexico

23 Netherlands

24 New Zealand

25 Norway

26 Poland

27 Portugal

28 Spain

29 Sweden

30 Switzerland

31 Taiwan

32 Turkey

33 United Kingdom

34 United Nations

35 USA

36 USSR

37 Yugoslavia

MAPS.PPT (Map Slides)

2   World

3   Side View Globe

4   Top View Globe

5   Spiral Globe

6   World Map

7   Africa

8   Asia

9   Central America

10 Europe

11 Middle East

12 South America

13 USA—Multicolor States

PEOPLE_1.PPT (People Slides—Set 1)

PEOPLE_2.PPT (People Slides—Set 2)

4   Silhouette of Four

5   Silhouette at Podium

6   Businessmen Reviewing

7   Woman on Phone

8   Da Vinci's Modern Man

9   Multicolor Running Figure

10   Four Dancers

11   Figure at Computer

12   Crowd of Businesspeople

13   Crowd of Workers

14   Man in Front of Graph

15   Man with Briefcase

16   Businesswomen

17   Woman with Extended Arm

18   Press Conference

19   Man at Desk

20   Man at Desk—Side View

PRESHELP.PPT (Presentation Helper)

2   Painting Hand, Signs 1–5

3   Painting Hand with String

4   Handshake

5   Businessmen Handshake

6   3-D Arrows from Center Point

7   Diagonal 3-D Arrows

8   3-D Arrows

9   Arrows

10   Arrows around in Circle

11 Curved 3-D Arrows

12 Diagonal Curved 3-D Arrows

13 Diagonal Curved Arrows

14 One-to-Three Arrows

15 3-D Arrows around 3-D Box

16 3-D Star

17 Star

18 Crystal Star

19 Sphere

20 Check Mark

21 X Mark

22 Pyramid

23 Cubes

24 Cube

25 Stairs

26 Blue Ribbon

SCIENTFC.PPT (Scientific Slides)

2 Match

3 Gasoline Nozzle

4 Gasoline Pump

5 Nuclear Power Plant

6 Eye Opened

7 Eye Closed

8 Ear

9 Lightbulbs

10 Shaded Lightbulb

11 Power Plug

12 Electric Outlet

13 Power Lines

14 Medical Symbol

15 Pills

16 Poison

17 Figure on Crutch

18 Figure in Wheelchair

19 Doctor with Stethoscope

20 Hospital Bed

21 Hospital Bed with Patient

22 Microscope

23 Magnifying Glass

24 Measuring Tubes

25 Container with Liquid

26 Liquid over Hot Plate

27 Scientist

28 Thermometer

29 Liquid over Heat

SPORTS.PPT (Sports Slides)

2 Football

3 Baseball

4 Baseball Catcher

5 Soccer

6 Volleyball

7 Basketball

8   Tennis

9   Boxing

10 Golf

11 Skiing

12 Horse Racing

13 Sailing

14 Canoeing

15 Archery

16 Racecar

TECHNAL.PPT (Technical Slides)

2   Television

3   Movie Projector with Screen

4   Slide Projector

5   Slide Projector with Screen

6   Slides Stacked

7   Slides Scattered

8   Film

9   Camera

10 Telephone Receiver

11 Telephone

12 Multiple-Line Telephone

13 Man on Phone at Desk

14 Close-up Man on Phone

15 Telephone Poles

16 Satellites

17 Satellite Dish

18   Billboard

19   Computer Card

20   Prom

21   Button

22   PC1

23   PC2

24   PC3

25   PC4

26   Laptop PC1

27   Laptop PC2

28   Computer 1

29   Computer 2

30   Computer 3

31   Computer 4

32   Printer

33   Digitizer

TRANSPOR.PPT (Transportation Slides)

2   Handicapped Sign

3   Warning Cones

4   One Way

5   Stop

6   Traffic Light

7   Crosswalk Sign

8   Gender Signs

9   No Smoking

10 Bicycle

11 Old-Fashioned Car

12 Two-Door Car

13 Transportation Collage

14 Taxi

15 Truck Cab

16 Truck

17 Train

18 Cable Cars

19 Stagecoach

20 Steamboat

21 Blimp

22 Hot Air Balloon

23 Airplane

24 Locomotive

25 Fighter Jet

Index

D

H

I

J–K

L

M

X-Z